THE INCREDIBLE HULK

HEART OF THE ATOM

WRITERS

HARLAN ELLISON, ROY THOMAS, ARCHIE GOODWIN, LEN WEIN, BILL MANTLO & PETER GILLIS

PENCILERS

HERB TRIMPE & SAL BUSCEMA

INKERS

SAM GRAINGER, JOHN SEVERIN, SAL TRAPANI, JOE STATON, SAL BUSCEMA & MIKE ESPOSITO

COLORISTS

GLYNIS WEIN, BEN SEAN & CARL GAFFORD

LETTERERS

ART SIMEK, IRVING WATANABE, JOHN COSTANZA, DIANA ALBERS, JIM NOVAK & TOM ORZECHOWSKI

EDITORS

STAN LEE, ROY THOMAS, LEN WEIN, AL MILGROM, DENNY O'NEIL & MARK GRUENWALD

COVER ARTISTS

DAVE COCKRUM & HERB TRIMPE

COVER COLORIST

CHRIS SOTOMAYOR

HULK: HEART OF THE ATOM. Contains material originally published in magazine form as INCREDIBLE HULK #140, #148, #156, #202-203, #205-207 and #246-248; and WHAT IF? #23. First printing 2012. ISBN# 978-0-7851-6212-4. Published by MARVEL WORLDWIDE, INC., a subsidiary of MARVEL ENTERTAINMENT, LLC. OFFICE OF PUBLICATION: 135 West 50th Street, New York, NY 10020. $24.99 per copy in the U.S. and $27.99 in Canada (GST #R127032852); Canadian Agreement #40668537. **Printed in the U.S.A**. ALAN FINE, EVP - Office of the President, Marvel Worldwide, Inc. and EVP & CMO Marvel Characters B.V.; DAN BUCKLEY, Publisher & President - Print, Animation & Digital Divisions; JOE QUESADA, Chief Creative Officer; TOM BREVOORT, SVP of Publishing; DAVID BOGART, SVP of Operations & Procurement, Publishing; RUWAN JAYATILLEKE, SVP & Associate Publisher, Publishing; C.B. CEBULSKI, SVP of Creator & Content Development; DAVID GABRIEL, SVP of Publishing Sales & Circulation; MICHAEL PASCIULLO, SVP of Brand Planning & Communications; JIM O'KEEFE, VP of Operations & Logistics; DAN CARR, Executive Director of Publishing Technology; SUSAN CRESPI, Editorial Operations Manager; ALEX MORALES, Publishing Operations Manager; STAN LEE, Chairman Emeritus. For information regarding advertising in Marvel Comics or on Marvel.com, please contact John Dokes, SVP Integrated Sales and Marketing, at jdokes@marvel.com. For Marvel subscription inquiries, please call 800-217-9158. **Manufactured between 5/30/2012 and 6/18/2012 by R.R. DONNELLEY, INC., SALEM, VA, USA.**

10 9 8 7 6 5 4 3 2 1

COLLECTION EDITOR
NELSON RIBEIRO
ASSISTANT EDITOR
ALEX STARBUCK
EDITORS, SPECIAL PROJECTS
MARK D. BEAZLEY & JENNIFER GRÜNWALD
SENIOR EDITOR, SPECIAL PROJECTS
JEFF YOUNGQUIST
SENIOR VICE PRESIDENT OF SALES
DAVID GABRIEL
SVP OF BRAND PLANNING & COMMUNICATIONS
MICHAEL PASCIULLO
RESEARCH & TEXT RECAPS
MARK O'ENGLISH
PRODUCTION
JERRON QUALITY COLOR & RODOLFO MURAGUCHI
COLOR RECONSTRUCTION
JERRON QUALITY COLOR
EDITOR IN CHIEF
AXEL ALONSO
CHIEF CREATIVE OFFICER
JOE QUESADA
PUBLISHER
DAN BUCKLEY
EXECUTIVE PRODUCER
ALAN FINE

SPECIAL THANKS TO POND SCUM, JEFF CHRISTIANSEN & MIKE FICHERA

HEART OF THE ATOM

INCREDIBLE HULK

15¢ 140 JUNE

CC

TM

MARVEL COMICS GROUP

THE INCREDIBLE HULK

TM

HULK! YOU HAVE RULED THIS WORLD *LONG* ENOUGH!

NOW-- IT IS TIME TO *DIE!*

THE BRUTE THAT SHOUTED LOVE AT THE HEART OF THE ATOM!

HARLAN ELLISON STRIKES AGAIN!

TRIMPE

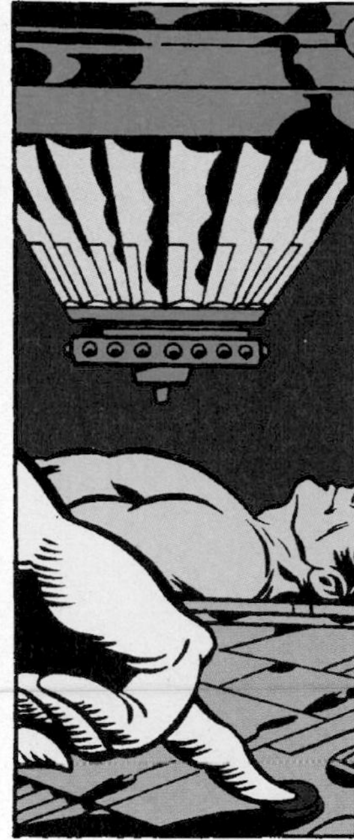
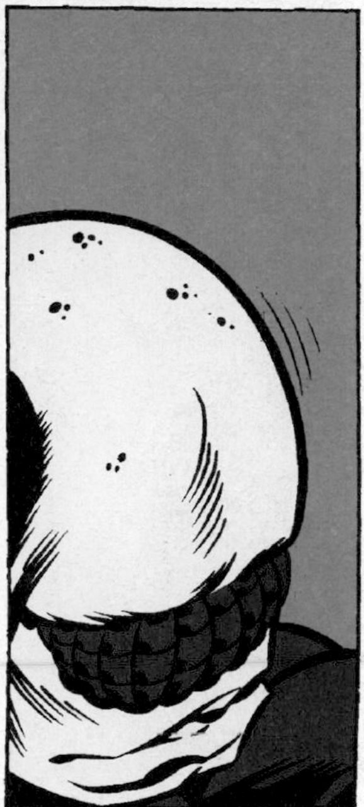

AND THUS IT GOES, THIS DANGEROUS VISION WHICH BEGAN *LAST ISSUE* : A STUNNED **HULK** LIES, SEMI-CONSCIOUS, IN THE PORTAL OF THE GREAT MACHINE OF **PSYKLOP**, THAT ELDRITCH ALIEN WHO PLANS TO **REDUCE** THE GREEN BEHEMOTH IN **SIZE**--TO SHRINK HIM AND COMPRESS HIM FOR CLOSER STUDY. EERILY, THE MOLECULAR RAY BEGINS TO **BATHE** THE COMATOSE GIANT IN ITS RUBY GLOW, AND THEN... **ENTER THE MIGHTY AVENGERS!**

THE BRUTE...

HOW IT **SHUDDERS**, THIS SUBTERRANEAN LABORATORY, WITH THE FULL FURY OF PITCHED COMBAT BETWEEN THE UNCANNY, EONS-OLD PSYKLOP AND THE MASSED POWER OF FIVE AVENGERS ASSEMBLED. AND ALL THE WHILE, THE HULK SHRINKS DOWN, **DOWN...** UNTIL HE EMERGES GIGANTICALLY IN **ANOTHER WORLD**, WHICH HE FIRST BESTRIDES LIKE A COLOSSUS, THEN FINDS **TOWERING OVER HIM** AS IF HE WERE BUT A CHILD'S DISCARDED TOY...

...THAT SHOUTED LOVE...

AND NOW, THE QUASI-HUMAN PSYKLOP **BREAKS FREE,** REACHES THE TELEPORTATIONAL DEVICE HE USED TO ENSNARE THE HULK. BEFORE ITS IRRESISTIBLE HUM, THE AVENGERS BLINK OUT OF EXISTENCE... TO REAPPEAR, MEMORY-LESS, ON A NEW YORK **SUBWAY PLATFORM.** IN A SUB-MOLECULAR UNIVERSE, A PERPLEXED **HULK** FIRST IS DWARFED BY FEATHER-TOPPED **TREES**... NOW, HE IS SMALLER THAN THE DIAMOND, ONYX-STRIATED **ROCKS**...

...AT THE HEART OF THE ATOM!

AND, MOST OMINOUS OF ALL...
...HE IS FAR, FAR TINIER THAN THE LUMBERING, LUPINE BEAST-THING WHICH COMES SNORTING AND SNUFFLING AT HIM THRU THE BIZARRE UNDERBRUSH!
RRONNKK RRONNK
WHAT'S GOING ON?
FIRST, HULK KEEPS SHRINKING --TILL HE WINDS UP HERE, LIKE A BUG IN THE GRASS.
THEN, HULK HEARS SOUNDS--LIKE SNARLING OF A DOG--OR GRUNTING OF A PIG--
4

RRONNK
--OR MAYBE SOMETHING--
--THAT LOOKS LIKE BOTH OF THEM!

HUNNHH! NOW HULK CAN TELL ONE THING, ANYWAY.
HULK IS NOT ANYPLACE HE'S EVER BEEN BEFORE.

SNAP!
BUT, WHEREEVER HE IS--

ONE THING HULK KNOWS FOR SURE--

HE IS STILL--THE HULK!

IMPALED ON ITS OWN SABRE-LIKE TUSK! A GRISLY WAY FOR EVEN A WOLF-THING TO DIE, HULK--

BUT NO WORSE, PERHAPS, THEN LIVING OUT THE REST OF YOUR LIFE IN A SUB-COSMOS YOU NEVER KNEW EXISTED--

--AND FROM WHICH AN INFINITY OF SEVEN-LEAGUE LEAPS WILL NEVER RELEASE YOU.

DEEPER THAN THE DARKNESS ARE YOUR THOUGHTS, HULK--A WONDER, REALLY, THAT YOU CAN HEAR ANYTHING--
--LET ALONE THE FAINT SHRIEKS OF TERROR WHICH RIPPLE THE MORNING IN THE PLACE WITH NO NAME!

ONE MORE MIGHTY THOOM--CARRYING YOU HIGH ABOVE THE WAVING FEATHER-FRONDS THAT PASS FOR TREES--AND YOU SEE IT--
A CITY! JUST LIKE ONES WHERE HULK CAME FROM!
THAT MUST MEAN--THERE ARE PEOPLE HERE. HUMANS!
BUT--WHY DO THEY SCREAM LIKE THAT?
THEY HAVEN'T EVEN SEEN HULK YET.

HAH! MORE OF THE PIG-DOGS--ATTACKING THE CITY.
PEOPLE THERE JUST FIGHT THEM WITH STICKS AND STONES.
6

BUT-- THEY NEED MORE.
POK!

THEY NEED-- HULK!

ARE YOU LISTENING, HULK? IF SO, THOSE BESTIAL BLEATS OF FEAR MUST TELL YOU SOMETHING--
--THAT, TO THE WOLF-THINGS, YOU ARE MONSTER--YOU ARE DEVIL--YOU ARE PAINGOD!

THEY DO KEEP COMING, DON'T THEY, HULK--LIKE THE PHOENIX, RISING ETERNAL ON ITS ASH--
GROK!

--THOUGH, SOON, THINGS COME DOWN TO JUST--
BLUDD!
--A BOY AND HIS DOG!

AND THEN--THERE ARE NONE.
HUH? WHAT'S THAT SOUND BEHIND HULK?
SCREAMING-- EVEN LOUDER THAN BEFORE!
7

PEOPLE--HUNDREDS OF PEOPLE--RUNNING OUT OF THE CITY--RUNNING THIS WAY.
THEY SCREAM LOUDER--LOUDER--LIKE THEY WANT TO HURT HULK.
MAYBE--HULK FOUGHT ON THE WRONG SIDE.
MRMEEEEEEE
MRMEEEE
MRMEEEE
WELL, IF THEY WANT A FIGHT--HULK WILL BATTLE THEM ALL.

SO NOW IT IS MEN WHO COME AT YOU, GIANT--COME AT YOU LIKE THE WAVES IN RIO--LIKE A PLAGUE OF SHRILLY SHRIEKING LOCUSTS--

AND YOU BRACE YOURSELF TO LASH OUT AGAINST THEM WITH FULL, UNFETTERED FURY--TILL YOU SUDDENLY SENSE THAT THEY ARE NOT CRYING FOR YOUR BLOOD. NO--

--THEY ARE MERELY--CHEERING.

THEN, AS THE JOYFUL MULTITUDES STRAIN UNACCUSTOMED MUSCLES LIFTING YOU UPON THEIR SHOULDERS, SUDDENLY THEIR SCREAMS ARE SCREAMS NO LONGER--
MRMEEEEEEEEE
MRMEEEEEE
--BUT MUSIC TO YOUR EMERALD EARS.

AND NOW, FINALLY, YOUR DIM BRAIN REGISTERS WHAT YOUR BRIGHT EYES HAVE LONG SINCE RECORDED--
YOU ARE GREEN.
ALL OF YOU--GREEN.
GREEN--LIKE THE HULK!
WE DO NOT UNDERSTAND YOUR WORDS, OUTSIDER...
8

...BUT WE ARE MOST GRATEFUL TO YOU FOR YOUR AID AGAINST THE WARTHOS, AND SHALL GLADLY GRANT YOU ANY BOON YOU MAY ASK.
BEWARE, JARELLA! HE IS AN ANIMAL... A MAN-MONSTER...
'TIS ONLY HIS EXTERIOR WHICH IS GRUFF AND BEAST-LIKE, COUSIN VISIS.
BENEATH THAT SEETHING SURFACE, MY QUEENLY POWERS CAN SENSE A SOUL AS HUMAN AS ANY.

SPEAK ON IN BELL-LIKE TONES, JARELLA... YOU WHO ARE EMPRESS BORN OF THIS SUB-ATOMIC SPHERE...

FOR, THOUGH THE SLOW-WITTED BEHEMOTH BEFORE YOU CANNOT DECIPHER YOUR WORDS, THEIR WARMTH SEEMS CLEAR ENOUGH...

...AND SOME THINGS SPEAK A TRANS-UNIVERSAL LANGUAGE.

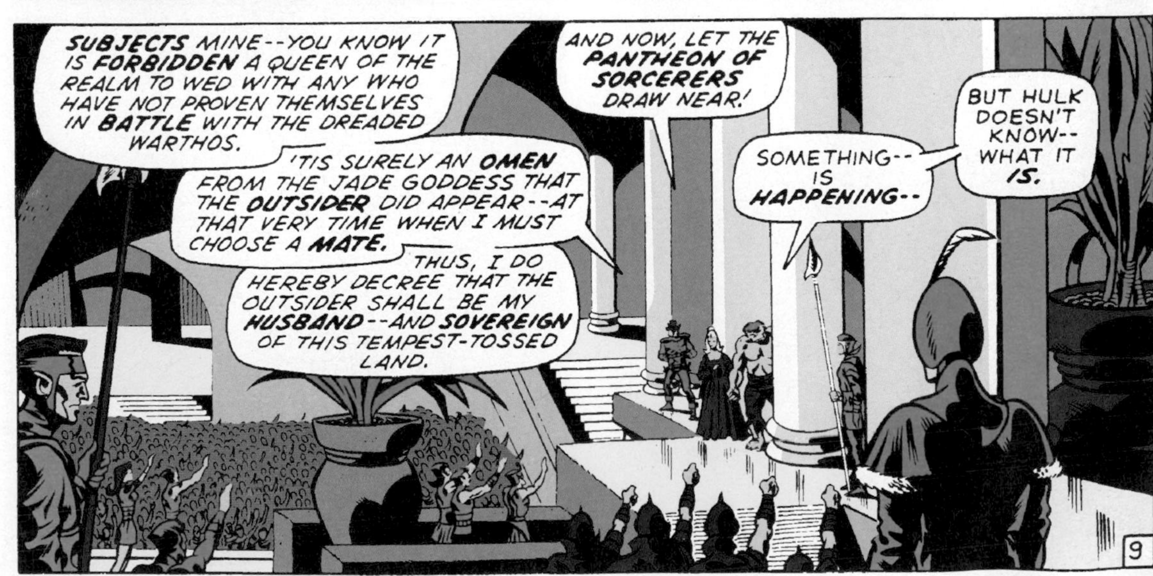
SUBJECTS MINE--YOU KNOW IT IS FORBIDDEN A QUEEN OF THE REALM TO WED WITH ANY WHO HAVE NOT PROVEN THEMSELVES IN BATTLE WITH THE DREADED WARTHOS.
'TIS SURELY AN OMEN FROM THE JADE GODDESS THAT THE OUTSIDER DID APPEAR--AT THAT VERY TIME WHEN I MUST CHOOSE A MATE.
THUS, I DO HEREBY DECREE THAT THE OUTSIDER SHALL BE MY HUSBAND--AND SOVEREIGN OF THIS TEMPEST-TOSSED LAND.
AND NOW, LET THE PANTHEON OF SORCERERS DRAW NEAR!
SOMETHING--IS HAPPENING--
BUT HULK DOESN'T KNOW--WHAT IT IS.
9

HEAR WE DO--AND OBEY WE DO, O JARELLA.
I KNOW THAT YOU ALL WILL TRY TO OBEY, GOOD TORLA.
I ONLY PRAY--THAT YOU SUCCEED IN WHAT I SHALL ASK.

THIS IS MY CHOSEN ONE--BUT HE SPEAKS NOT OUR TONGUE.
I KNOW WELL THAT IT IS WITHIN YOUR POWERS TO--TEACH HIM.
DO SO.
ATTEMPT WE SHALL, DEAR LADY.
BUT--A MOST DISTRACTED, A MOST DIFFICULT SUBJECT HE SEEMS.
HOLI--MOLI--FORM WITH ME THE TRIAD.

READY WE ARE, FRIEND TORLA.
BUT--RESTLESS THE STRANGE ONE GROWS.
HUH? NOW THESE THREE--AND THE GIRL--MAKE A CIRCLE AROUND HULK.
IF THEY TRY TO KILL HULK--
HASTEN! THE CHANT WE MUST BEGIN--!

POWERS THAT WALKED OUR WORLD WHEN YOUNG--LET THIS ONE NOW SPEAK OUR TONGUE--
GO ON. SOMETHING WILL HAPPEN. IT MUST.
AND CONTINUE THEY DO--AS THREE LONG- AND SPECIALLY-TRAINED MINDS ARE LINKED--AND A CRACKLE OF MENTAL ELECTRICITY BEGINS TO SET THE AIR TO SMOULDERING--

"ANY SMOOTHLY-FUNCTIONING TECHNOLOGY WILL HAVE THE APPEARANCE OF WITCHCRAFT."
ARTHUR C. CLARKE SAID THAT.

"SHAZAM!"
BILLY BATSON SAID THAT.
10

HOLY HANNAH!
THAT WAS-- QUITE A CLOUT.

BUT NOW--I CAN UNDERSTAND THE CHEERING VOICES I--
WAIT! SOMEHOW-- SOME WAY--THAT THREE-WAY BRAIN-BATH DID SOMETHING ELSE TO MY HEAD.

I'VE GOT BRUCE BANNER'S MIND AGAIN--EVEN THOUGH I'M IN THE BODY OF-- THE HULK.

AND--IT FEELS JUST FINE!

YOU'VE BEEN THRU A LOT, ROBERT BRUCE BANNER--AND SO YOU ADJUST QUICKLY TO YOUR NEWFOUND SITUATION--
--YES, EVEN TO BEING FITTED AS BECOMES A MIGHTY-MUSCLED KING-TO-BE.

YOU DON'T EVEN MIND BEING THE CENTER OF ATTENTION--STRIDING ALONG THE SCENIC ROUTE TOWARD THE PALACE ROYAL --ALL EYES UPON YOU--

--AND WE DO MEAN ALL.
YOU THINK YOU'VE FOILED MY PLAN TO SUCCEED YOU ONE DAY, DON'T YOU, JARELLA?
WELL, I'VE A THRONE TO WIN--AND WORLDS TO KILL AFTER I DO.
AND NOTHING SHALL STAND IN MY WAY --FOR LONG.

...THIS FAR-OFF WORLD YOU SAY YOU COME FROM, BRUCE, MY BELOVED...DO YOU MISS IT?
I--WON'T LIE TO YOU, JARELLA. YES--I DO.
BUT, IT'S CLEAR THAT YOUR WORLD'S TECHNOLOGY WON'T EVER BE ABLE TO SEND ME BACK.
SO, I'LL BE VERY PROUD TO BE YOUR KING...YOUR PROTECTOR... YOUR HUSBAND.
11

TIME GROWS SHORT. TOO SHORT. THE STRANGER MUST DIE-- JARELLA ALSO!
TONIGHT!
YOU KNOW WHAT YOU ARE TO DO-- WHAT YOU MUST SAY?
YES, LORD VISIS. OUR SWORDS WILL BE SHARP--
--OUR MOTIVES APPEAR NOBLE.
EXCELLENT. I KNOW YOU ASSASSINS OF THE PITLL PAWOB DIVISION ARE SKILLED IN YOUR-- CRAFT.
PRACTICE IT WELL TONIGHT-- AND YOU'LL FIND YOUR FUTURE KING NOT UNGENEROUS.

--BETTY--!
YOU MUST KNOW THAT I'M DOING--THE ONLY THING I CAN DO--WHAT I'D WANT YOU TO DO, IN MY PLACE.
YOU DON'T NEED ME ANY LONGER. THESE PEOPLE DO.
AND--THAT'S SOMETHING NEW FOR THIS GREEN-SKINNED GALOOT--EVEN FOR BRUCE BANNER--
--BEING NEEDED.
12

MAYBE, WITHOUT THE HULK RAMPAGING AROUND, SOMEONE WILL BE ABLE TO CURE YOU OF BEING --TURNED INTO CRYSTAL.
IF I CAME BACK-- TRIED TO HOLD YOU CLOSE--YOU'D JUST BE SHATTERED-- LIKE A GLASS GOBLIN.
SO, I--
WHO--?
FRIENDS OF THE REALM, YOU BRUTISH CLOWN--WHO WANT TO SEE YOU AND JARELLA PAY FOR YOUR MANY SINS.
REPENT, HARLEQUIN--
--SAID THE TICKTOCKMAN.
SEEMS TO ME I READ THAT SOMEPLACE.

BUT, IF YOU CREEPS THINK YOU CAN TAKE THE HULK WITH THOSE PIG-STICKERS--
MMMFF! YOU BOYS MEAN BUSINESS, DON'T YOU?
GET HIM! HE FALLS TO THE PAVING BELOW!
NO MATTER. WHERE HE GOES, WE FOLLOW-- AND WE DESTROY!
13

YOU FALL HEAVY, OUTSIDER--BUT EVEN AS YOU DO, YOU FEEL NOTHING SAVE PITY FOR THOSE WHO WOULD TRY A DULL KNIFE TO SLAY YOU.

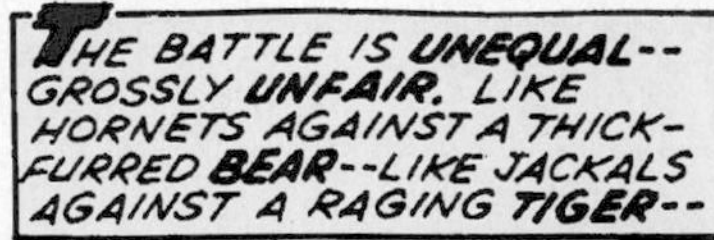
THE BATTLE IS UNEQUAL--GROSSLY UNFAIR. LIKE HORNETS AGAINST A THICK-FURRED BEAR--LIKE JACKALS AGAINST A RAGING TIGER--

--LIKE SANTA CLAUS VS. SPIDER-MAN!
WELL, THAT LITTLE PALACE REVOLT DIDN'T LAST LONG, DID IT?
NOW, AS FOR YOU--
N-NO--DON'T KILL ME--PLEASE--

KILL YOU? WHY, I WOULDN'T THINK OF KILLING YOU, LITTLE MAN.
I'LL JUST DO IT!
A SON OF THE ASSASSINS --NEVER R-REVEALS --
--UNLESS, OF COURSE, YOU TELL ME WHO PUT YOU UP TO THIS STUNT.

NEVER, HARVEY? NOT EVEN WHEN THE MOST POWERFUL HAND IN THE UNIVERSE IS ABOUT TO GIVE YOU A MEAN MASSAGE?
PLEASE, I--I HAVE RECONSIDERED.
AFTER ALL--WHAT DO I OWE A TRAITOR LIKE VISIS?
BROTHER VISIS, EH? I FIGURED AS MUCH.
WELL, I'VE GOT OTHER FISH TO FRY NOW, CHUM...

BY THE WAY, YOU'RE WANTED IN SURGERY...
...AS A PATIENT...!
14

THE CITY HAS BEEN ASLEEP-- WITH STILL HANDS. BUT NOW, IT'S S.R.O. IN THE GREAT HALL OF ASSEMBLY, AS--
--I SPEAK THE TRUTH, MY ADOPTED PEOPLE! A PLOT TO ASSASSINATE YOUR QUEEN AND HER CHOSEN MATE--
--AND SEAT ANOTHER ON THE THRONE OF THRONES!
BASE BETRAYAL! WHO IS GUILTY OF THIS MURDEROUS OUTRAGE?
TELL US-- TELL US-- THAT WE MAY METE OUT JUSTICE-- AND VENGEANCE!

WHY, WHO ELSE--BUT THE MAN WHO HOPED ONE DAY TO SIT UPON THAT THRONE?
WHO BUT THE MAN NAMED-- VISIS?
THEY TOLD YOU! THE SWINE TOLD YOU!

BUT, THERE WILL BE OTHER DAYS-- OTHER WAYS--IF ONLY I CAN--
RUN FOR THE STARS, VISIS-- YOU'LL NOT ESCAPE.
GUARDS!

WE AWAITED BUT YOUR SIGNAL, MAJESTY-- AND NOW WE HAVE HIM.
UNHAND ME, YOU CRETINOUS CLODS!
LET ME FACE MY FATE WITH DIGNITY, AT LEAST.

WELL, OUTSIDER? YOU HAVE USURPED THE THRONE THAT WAS MINE BY RIGHTS.
TAKE MY LIFE, AND WELCOME TO IT. IT MEANS NOTHING TO ME NOW.
THE VERY REASON WHY YOU SHALL HAVE IT, VISIS.
YET, IN ETERNAL EXILE-- IN THE WARTHO-HAUNTED OUTLANDS.
YOU COULD HAVE BEEN A NOBLE, VISIS--AN HONORED PRINCE OF A PROUD PEOPLE.
NOW YOU ARE MERELY ONE OF-- THE DISCARDED.
15

THEN, AS THE ARCH-TRAITOR IS LED AWAY...
FUNNY, I SHOULD FEEL GLAD VISIS GOT WHAT WAS COMING TO HIM.
BUT, I FEEL ONLY PITY... PITY FOR A MAN, LIKE MYSELF, WITHOUT A COUNTRY...WITHOUT A WORLD.
THIS IS YOUR WORLD NOW, MY LOVE...NOW, AND FOREVER.
WILL YOU SPEAK TO THE PEOPLE... OF THE OTHER THING?
YES... I GUESS I WILL.

HEAR ME, CITIZENS! I HAVE... SOMEWHAT BRIGHTER NEWS.
HER HIGHNESS JARELLA HAS CONSENTED TO BECOME, ON THE MORROW, MY WIFE.
FROM THAT DAY, YOUR LAND WILL BE MINE...YOUR CARES, MY CARES!
HAIL HULK!

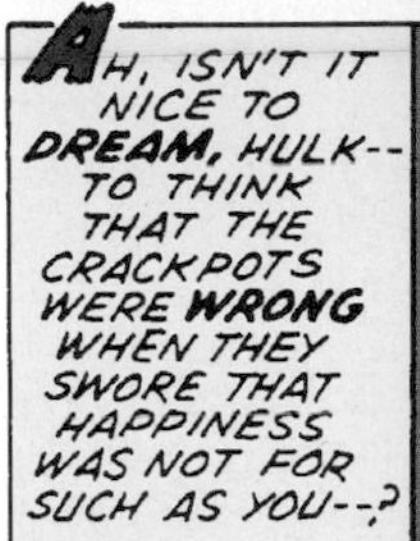
AH, ISN'T IT NICE TO DREAM, HULK-- TO THINK THAT THE CRACKPOTS WERE WRONG WHEN THEY SWORE THAT HAPPINESS WAS NOT FOR SUCH AS YOU--?

SKRUTTCH!
BUT, IT DOESN'T TAKE MUCH TO END A DREAM, DOES IT? NOT MUCH AT ALL--!
HUH? WHAT THE DEVIL IS THAT--?

DON'T YOU RECOGNIZE IT, HULK--BRUCE BANNER? THAT'S THE SOUND OF REALITY PRESSING IN UPON YOU--THE THUNDER OF DREAMS CRASHING INTO RUINED SHARDS ABOUT YOUR FEET!
PREPARE YOURSELF, HULK! YOUR TIME HERE IS ENDED!
THAT VOICE-- NO! IT CAN'T BE--NOT HERE--
NOT NOW! NOT NOW!!
WHAT IS IT, MY BELOVED? WHAT?
16

IT'S PSYKLOP!
HE HAS-- COME FOR ME!
17

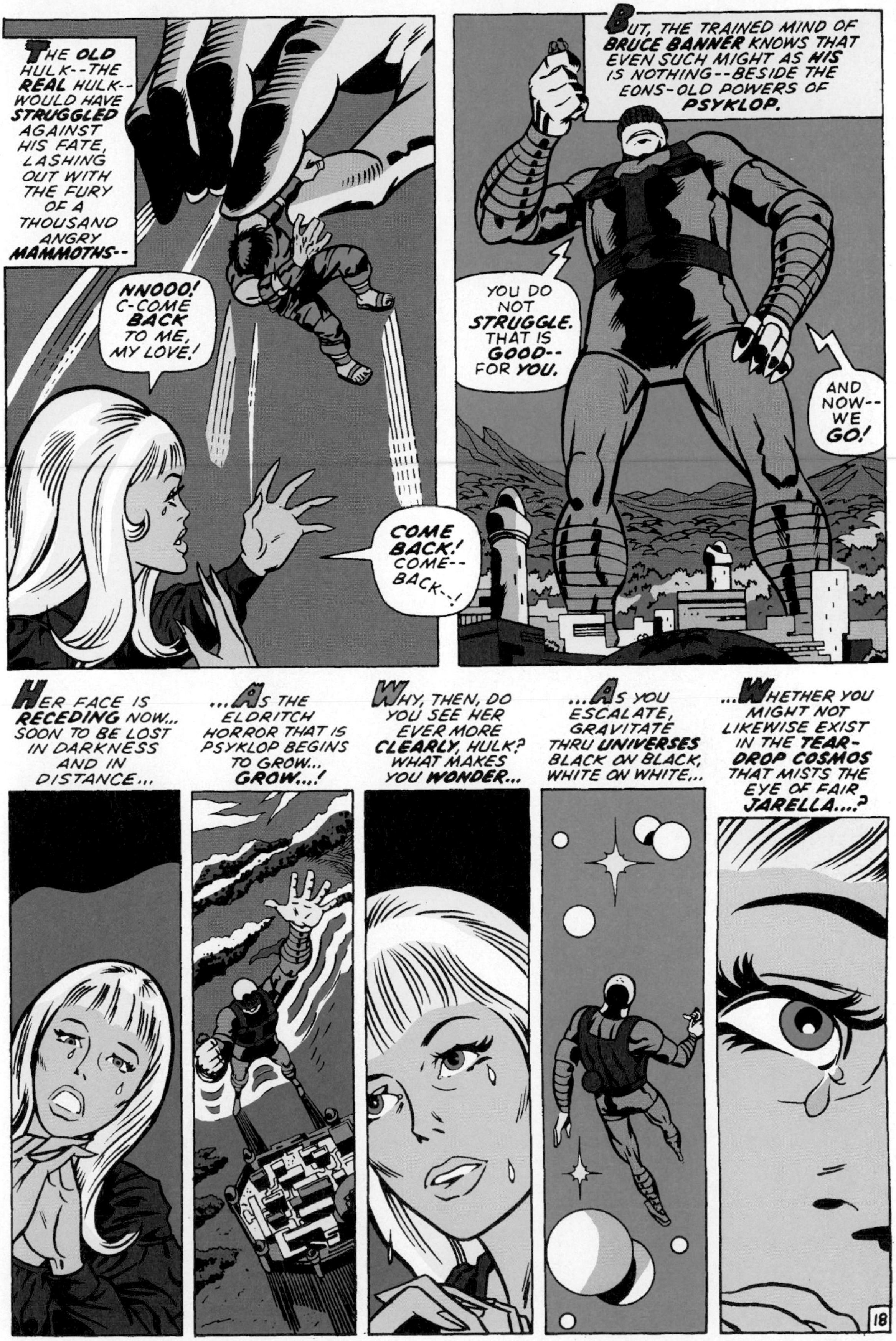

THE OLD HULK--THE REAL HULK--WOULD HAVE STRUGGLED AGAINST HIS FATE, LASHING OUT WITH THE FURY OF A THOUSAND ANGRY MAMMOTHS--

NNOOO! C-COME BACK TO ME, MY LOVE!

COME BACK! COME--BACK--!

BUT, THE TRAINED MIND OF BRUCE BANNER KNOWS THAT EVEN SUCH MIGHT AS HIS IS NOTHING--BESIDE THE EONS-OLD POWERS OF PSYKLOP.

YOU DO NOT STRUGGLE. THAT IS GOOD--FOR YOU.

AND NOW--WE GO!

HER FACE IS RECEDING NOW... SOON TO BE LOST IN DARKNESS AND IN DISTANCE...

...AS THE ELDRITCH HORROR THAT IS PSYKLOP BEGINS TO GROW... GROW...!

WHY, THEN, DO YOU SEE HER EVER MORE CLEARLY, HULK? WHAT MAKES YOU WONDER...

...AS YOU ESCALATE, GRAVITATE THRU UNIVERSES BLACK ON BLACK, WHITE ON WHITE...

...WHETHER YOU MIGHT NOT LIKEWISE EXIST IN THE TEAR-DROP COSMOS THAT MISTS THE EYE OF FAIR JARELLA...?

AND NOW, A FINAL WRENCHING...ONE LAST THRUST UP THRU TIME AND INFRA-SPACE...AND YOU ARE BACK WITHIN THE ALIEN'S PULSING LAB ONCE MORE...
SO--YOU SOMEHOW REGAIN YOUR FORMER SIZE, MONSTER--BUT IT DOES NOT MATTER.
FOR, AS SOON AS I HAVE SEDATED YOU ANEW--
NO!
YOU'RE NOT GOING TO TREAT ME LIKE A GUINEA PIG AGAIN--NOT EVER!

MISSHAPEN MAN-BEAST! I WATCHED YOU IN YOUR SUB-ATOMIC EDEN...WATCHED YOU GROW THOUGHTFUL, AND SOFT, AND WEAK.
CAN SUCH A CREATURE HOPE TO STAND AGAINST ONE WHO HAS SWORN TO SERVE THE DARK GODS?
UNNH

AND PSYKLOP IS RIGHT, HULK--AT LEAST, HE WOULD BE RIGHT, IF YOU STILL POSSESSED THE MIND OF BRUCE BANNER--

BUT, EVEN AS YOU CROUCH THERE, YOU FEEL THE SORCERER'S SPELL SLIP FROM YOU--AND WITH IT, THE LAST VESTIGE OF BANNER'S PERSONALITY--HIS HUMANITY--

FOR, TORLA'S WAS A LITTLE SPELL, CAST IN A LITTLE WORLD--AND NOW IT FADES FROM YOUR GREAT SHOULDERS LIKE THE MORNING DEW--

--AND YOU ARE THE BECLOUDED HULK ONCE MORE--

--WITH THE HULK'S BRUTAL, MINDLESS STRENGTH!
NOW HULK WILL GET YOU--MAKE YOU PAY!

THIS CANNOT BE! IT CANNOT!
ALL MY PREPARATIONS--MY SUBTLE CALCULATIONS--
MAYBE THINGS LIKE THAT WORK--WITH PUNY HUMANS--
BUT YOU ARE FACING THE HULK NOW--DO YOU HEAR--?
19

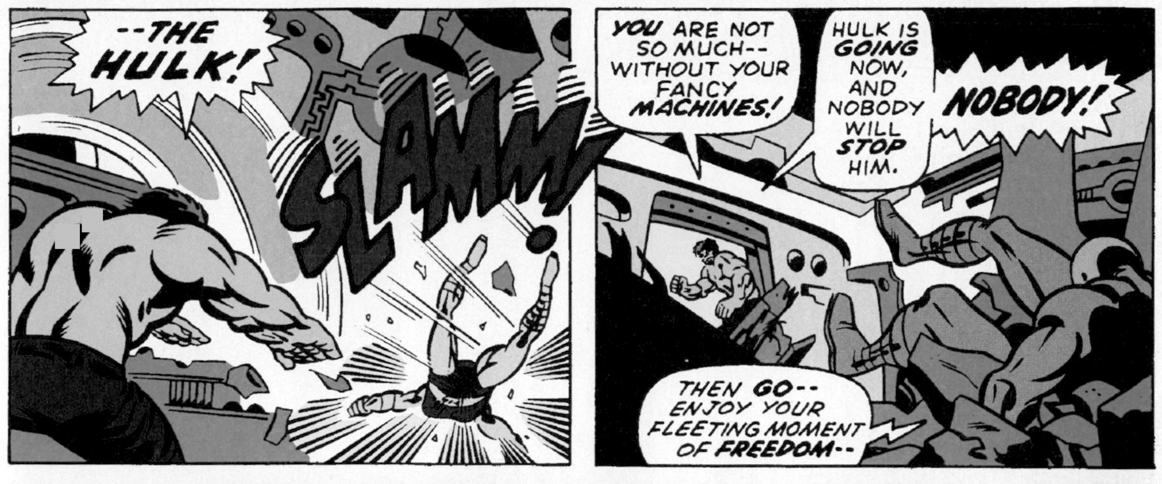

NEXT: DOC SAMSON!

INCREDIBLE HULK

MARVEL COMICS GROUP™

20¢ CC

148 FEB 02456

APPROVED BY THE COMICS CODE AUTHORITY

THE INCREDIBLE HULK™

YOU!! YOU KILLED JARELLA.. THE GIRL HULK LOVES!

FOR THAT... YOU DIE!!

TRIMPE & SEVERIN

THE GIRL IN THE EMERALD ATOM!

THE INCREDIBLE HULK!™
BUT TOMORROW-- THE SUN SHALL DIE!
PROJECT: GREENSKIN BASE MAY BE A GIRDER OR TWO SHY OF COMPLETION...
BUT THAT V.T.O.L.* TRANSPORT AND THE REST OF COMBAT FORCE ONE ARE READY TO MOVE!
WE'LL NAIL THE HULK FOR YOU, CORBEAU...
*V.T.O.L.--VERTICAL TAKE-OFF AND LANDING. --STAN.
AND PETER CORBEAU, DOCTOR OF PHYSICS, NOBEL PRIZE WINNER, SMILES... HE IS USED TO PEOPLE WHO DOUBT, WHO DON'T UNDERSTAND. HADN'T THEY REFUSED TO BELIEVE IN HIS GREATEST TRIUMPH, STARCORE ONE...?
BUT HANGED IF I SEE HOW THAT ORBITING WHOSIS OF YOURS OUT IN SPACE CAN TURN HIM BACK INTO BRUCE BANNER PERMANENTLY!
STAN LEE, EDITOR
ARCHIE GOODWIN, WRITER
HERB TRIMPE, ARTIST
JOHN SEVERIN, INKER
ARTIE SIMEK, LETTERER
WITH A WELCOME PLOTTING ASSIST FROM CHRIS CLAREMONT.
777 Z

YET NOW IT WAS FACT--THE WORLD'S FIRST ORBITING SOLAR REACTOR! A FACT THAT MIGHT BE THE SALVATION OF A COLLEAGUE, A FRIEND...ROBERT BRUCE BANNER!
OF COURSE YOU'RE SKEPTICAL, GENERAL. YOU, YOUR DAUGHTER, AND MAJOR TALBOT HAVE HEARD MANY SUCH THEORIES...AND SEEN THEM FAIL.
BUT ONCE THIS RECEIVER UNIT IS SET UP, I THINK WE'LL SEE MINE SUCCEED...

...PROVIDED, NATURALLY, THAT YOU CAPTURE THE HULK.
EASE YOUR MIND ABOUT THAT, DOCTOR. MY "HULK-BUSTERS" CAN DELIVER!

FUNNY THING IS, IF THEY DO, AND YOUR IDEA WORKS...THIS WHOLE BASE'LL BE OBSOLETE BEFORE IT'S COMPLETED! STILL--
WHAT IS IT, AIRMAN?
THE HULK, SIR! WE'VE GOT A FIX ON 'IM!

SCANNER HAS HIM VECTORED AT COORDINATES TWO-THREE-ZERO-NINER!
GET ALPHA SECTION OF OUR SEARCH-AND-STRIKE SQUADRON ALOFT--
RIGHT NOW!

AND, IN MOMENTS, THE BRIGHT MORNING SKY ABOVE NEW MEXICO IS ALIVE WITH THE WHINE AND THUNDER OF JETS...
BUT THE SOUND MIGHT WELL BE THE BAY OF THE HOUND, THE SHRILL OF THE HORN...
HB 1
A
FOR THESE ARE HUNTERS. THE HUNTERS OF GENERAL "THUNDERBOLT" ROSS...
2

AND THIS LONE FIGURE STRIDING ACROSS THE SOUTHWESTERN WASTELANDS IS THEIR PREY...

...MUCH LESS THE IMPACT OF THEIR SONIC BOOM?!

BUT THERE ARE OTHER WORLDS, OTHER EXISTENCES, OF WHICH WE NEVER DREAM...

AND HERE, AS IN OUR WORLD, THERE ARE HUNTERS. HUNTERS WHO HAUNT THE SKIES...

THEIR TARGET IS THE COLUMN, AND THE WARRIOR-QUEEN WHO RIDES AT ITS HEAD...

BUT NOT TRULY ALONE. FOR, AS SHE FIGHTS, A MEMORY IS WITH HER... OF A GIANT FROM WORLDS BEYOND HERS, WHOSE GROTESQUE FORM MASKED A CHAMPION'S SOUL, WHOSE GREAT COURAGE SAVED K'AI FROM THE PLOTTER, VISIS, AND WON HER HEART...*

AND AS THE THOUGHT OF THIS MAN LONG LOST HAS SUSTAINED AND DRIVEN HER THROUGH ONE ORDEAL...
SO IT CARRIES HER THROUGH MANY AS SHE RETREATS FROM THE WILDS...

UNTIL AT LAST THE PERILOUS TRAVELS END...
AND JARELLA ARRIVES AT THE MOUNTAIN RETREAT OF TORLA, CHIEF SORCERER OF THE REALM.

--BUT OUR REALM MAY CRUMBLE FROM THE FORCES VISIS ARRAYS AGAINST US, TORLA.
REST, MY LADY. LATER WE MAY PLAN.
FOR NOW... A POTION TO REVIVE YOU.

SOON...
ALL BEGAN TO GO AMISS WHEN BRUCE BANNER WAS TAKEN FROM US.
I KNOW NOT WHAT INCREDIBLE REALM NOW HOLDS HIM...
YET IF I COULD FIND IT, AND BRING HIM BACK...
AY. MANY READ IT AS A SIGN AGAINST YOU WHEN THAT ONE CHOSEN TO BE YOUR KING WAS SNATCHED AWAY BY THE HAND OF THE GODS...
I WILL CALL A GATHERING OF THE PANTHEON OF SORCERERS.
BUT A CONJURING OF THE MAGNITUDE YOU REQUIRE COULD WELL SHAKE OUR WORLD...AND THE COSMOS!

AND WHAT OF OUR PART OF THAT COSMOS? HERE TIME MOVES MORE SLOWLY. HERE, PROJECT GREENSKIN BASE IS ABOUT TO RECEIVE THAT WHICH GIVES IT ITS REASON FOR BEING...
AS THE RETRACTABLE ROOF OF THE RADIATION RESEARCH COMPLEX YAWNS WIDE...

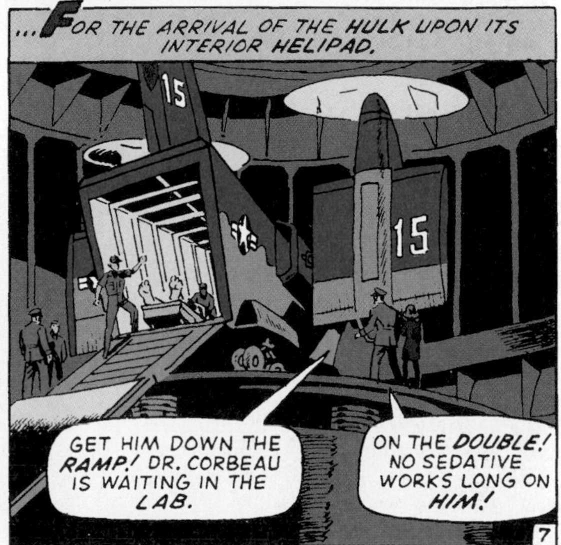
...FOR THE ARRIVAL OF THE HULK UPON ITS INTERIOR HELIPAD.
15
GET HIM DOWN THE RAMP! DR. CORBEAU IS WAITING IN THE LAB.
ON THE DOUBLE! NO SEDATIVE WORKS LONG ON HIM!
7

But for now, the effect ***holds.*** *The Hulk sleeps, and perhaps...* ***dreams.*** *Of a lost, tiny world, a brief moment of happiness... and a girl named* ***Jarella...***

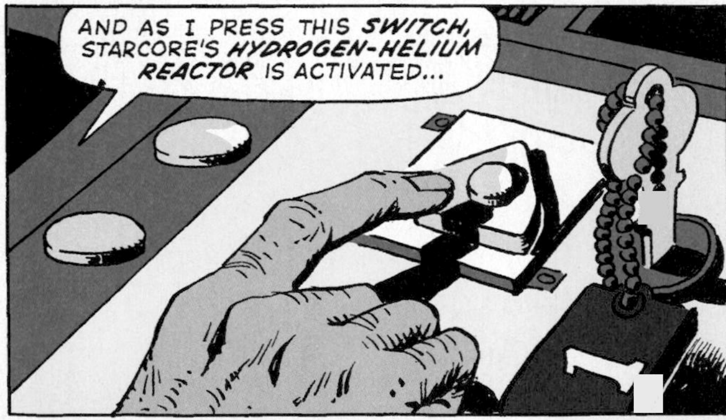

"...IN ONE FANTASTICALLY CONCENTRATED BEAM THAT NOW STRIKES OUR SOLAR-WAVE RECEIVER..."

WHICH FILTERS IT DOWN HERE... TO PLAY OVER THE HULK!
SHEER SOLAR ENERGY PENETRATING EVERY ATOM OF HIS BODY...

ATTACKING AND NEUTRALIZING THE GAMMA RADIATION THAT MADE HIM WHAT HE IS!
WHAT HAPPENS?! SOMETHING HITS HULK... LIKE SHOWER OF FIRE!

IT IS HURTING HULK... CHANGING HULK!
NO! DON'T WANT TO CHANGE...!
DON'T WANT...
CHANGE...
I'M...
I'VE...

C-CHANGED....!
I-IT'S DONE....!
AND HE'S BRUCE AGAIN... MY DARLING, BRUCE!
BUT, CORBEAU... CAN YOU BE CERTAIN IT'S PERMANENT?
9

EVERY-THING CHECKS OUT!
GAMMA RADIATION SENSORS REGISTER ZERO. YOU'VE DONE IT, DR. CORBEAU!
YOU'RE SAFE, BRUCE. WE'VE COMPLETELY NEUTRALIZED THE FORCE THAT TURNS YOU INTO THE HULK!
WELCOME BACK, MY BOY! I MAY HAVE LOST A HULKBUSTER'S BASE, BUT I'VE REGAINED A FUTURE SON-IN-LAW, EH?

GENERAL ROSS! STARCORE ONE IS SIGNALLING SOME KIND OF... SOLAR DISTURBANCE!
CAN YOU GET ANYTHING ON THE LASER-BEAM TRANSVIEWER?
DOWNES USAF

GOOD LORD! A FLARE! LOOK AT IT SHOOTING UP OFF THE SUN'S SURFACE!
IT'S GIGANTIC!
NO ORDINARY SOLAR STORM EVER BEHAVED LIKE THAT! WHY, IF EARTH HAD BEEN IN LINE WITH IT...

...THE HEAT AND RADIATION COULD HAVE KILLED MILLIONS!
YOU'RE THE PRIZE-WINNER IN SOLAR PHYSICS, CORBEAU...

ANY QUICK, INCISIVE THOUGHTS?
ONLY THE MOST OBVIOUS, GENERAL.
SOMEWHAT, SOMEHOW...
IT'S CONNECTED WITH OUR CHANGING BRUCE BANNER FROM BEING THE HULK!
10

AND GREAT MAGIC IT IS. FOR THE DESTINATION OF JARELLA IS INCREDIBLY DISTANT. FOR, HER WORLD IS LOST WITHIN OURS, ONE PARTICLE OF A UNIVERSE LOCKED INSIDE AN ATOM OF OUR OWN! THIS THEN IS THE BARRIER THROUGH WHICH THE SORCERY NOW MOVES JARELLA...

TWO MORE BURSTS OF THE SOLAR FLARE, DR. CORBEAU...PRACTICALLY ON TOP OF EACH OTHER!
IT'S LIKE SOMETHING GIVING THE SUN A SWIFT, HARD KICK!
WHICH BEGS THE QUESTION: WHAT HAPPENS WHEN THE SUN KICKS BACK?

AND IF MY HIGH SCHOOL PHYSICS INSTRUCTOR WAS RIGHT ABOUT ACTIONS HAVING EQUAL AND OPPOSITE REACTIONS...
THAT'S A FRIGHTENINGLY REAL POSSIBILITY!
IN TRANSFERRING SOLAR ENERGY TO THE HULK, WE MAY HAVE SET SOMETHING IN MOTION...
I DON'T LIKE CONTEMPLATING HOW FAR IT COULD GO.

PETE, I'M STILL GROGGY FROM THE CHANGE, BUT IF I READ YOU...IF WHAT YOU SAY IS TRUE...THERE'S ONLY ONE ANSWER.
REVERSE THE PROCESS...MAKE ME THE HULK AGAIN!
HOLD IT, BRUCE... CALM DOWN!
DON'T BE SO QUICK TO PLAY MARTYR...I CAN'T BELIEVE YOU'RE THAT FOND OF GREEN-SKIN AND A TWO-SYLLABLE VOCABULARY.

WE'RE STILL TALKING IN TERMS OF IF, OLD FRIEND.
BEFORE EVEN THINKING OF GIV-ING AWAY THE NEW LIFE WE'VE WON YOU, THIS PHENOMENON GETS CHECKED AND RECHECKED BY EVERY AVAILABLE SOURCE!

THERE'S NO POINT IN YOU SWEATING IT OUT HERE UNTIL WE HAVE.
TAKE THE KEYS TO MY PLACE ON THE COAST, BRUCE.
IT'S PRETTY ISOLATED... BUT THAT CAN BE A BLESSING AT A TIME LIKE THIS.
12

A HOP FROM AN AIR FORCE JET... A RENTED CAR... A RIBBON OF BLACKTOP TWISTING PAST OCEAN-WASHED ROCK AND SAND...

AND BRUCE BANNER IS BROUGHT TO A PLACE LONELY AND REMOVED. A PLACE OF SILENCE, SAVE FOR THE ROLLING WAVES, THE CRYING GULLS... AND, CURIOUSLY FOR ONE WHOSE LIFE, WHOSE SANITY, MAY BE IN THE BALANCE...
...A PLACE OF PEACE.

PETE WAS RIGHT ABOUT THIS SPOT. THERE'S AN APARTNESS, A TIMELESSNESS, A MAN CAN LOSE HIMSELF IN...
PERHAPS I SHOULD HAVE BROUGHT BETTY... BUT SOMETHING KEPT ME FROM IT...
SOME VAGUE THOUGHT OR MEMORY. BUT WAS IT MINE... OR THE HULK'S?

OR PERHAPS BOTH, AND ONE THING MORE...
...THE TOUCH OF MAGIC.
THAT WEIRD GLOW ON THE BEACH--!
FORMING INTO SOMETHING...

A GIRL! NO... NOT JUST A GIRL, BUT--
MY LAST FEAR PASSES... YOU REMEMBER ME, BRUCE BANNER!
EVEN AS I RECOGNIZE YOU...
THOUGH YOUR FORM IS NOT THAT OF THE MIGHTY ONE WHO STRODE MY WORLD!*
JARELLA!
*DURING THAT SUB-ATOMIC SOJOURN, THE HULK'S BODY HAD BANNER'S MIND-- STAN.
THE MEMORY WAS HIDDEN, JARELLA, BUT I COULDN'T TRULY FORGET OUR BRIEF TIME TOGETHER...
THE ONLY TIME THE HULK AND I--
--EXISTED HAPPILY AS ONE!
13

BUT SUCH TIMES ARE NOT EASILY RECAPTURED. MANY SHADOWS LOOM TO SPOIL THIS ONE...
NOT THE LEAST IS THAT CAST BY FIALAN, ASSASSIN SUPREME!
I HAVE BEEN CARRIED AFTER THE EMPRESS, AS LORD VISIS PREDICTED.
MY TASK WILL BE ABSURDLY SIMPLE.

OBVIOUSLY TORLA WORKED FURTHER MAGIC TO ENABLE JARELLA TO UNDERSTAND THIS WORLD'S TONGUE...
BUT NO SORCERER'S SPELL SHALL SHIELD HER FROM MY WEAPON, OR--
BUT HARK--! THAT SOUND...

SOME MANNER OF FLYING CRAFT DESCENDS!
IT IS AS AWESOME AS THE GIANT WARTHOS OF OUR WORLD!
NO MASTER OF THE ASSASSIN'S ART STRIKES IN THE FACE OF UNKNOWN FACTORS. I MUST WAIT...FOR NOW.

BANNER, I'M SORRY, BUT I'VE BEEN SENT TO--
YOU NEEDN'T SAY IT, MAJ. TALBOT. THUNDERBOLT ROSS WOULDN'T SEND A CHOPPER AND HIS TOP SECURITY OFFICER JUST TELL ME EVERYTHING'S PEACHY...
THE LADY AND I WILL BE RIGHT WITH YOU.

AND...
ABOUT THAT GIRL, BANNER. I DIDN'T WANT TO SAY ANYTHING IN FRONT OF HER, BUT--
CONGRATULATIONS, TALBOT.
I WAS AFRAID THE MILITARY HAD DRUMMED ALL THE CURIOSITY OUT OF YOU.
IF A BEAUTIFUL GIRL WITH GREEN SKIN DIDN'T PROMPT A QUESTION OR TWO...
WELL, I'M ASKING THEM, MAN. WHAT'S THE STORY...?!
14

AND THAT STORY OF THE HULK IN A MICRO-UNIVERSE IS TOLD SEVERAL TIMES...
INCREDIBLE! I CAN'T BLAME YOU, BANNER...BUT WHAT ABOUT BETTY? HAVE YOU CONSIDERED HER FEELINGS IF SHE LEARNS OF THIS JARELLA?
I'VE SCARCELY HAD TIME TO EXAMINE MY OWN, GENERAL.
RIGHT NOW, I GATHER DR. CORBEAU HAS A PROBLEM THAT MAKES ANY OF OUR INDIVIDUAL ONES PRETTY PETTY!

AND, IN A WORD, THAT PROBLEM IS...
--NOVA, PETE? AS A REACTION AGAINST THOSE SOLAR FLARINGS, OUR SUN'S GOING NOVA?!
STUDY THESE INFRA-DIAGRAMS STARCORE ONE'S BEEN SENDING...
OL' SOL HAS FOUND A WAY OF KICKING BACK ALL RIGHT... BY BLOWING ITSELF UP!

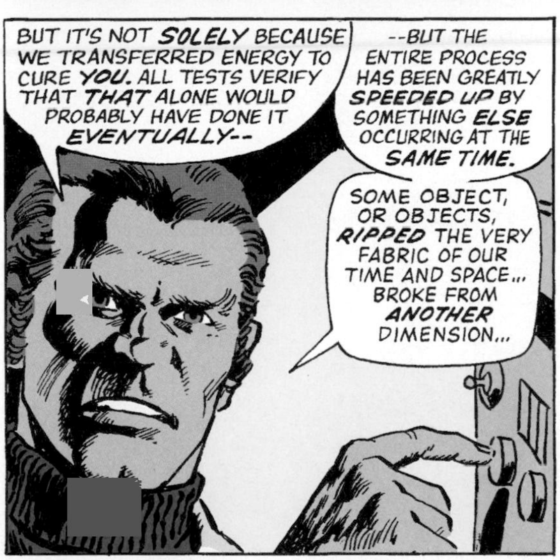
BUT IT'S NOT SOLELY BECAUSE WE TRANSFERRED ENERGY TO CURE YOU. ALL TESTS VERIFY THAT THAT ALONE WOULD PROBABLY HAVE DONE IT EVENTUALLY--
--BUT THE ENTIRE PROCESS HAS BEEN GREATLY SPEEDED UP BY SOMETHING ELSE OCCURRING AT THE SAME TIME.
SOME OBJECT, OR OBJECTS, RIPPED THE VERY FABRIC OF OUR TIME AND SPACE... BROKE FROM ANOTHER DIMENSION...

...INTO OUR OWN! THE SUN'S REACTION IS THE RESULT.
PETE!
B-BUT... THAT SOUNDS MUCH LIKE THE JOURNEY TORLA'S SPELL--
YES. I'M SORRY...

HAVING HEARD THE STORY OF YOUR COMING, JARELLA, I CAN'T BELIEVE ANYTHING ELSE. BUT THE SUN IS A DAY FROM CRITICAL POINT...
IF A RETURN IS AFFECTED BEFORE THEN... THE BALANCE MIGHT BE RESTORED, THE TIME-SPACE FISSURE HEALED!
PETE, THERE'S A MADMAN AND HIS ARMY WAITING IN THAT WORLD TO DESTROY JARELLA!

I KNOW, BRUCE, AND I'M WORKING ON SOMETHING...
BUT IF OUR SOLAR SYSTEM BURNS TO A CRISP...HER SUB-ATOMIC COSMOS GOES WITH IT AS WELL!
BASE COMMUNICATIONS? I WANT A PRIORITY LINE TO NICK FURY OF SHIELD!
15

SHIELD! ELITE AMONG AMERICA'S TOP SECRET DEFENSE ORGANIZATIONS...
WHY ELITE? PERHAPS FOR ITS ABILITY TO DO SUCH AS WE SEE HAPPENING NOW. WHAT SOME MIGHT CALL...
IMPOSSIBLE! I DON'T BELIEVE ANYTHING SUCH AS YOU ASKED FOR COULD EXIST, CORBEAU...
LET ALONE THAT AN OUTFIT COULD HAVE IT READY IN JUST OVER EIGHTEEN HOURS!
DON'T FORGET, GENERAL ROSS...
THEY'VE GOT THE SERVICES OF AN INVENTIVE GENIUS LIKE TONY STARK...

"...AND A HOWLING DYNAMO OF A RAMROD!"
NICK FURY! SINCE WHEN DOES SHIELD'S DIRECTOR PLAY DELIVERY BOY?
COULDN'T RESIST GETTIN' TOGETHER AGAIN WITH A FELLA STOGIE-CHOMPER, GENERAL.*
*THEY FIRST MET IN HULK #106.--STAN

AND I WANTED TA PERSONALLY MAKE SURE THIS LIFE MODEL DECOY DOC CORBEAU WANTED MADE IT.
WITH THE WHOLE BLASTED SUN AT STAKE, WHO TAKES CHANCES?
T-THIS IS SORCERY AS GREAT AS TORLA'S...!

ONLY HERE WE CALL IT SCIENCE, JARELLA. TO REPAIR THE SPACE-TIME RIFT, WE HAVE TO RESTORE EXACTLY WHAT WAS TAKEN FROM YOUR WORLD.
BUT SINCE THIS LMD DUPLICATES YOU PERFECTLY, WE CAN RETURN IT IN YOUR PLACE!
TIME'S GETTING SHORT, CORBEAU. HOW'S BANNER COMING WITH THOSE LAB EQUIPMENT MODIFICATIONS?

--DONE! WHAT WITH REED RICHARDS AND HENRY PYM CONTRIBUTING THEIR EXPERTISE...
PLUS MY KNOW-HOW COMBINED WITH PETE'S...
THERE'S NO QUESTION WE CAN MAKE THE INTER-DIMENSIONAL TRANSFER.
IT LOOKS LIKE WE MAY PULL THIS OFF!
AND WITHOUT MY BECOMING THE HULK AGAIN--
16

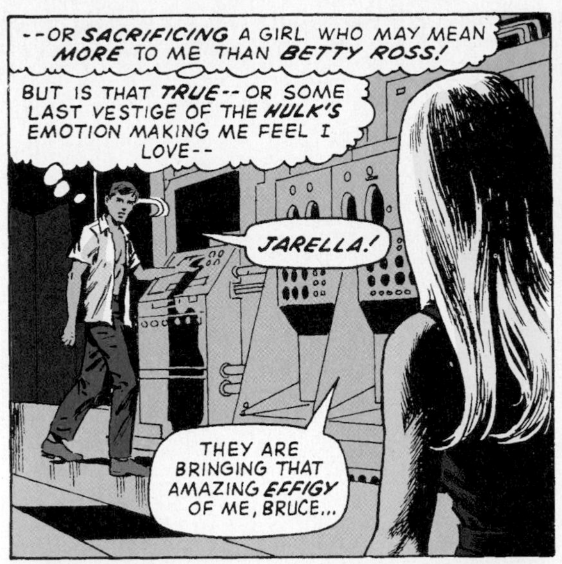
--OR SACRIFICING A GIRL WHO MAY MEAN MORE TO ME THAN BETTY ROSS!
BUT IS THAT TRUE--OR SOME LAST VESTIGE OF THE HULK'S EMOTION MAKING ME FEEL I LOVE--
JARELLA!
THEY ARE BRINGING THAT AMAZING EFFIGY OF ME, BRUCE...

YOU MUST HAVE BEEN ANXIOUS TO SPEAK ALONE TO THIS MAN, O QUEEN OF K'AI.
YOU RUSHED AHEAD OF THOSE OTHERS WHOSE PRESENCE STAYED MY HAND.
BUT NOTHING DELAYS ME NOW! I NEED BUT RELEASE MY WEAPON'S SAFETY DEVICE AND--

AND THE SENSES OF A MAN WHO HAS BEEN HOUNDED AND HUNTED FOR YEARS ARE SUDDENLY STIRRED BY THAT SLIGHTEST OF NOISES!
ZTAK!
DOWN, JARELLA!

ZRRAP!
I KNOW THAT SOUND, BRUCE BANNER!
THE FORCE BLASTER OF A PTILL PAWOB ASSASSIN!
STAY LOW! THOSE BURSTS CAN'T BE BROUGHT TO BEAR ON US!

YOUR WORDS ARE MEANINGLESS, OTHERWORLDER. BUT IF YOU SPEAK OF HIDING...
KNOW THAT SUCH IS IMPOSSIBLE FROM ONE WHO WEARS THE BANDS OF LEVITATION!
MASTER ASSASSINS CARRY WEAPONS LOST TO THE REST OF MY WORLD--WE ARE FINISHED, BRUCE!

BUT THOUGH LEVITATION HAS BROUGHT FIALAN INTO PROJECT GREENSKIN UNDETECTED, THE BLASTS FROM HIS WEAPON HAVE SET OFF SENSOR-ALARMS.
WHICH QUICKLY BRING...
17

GUARDS!
BUT EVEN THEY CANNOT STAND BEFORE MY BLASTER'S FORCE.
IF ONLY MORE SUCH ARMAMENT HAD SURVIVED FROM THE GREAT CIVILIZATIONS OF MY PLANET'S PAST--
--WE ASSASSINS ELITE WOULD BE NOT HIRELINGS ...BUT RULERS!

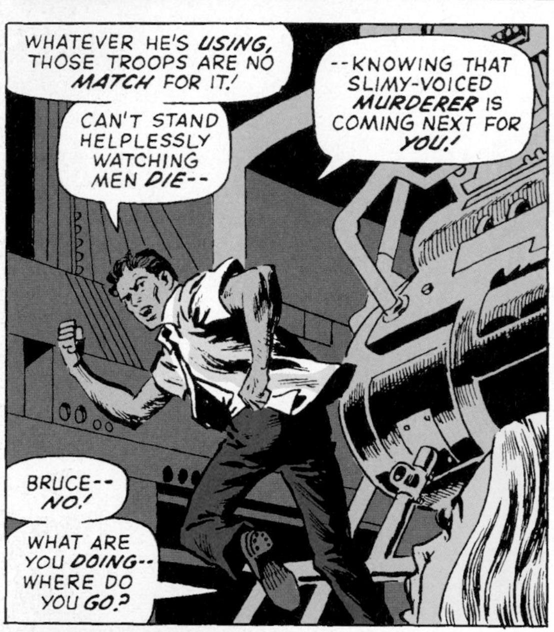
WHATEVER HE'S USING, THOSE TROOPS ARE NO MATCH FOR IT!
CAN'T STAND HELPLESSLY WATCHING MEN DIE--
--KNOWING THAT SLIMY-VOICED MURDERER IS COMING NEXT FOR YOU!
BRUCE-- NO!
WHAT ARE YOU DOING-- WHERE DO YOU GO?

SO! JARELLA'S OTHERWORLDER FLEES! THAT CHAMBER WILL BE NO PROTECTION. ONE BLAST AND--
BUT IN BATTLING, I HAVE LOST SIGHT OF MY TRUE VICTIM! IT MATTERS NOT WHERE THIS ONE SCURRIES.
IT IS THE QUEEN WHO NOW MUST DIE!

YOU HAVE MOVED SWIFTLY THROUGH THIS MAZE-LIKE COMPLEX, EMPRESS...
BUT HARDLY FAST ENOUGH TO ESCAPE THE VENGEANCE OF LORD VISIS--

--AS DELIVERED BY THE ARTFUL HAND OF THE ASSASSIN SUPREME...
FIALAN!
18

BUT FOR THE FIRST TIME IN COUNTLESS KILLS, THAT HAND SHAKES...
AS THE VERY AIR SEEMS TO VIBRATE WITH A HIGH-PITCHED WHINE.
W-WHAT?! IT COMES FROM--

FROM THE CHAMBER WHERE YOU SAW BRUCE BANNER SCURRY, FIALAN...
THE CHAMBER WHERE, A DAY AGO, SOLAR ENERGY FROM THE STARCORE ONE REACTOR MADE HIM AN ORDINARY MAN AGAIN...
THE CHAMBER WHERE, DESPITE MISGIVINGS AND FEARS, THE PROCESS HAS BEEN REVERSED...

...AND ROBERT BRUCE BANNER IS ORDINARY NO LONGER!
THWOM!
HULK LIVES!

THE BRUTE JARELLA CHOSE OVER LORD VISIS!
IF YOU LIVE, MONSTER--
--IT IS BUT TO BE SLAIN!
THE WEAPON PAINS BUT DOES NOT STOP THE HULK...THAT IS DONE BY WHAT HE SEES AS FIALAN LEVITATES UPWARD!
YOU ARE...JARELLA! YOU...LOVED HULK!
HULK REMEMBERS NOW. YOU ARE IN DANGER!
THAT'S WHY PUNY BANNER LET HULK COME BACK.
BUT WHY DO YOU LOOK LIKE THAT? HULK IS HERE TO HELP YOU, SAVE YOU!
BUT THOUGH THE EMERALD-HUED GIRL STARES...
SHE CANNOT SEEM TO SPEAK, TO SHOUT, OF THE FORGOTTEN ENEMY...
CAUTION
RADIO-ACTIVE ELEMENT
ACCESS PANEL

19

...OR OF HIS WEAPON LEVELED AT THE ARRAY OF EQUIPMENT BEHIND THEM...
ZRAK!

...VOLATILE EQUIPMENT!

I THOUGHT SUCH VAST MACHINERY MIGHT REACT THUSLY...
YET IT WAS POTENT BEYOND MY EXPECTATIONS!
AND WELL PERHAPS THAT IT WAS.
FOR NOW IT IS CERTAIN. NEITHER QUEEN NOR HER BRUTE SURVI--

BUT THERE ARE FEW CERTAINTIES, FIALAN. AND MOST UNCERTAIN OF ALL IS--
THE HULK!
SHE IS DEAD. HULK FINALLY FINDS JARELLA... AND YOU KILL HER!
GODS OF K'AI...!
YOU!

MY BANDS OF LEVITATION...! THE BLAST DAMAGED THEM!
YOU!

YOU KILL THE ONE GIRL WHO LOVES HULK FOR WHAT HE IS!
AND NOW--

HULK KILLS YOU!
20

HULK DID IT...
BUT...
IT DOES NOT BRING JARELLA BACK...!

HULK IS ALONE AGAIN.
MORE ALONE THAN EVER.
NO... NO, MY LOVE!

WHAT YOU SAW DIE WAS A REPLICA... A MACHINE... THAT WAS LIKE ME.
FIALAN MADE THE SAME MISTAKE.
HULK DOESN'T UNDERSTAND. BUT YOU ARE REAL... YOU ARE BACK. AND HULK WILL SEE NOBODY TAKES YOU AWAY AGAIN!
GET CORBEAU... AND MORE HELP, TALBOT! WE SAVED THE GIRL BY TURNING LOOSE THAT LMD DURING THE ASSASSIN'S ATTACK...
BUT WHO KNOWS WHAT WILL HAPPEN NOW?

HULK, LISTEN... YOU MUST LET JARELLA COME WITH US. SOMETHING TERRIBLE IS HAPPENING TO THE SUN... IT COULD DESTROY YOU, THE WORLD.
WITH THE LMD GONE, ONLY JARELLA CAN SAVE US.

TIME IS VANISHING. CAN YOU COMPREHEND, TRY TO SEE...?
HULK SEES YOU WANT TO TAKE ONLY GOOD THING IN HIS LIFE!
DON'T CARE ABOUT THE SUN... THE WORLD... ONLY JARELLA!
TOUCH HER AND SEE HOW FAST THE HULK CAN SMASH!
21

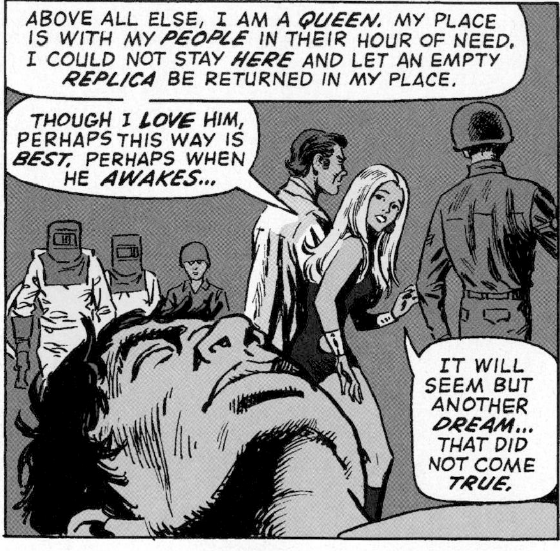

AND IT IS BUT MINUTES LATER THAT WORD IS DELIVERED TO GENERAL ROSS...

NEXT: HIS LEGACY IS OUR EARTH--"THE INHERITOR!"

Despite Jarella's prediction, she remained far more than a simple dream in the mind of both the Hulk and Bruce Banner. The Hulk's memories of her drove him into conflicts with the green-haired Polaris and others, and Banner's love for Jarella caused him to end his relationship with his fiancée, Betty Ross, driving her into the arms of his long-time rival, Glenn Talbot. Banner sought out the assistance of Dr. Henry Pym (Ant-Man) in returning to Jarella's subatomic world, but the interference of the Chameleon resulted in Bruce's becoming trapped on the Microversal planetoid Moto, apparently an Earth-like world conquered by time-lost Nazis. In reality, the world was actually a plaything of the dream-granting Shaper of Worlds, who had given Nazi Otto Kronsteig his heart's desires. By defeating Kronsteig's "Captain Axis" alter ego, the Hulk destroyed the Nazi's dreams, and the angry Shaper demanded that Hulk realize his own dreams as compensation. At last the Hulk was presented with his longed-for Jarella, but knowing her to be nothing more than a dream the monster angrily rejected this false Jarella, preferring the eternal pursuit of his true love over a mere facsimile.

Incredible Hulk #155 — Art by Herb Trimpe

Faced with the unprecedented rejection of his gifts, the Shaper focused his energies on the emerald behemoth, transporting him away into interdimensional space. This was "the power of the Shaper, Hulk, being used as it has never been used before... to bring another to his dream, instead of another's dream to me."

INCREDIBLE HULK
MARVEL COMICS GROUP
20¢ 156 OCT 02456
APPROVED BY THE COMICS CODE AUTHORITY
THE INCREDIBLE HULK
YOU!! YOU LOOK LIKE HULK-- BUT I AM HULK! I AM!
NO!! WE'RE BOTH THE HULK--BUT AT LAST, I'VE GOT BRUCE BANNER'S BRAIN!
AND IF ONE OF US HAS TO DIE.. IT WON'T BE ME!
IT'S HULK VS. HULK.. AT THE HEART OF THE ATOM!

THE INCREDIBLE HULK!

HENRY PYM'S SIZE-REDUCTION SERUM...THE AWESOME POWER OF THE SHAPER.* IT TOOK BOTH--
--PLUS A LOT OF STRIFE TO GET FROM THAT BIG, BLACK BEYOND TO HERE.
*STRANGE BEING OF YET ANOTHER MICRO-WORLD INTRODUCED LAST ISH-- ROY.

BUT TO RETURN TO THE ONE PLACE WHERE PHYSICIST BRUCE BANNER AND HIS GREEN, GAMMA-RAY SPAWNED ALTER-EGO CAN PEACEFULLY CO-EXIST--
--IT WAS WORTH IT!
AND THIS TRIP... I'M HERE TO STAY.

BETTY ROSS, JIM WILSON, ALL THE OTHERS OF EARTH WHO CARED, WHO TRIED TO HELP-- YOU'LL BE REMEMBERED... AND MISSED.
BUT FREE FROM THE SHADOW OF THE HULK, YOU'LL BE SAFER...HAPPIER.
AND IF THIS FAMILIAR LOOK-ING TRAIL LEADS WHERE I THINK-- TO A CITY CALLED K'AI, A LOVELY LADY NAMED JARELLA--
A CUT OF THAT HAPPINESS MAY JUST BE MINE!

YES! HERE'S WHERE THE HULK BATTLED THOSE GREAT BEASTS-- WHAT WERE THEY CALLED--?
--WARTHOS. AND FROM THIS POINT I SHOULD BE ABLE TO SEE--
THE CITY!
OH, LORD...!

JARELLA'S HOME!
THE GREAT JADE CITY WHERE SHE RULED AS QUEEN--
NOTHING BUT RUIN... RUIN AND UTTER DESOLATION!
2.

PERHAPS IF YOU WERE THE OLD--THE TRUE--HULK, THIS GRIM SCENE MIGHT NOT HOLD YOU SO. YOU MIGHT BE LOOKING WARILY, IMPATIENTLY ABOUT--
--AND SEE THE SILENT RIDERS CROSSING THE MOON'S BRIGHT FACE--

--AS YOU HAVE BEEN SEEN, AND SINGLED FOR ATTACK!
TO ME, NIGHT PATROL--!
WRAK!
UNGHHH!
K'AI'S RUINS YIELD ANOTHER TRAITOR TO LORD VISIS!
HA! SEE HOW THE FOOL IS SHOCKED... HURT!

YOU MILK-BLOODED FOLLOWERS OF JARELLA ARE ALL THE SAME.
EVEN A GREAT-BODIED LUMP SUCH AS YOU HAS NO TASTE FOR BATTLE!
BOK!
ONLY FOR COMING TO THIS PLACE BY NIGHT TO MOURN HER DEFEAT!

YEAH, BALDY... YOU CAUGHT ME SHORT.
FORGOT FOR A MOMENT WHO I WAS, WHAT I'D BECOME.
THOM!
BUT A FEW WHACKS ON THE HEAD TEND TO REMIND YOU!
BRUCE BANNER'S GENTLE, CIVILIZED MIND NOT WITHSTANDING--

--I'M STILL VERY MUCH THE HULK!

3.

AND I WON'T FORGET IT AGAIN... EVER!
NOW LET'S DISCUSS THAT "NO TASTE FOR BATTLE" BUSINESS, GUYS--

--OR DID YOU SUDDENLY RECALL A PREVIOUS ENGAGEMENT?
FOR A FORMERLY MILD-MANNERED SCIENTIST, HASSLING A FEW BAD GUYS MAY BE FUN, BANNER--
BUT IT ISN'T FACING THE BIG PROBLEM.
NAMELY: WHAT'S HAPPENING ON THIS WORLD YOU WERE SO HAPPY TO REACH AGAIN?

THERE WAS WAR BETWEEN JARELLA AND THE EXILED TRAITOR, VISIS.
SHOULD HAVE REMEMBERED THAT FROM HER VISIT TO EARTH.*
NOW THAT SEEMS TO HAVE ENDED... FOR THE WORSE! BUT WHAT--
SNAP!
UH-OH! SOUNDS LIKE NEW PLAYMATES...
*HULK #148-- RASCALLY.

GUESS AGAIN, LEADFOOT! SNEAKING FROM THE WOODS--
--WON'T WORK AGAINST ME ANY BETTER THAN THAT LITTLE AERIAL JOBBY.
IN FACT, IT'S GOING TO BE A LOT WORSE FOR Y--

GODS OF K'AI! A MIRACLE! 'TIS YOU... BRUCE BANNER.
CHOSEN ONE OF THE QUEEN!
DO YOU NOT RECALL TORLA, O HERO OF THE REALM?
--CHIEF SORCERER OF OUR GRACIOUS LADY?
4.

TORLA...OF COURSE. BUT... THE QUEEN, MAN! BEFORE WE TALK OF ANYTHING ELSE--
TELL ME WHAT'S HAPPENED TO JARELLA!
YOU ASK ME TO SPEAK OF SITUATIONS SHAMEFUL INDEED, BRUCE BANNER.

FOR THIS MOTLEY BAND-- AND A FEW SCATTERED OTHERS --ARE WHAT REMAINS OF K'AI'S LEGIONS. HARRIED, HARASSED OUTLAWS IN OUR OWN REALM!
AND THE QUEEN HAS BEEN TAKEN BY THE WREAKER OF THIS HAVOC--
VISIS!

"AY," SAYS TORLA--
"WITHIN HIS MOUNTAIN STRONGHOLD, THE TRAITOR HOLDS OUR LADY HELPLESS PRISONER--

"--SEEKING TO BEND, TO BREAK HER FOR HIS OWN DEVIOUS ENDS."
ANOTHER REFUSAL, O QUEEN? THIS GAME WEARIES ME.
THEN END IT, VISIS... AND MY LIFE AS WELL.
BEFORE I AGREE TO MARRY YOU, AND BY DOING SO MAKE LEGITIMATE YOUR USURPING OF MY THRONE--
I CHOOSE DEATH!
YOU CHOOSE, MADAM?
YOU'D BEST JOIN ME IN A SHORT WALK, JARELLA--

--AND LEARN THAT IF CHOICES DO EXIST IN THIS MATTER--
--THEY ARE FOR VISIS ALONE TO MAKE!

5.

NOW, JARELLA... OBSERVE.
THE DUNGEONS OF MY KEEP ARE VAST... NOT ALL ARE SO PLEASANT AS YOURS, EH?
THOSE MEN... I RECOGNIZE SOME OF THEM.
OF COURSE. ALL WERE ONCE SUBJECTS OF YOURS--
AND ALL WILL BE SLAIN WITH YOUR NEXT REFUSAL!

AND THIS IS NOT THE ONLY SUCH PIT. THERE ARE OTHERS. SOME WITH WOMEN, CHILDREN...
FOR EVERY NO YOU GIVE ME, ONE WILL BE EMPTIED, PROUD EMPRESS.
BUT A YES WILL SAVE THEM, FREE THEM... THAT IS THE CHOICE I OFFER, JARELLA!

VERY WELL, VISIS... I SHALL BE YOUR BRIDE.
BUT THE DOWRY I BRING WILL BE BITTER INDEED!
HATRED AND CONTEMPT FOR YOU... THAT IS MY DOWRY.
ALONG WITH LAUGHTER... THE DAY YOU DRAW YOUR FINAL BREATH!

LOOK NOW TO ANOTHER, LARGER WORLD. THE ONE THAT IS OUR OWN. AND HERE, AT THIS MOON-LIT RESORT, WE WILL SEE THE OFFERING OF A SIMILAR, AND AT ONCE VASTLY DIFFERENT CHOICE.
I NEEDED THIS TIME, TO RELAX, TO THINK... ABOUT ME, ABOUT BRUCE--
--AND YOU, GLENN. I'M GLAD YOU TOOK LEAVE TIME TO JOIN ME.
6.

I'M SORRY IT COULDN'T BE LONGER, BETTY. BUT BEFORE I RETURN TO THE BASE--
THERE'S SOMETHING I MUST ASK. MAYBE IT'S TOO SOON AFTER WHAT HAPPENED TO BANNER, BUT--
GLENN, EVEN BEFORE EVERYONE GAVE BRUCE UP AS LOST--
EVERYTHING SEEMED TO HAVE CHANGED BETWEEN US...PERHAPS PERMANENTLY.

BETTY, DOES THAT MEAN--?
GLENN, IT MEANS WHAT'S PAST IS PAST. I DON'T REGRET WHAT I ALMOST HAD WITH BRUCE--
BUT IT'S TIME NOW TO THINK OF THE FUTURE. AND IF THAT FUTURE MEANS MARRIAGE FOR YOU AND ME--

IT DOES, BETTY. BELIEVE ME, DARLING--
IT DOES!
ON EARTH THEN, THE BEGINNING OF A NEW RELATIONSHIP; WHILE IN JARELLA'S SUB-ATOMIC WORLD--

--A PLAN OF ACTION IS ABOUT TO BE LAUNCHED!
JUST WHAT I'VE BEEN LOOKING FOR.

AND WITH ONE MIGHTY THOOM A TINY TITAN CRASHES AMIDST A GATHERING OF GIANTS...
WARTHOS!
PART PIG, PART CANINE--ALL TROUBLE!
7.

AND JUST ABOUT IDEAL FOR WHAT I'VE GOT IN MIND--
WOM!
--ONCE I GET THROUGH REASONING WITH THEM!

DON'T CROWD-- EVERYONE GETS A TURN!
BA-DOM!
BUT WHAT I'M REALLY AFTER--

--IS YOU!
THE LEADER OF THE PACK!
KA-THUD!

LET HOURS PASS. SHIFT IN PLACE TO A CASTLE. GAZE INTO ITS GREAT HALL, WHERE...
THE BRIDE ARRIVES! STAND READY, PRIEST.
BUT BEFORE SHE IS WITHIN HEARING--
--CAPTAIN OF THE GUARD, DISPATCH PATROLS TO RECAPTURE OR SLAY ALL PRISONERS FREED THIS MORNING!

AH, JARELLA! YOU DO MERE WEDDING GARMENTS GREAT JUSTICE!
IN THE DUNGEONS, I MAY HAVE DWELLED OVERMUCH ON MATTERS POLITIC--
BUT FOR ALL MY ROUGH AND READY WAYS, I AM NOT BLIND TO BEAUTY.
YOU'LL COME TO LOVE ME, MADAM.

8.

BA-KOOM!
NO--! AND IT'S NOT A BIRD, OR A PLANE--
--OR THE FINALE OF AN OLD MGM TARZAN FLICK.
JUST THE HULK--AND HIS TROOP OF TRAINED WARTHOS!
DOING A VARIATION ON LOCHINVAR--
--OR MAYBE, THE GRADUATE!
NOT THAT MY CUTSEY REFERENCES HAVE MUCH MEANING HERE--

9.

IN DAYS THAT FOLLOW, MINSTRELS COMPOSE SONGS OF THE RAID, OF JARELLA'S RESCUE BY HER OTHER-WORLDLY HERO...

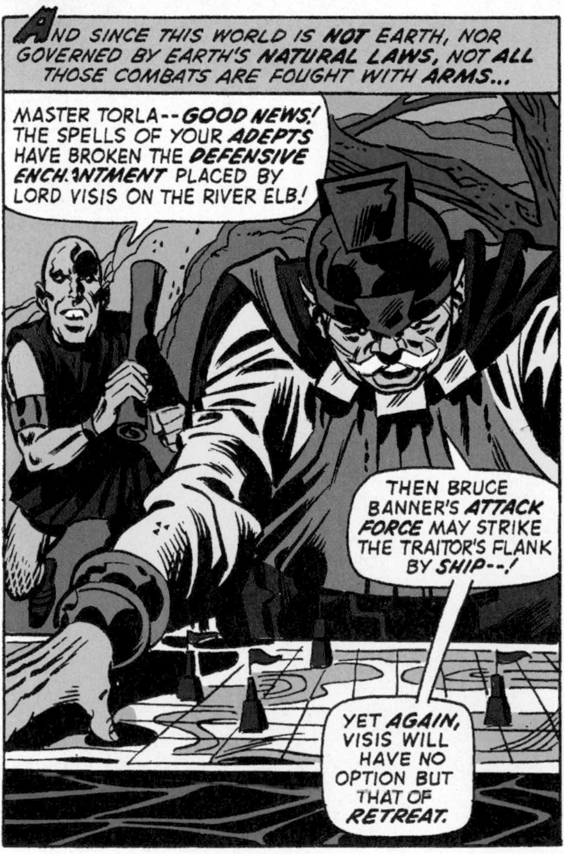

10.

A CIVILIZATION THAT CRUMBLED INTO THE SEA, WITH BUT FEW SURVIVING. NOW THEIR DESCENDENTS TRY TO MAINTAIN WHAT REMAINS OF THAT LOST TECHNOLOGY, HIRING OUT WEAPONS AND THEMSELVES--

YOU ARE ARROGANT, O STEWARD OF ALL ASSASSINS. AND IF I AM BESTED--
--HOW WILL YOU AND YOUR MERCENARIES FARE? WHO WILL HIRE YOU IN JARELLA'S WORLD OF PEACE--
--WHEN SHE NOW HAS HER INVINCIBLE MAN-MONSTER-- THE ONE CALLED BANNER-THE-HULK--TO INSURE THAT PEACE GOES FOREVER UNBROKEN?!
A CONVINCING POINT, WELL RAISED, VISIS. BUT YET ANOTHER OBSTACLE TO SUCH AN ALLIANCE OCCURS TO ME--

--IT TURNS ON THIS "HULK," AND THE TRUTH IN YOUR ACCOLADE OF--
--INVINCIBLE.
COME TO OUR RECONSTRUCTION SHOPS, LORD--
--I WOULD HAVE AN OPINION FROM YOU.

YOU ARE FAMILIAR WITH THE MORE STANDARD IMPLEMENTS WE HAVE SALVAGED FROM OUR DISTANT PAST.
FORCE BLASTERS... LEVITATIONAL BANDS...?
IF THESE WERE THE STUFF TO STOP YOUR HULKING ONE, I DOUBT YOU'D BE HERE TODAY.
BUT BEHOLD THIS, VISIS! FOUND AMID THE RUINS OF THE ANCIENTS NEARLY A CENTURY AGO!
IT HAS TAKEN THAT LONG TO LEARN ITS PURPOSE, TO RECLAIM IT...TO MAKE IT FUNCTION!
DEMONS OF THE EARTH AND SKY--!

--NEVER HAVE I SEEN SO MIGHTY AN ENGINE!
KRYLAR--! WHAT IS THIS INSTRUMENT?!
MERELY REMAIN WHERE YOU STAND, LORD.

I SHALL DEMONSTRATE WHAT NONE OUTSIDE THESE WALLS HAVE WITNESSED--
KLIK
--WHAT NONE BUT THE PITLL PAWOB COULD EVEN IMAGINE!

12.

GODS!
Z-DAK!
'TIS A SERPENT-BEAST OF THE GREAT KRELL JUNGLE!
HHHSSSSSSSSS
THE VERY IMAGE OF THE MONSTER THAT NEARLY SLEW ME AS A CHILD!
B-BUT IT CANNOT BE...! IT COULD NOT EXIST IN A CLIME SUCH AS THIS--

--YET I FEEL ITS REPTILIAN BREATH, AM FIXED BY ITS BURNING GAZE AS IT THRUSTS FOR THE KILL!
IN THE NAME OF ALL DEMONS! SOMEONE--ANYONE--SAVE ME!

ALLOW ME, LORD VISIS! FEW MEN COULD STAND FACING WHAT YOU DO.
FOR THAT IS NOT A MERE MONSTER, BUT SOMETHING WHICH HAS LONG HAUNTED YOU.
INDEED... THE THING YOU FEAR MOST! AND THAT IS THE MACHINE'S POWER, TO TAKE ANY BEING'S ULTIMATE FEAR--
--AND GIVE IT... LIFE!
KLIK

I-IT... VANISHES, AS THOUGH NEVER THERE!
AH, BUT IT WAS, LORD... UNTIL I STOPPED THE MACHINE. THERE... AND QUITE ABLE TO DESTROY YOU!
SUCH SORCERY COULD DEFEAT ANY FOE--
EVEN... THE HULK!

NOT SORCERY, VISIS... TECHNOLOGY. BUT THAT WAS THE OPINION I HOPED TO HEAR!
YOUR HAND, MAN... ALLIES WE SHALL BE!
UNTIL VICTORY. FOR WHY SHOULD ANY SUPERSTITIOUS BARBARIAN RULE... WHEN THE PITLL PAWOB CAN DO IT BETTER?!

13.

SO KRYLAR, STEWARD --LEADER--OF THE PITLL PAWOB COMES TO THE KEEP OF THE TRAITOR, VISIS.
HARD UPON HIS HEELS COME OTHERS...THE LEGIONS OF QUEEN JARELLA. AND BY THE FIRST MOON'S LIGHT, THEY ENCAMP... AND WAIT.
MUST YOU LEAVE MY SIDE SO SOON, MY BELOVED?
THIS NIGHT ABOVE OTHERS--THERE IS MUCH I WOULD SAY.
WE ATTACK AT DAWN, JARELLA...YOU SHOULD REST, TRY TO SLEEP.

OUTSIDE THE QUEEN'S TENT, A FAMILIAR FIGURE OVERTAKES THE MAN FROM ANOTHER WORLD...
FRIEND BANNER, I KNOW THE MIND OF OUR LADY. IT SEETHES WITH CONCERN.
ONCE, THE HAND OF THE GODS TORE YOU FROM HER--
WHO KNOWS WHAT THE 'MORROW OFFERS? SHE WOULD HAVE ONE NIGHT OF HAPPINESS--
--AND WANTS YOU TO MARRY US, TORLA. I KNOW--

--I SUSPECTED AS MUCH, AND IT TEMPTS ME.
I WANT HAPPINESS TOO...BUT NOT FOR A NIGHT, A MOMENT. I'VE HAD THAT...AND THE HURT THAT FOLLOWS WHEN IT BECOMES ASHES. JARELLA DESERVES SOMETHING BETTER, LASTING--
THAT CAN ONLY COME WHEN THE BATTLE ENDS--
--AND THERE'S PEACE.

DAYBREAK! AND WITH IT--BEFORE THE TRUMPETS OF ATTACK CAN SOUND--A CHALLENGE FROM THE CASTLE.
THEIR CHAMPION AGAINST OURS--
WHOSOEVER TRIUMPHS DECIDES THE BATTLE... AND THE WAR.
IF I DIDN'T KNOW BETTER--
--I'D SWEAR VISIS HAD SEEN TOO MANY MOVIES.

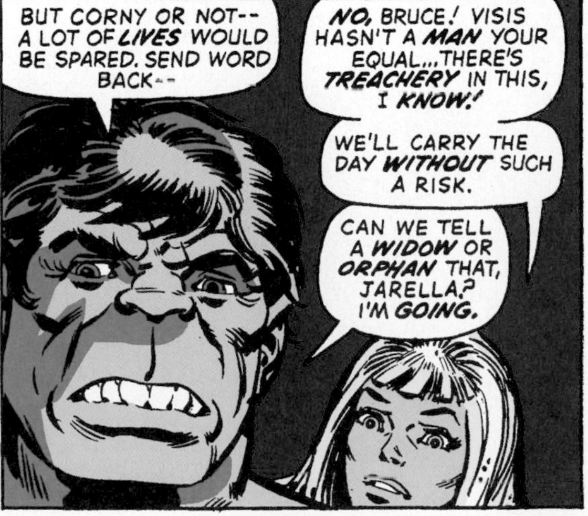
BUT CORNY OR NOT--A LOT OF LIVES WOULD BE SPARED. SEND WORD BACK--
NO, BRUCE! VISIS HASN'T A MAN YOUR EQUAL...THERE'S TREACHERY IN THIS, I KNOW!
WE'LL CARRY THE DAY WITHOUT SUCH A RISK.
CAN WE TELL A WIDOW OR ORPHAN THAT, JARELLA? I'M GOING.
14.

WE JUDGED OUR MAN WELL, LORD VISIS.
REALLY, KRYLAR--!
HE MAY BE GREEN AS WE--
BUT NO MAN-- ONLY A MISSHAPEN BRUTE!

VISIS! I KNOW IT WON'T BE YOU--
BUT WHOEVER YOU'VE GOT, SEND HIM TO ME!
THEY'RE HOLDING MY BREAKFAST BACK AT CAMP!

GROSS FREAK!
WE HAVE THIS FOR YOU!
F-ZAK!

W-WHAT?! SOME SORT OF RAY DEVICE--!
JARELLA WAS RIGHT ABOUT THIS BEING A TRICK. BUT...IT'S NOT HURTING ME, OR--
WAIT!
OUT OF THE CENTER OF THE RAYS-- SOMETHING'S FORMING--!

NO! IT CAN'T BE! N-NOT--!
YOU! WHO ARE YOU? YOU HAVE HULK'S FACE... BUT SPEAK WITH VOICE OF PUNY BRUCE BANNER!

--AND HULK HATES BRUCE BANNER!
BOM!
HATES HIM ENOUGH TO SMASH--
--TO KILL!
AND HERE IT IS, BRUCE BANNER, IN LIVING COLOR--
THAT NIGHTMARE ALWAYS TUCKED IN YOUR MIND'S NETHER CORNERS. THE DARK SIDE OF YOU--THE HULK SIDE--TOTALLY FREE, AMOK--

15.

--PITTED AGAINST SENSES UNRELIEVEDLY SAVAGE!

THAT HURTS HULK, MAKES HIM MAD.
AND THE MADDER HULK GETS--

16.

NOW, HULK WITH WEAKLING BANNER'S VOICE--
--YOU DIE!
AND AS YOUR ARMS FLAIL HELPLESSLY, AS THE WORLD SWIMS DIMLY BEFORE YOU... IT SEEMS THIS MUST BE TRUE.

IF YOU WERE ALONE, IT WOULD BE, BRUCE BANNER. BUT THE WOMAN WHO LOVES YOU HAS SEEN--
AND HAVING UNDERSTOOD...ACTS!
TORLA! WE NEED A SORCERERS' TRIAD...SWIFTLY!
YOUR SPELL WHICH FIRST LET THE HULK SPEAK OUR TONGUE--
--ALSO GAVE HIM BRUCE'S MIND.
BUT IF HE COULD BECOME AGAIN AS WHEN HE ARRIVED ON OUR WORLD--
THERE MIGHT STILL BE HOPE FOR HIM AGAINST HIS FOE!

A FIGHTING CHANCE. THAT IS WHAT THESE THREE CONJURERS PLAN TO GRANT AS THEY FORM THEIR MYSTIC LINK...
HARK, BROTHERS--
--WE BEGIN.
LET ECHO OUR CHANT THROUGH THE UNIVERSE--
THAT GODS MAY HEAR AND OUR SPELL REVERSE--

YOUR DEAD, BANNER. NO WAY TO BREAK FREE OR--
MY MIND! SOMETHING TOUCHING MY MI--
THE TOUCH OF SORCERY, THE TUG OF MAGIC... AND THAT IN THE HULK WHICH IS BRUCE BANNER--

--RECEDES FROM CONTROL! WHAT IS LEFT IS THE CREATURE OF OLD--
UFFF! WHAT HAPPENS TO HULK--?
WHAT HAPPENS TO ONE HULK WAS FIGHTING?
HE IS... GONE!
YES. THE CREATURE, THE BRUTE OF OLD... WHO KNOWS NO FEAR!
17.

KRYLAR! WHAT TRICKERY IS THIS?
VICTORY WAS OURS! WHAT BASE DECEIT MADE YOU STOP THE MACHINE?
SIMPLETON! THE WEAPON STILL FUNCTIONS.
BUT SOME STRANGE OTHER FORCE IS AT WORK NOW--

SUCH AS YOUR MEALY MOUTH, WHELP OF A WARTHO?
AM I A FOOL TO BELIEVE THE MONSTER SUDDENLY LOST ALL FEAR? RATHER I THINK YOU HAVE BETRAYED ME TO JARELLA!
AND MUST DIE FOR IT!
MEN OF PITLL PAWOB... TO YOUR STEWARD!
VISIS GOES MAD! LET YOUR BLASTERS SPEAK--

NOT BEFORE MY STEEL, O KRYLAR!
AS FOR YOUR MEN... MY GUARDS DISPATCHED THEM WHILE YOU MANNED THE MACHINE.
PERHAPS I PREMATURELY ANTICIPATED YOUR TREACHERY--
BUT YOU DID NOT DISAPPOINT ME, ALLY MINE!

BUT ANOTHER IS DISAPPOINTED...
WHERE HAS FOE WHO LOOKED LIKE HULK GONE?!
HE CANNOT THROW HULK TO GROUND, THEN JUST VANISH--
WILL FIND HIM... FINISH BATTLE!
AND HULK HAS FUNNY FEELING--

--FOE CAME FROM THERE!

YES! HULK REMEMBERS... BIG HOUSE IS PLACE OF ENEMIES! ENEMIES OF--
WHAT?! SOMETHING ELSE HAPPENS... HULK IS STARTING TO--
--GROW! BUT WHY... WHY?
BECAUSE, HULK, A SERUM YOU TOOK--DEVELOPED BY A MAN NAMED PYM--WAS UNSTABLE. SO UNSTABLE THAT ITS SHRINKING EFFECT IS NOW WEARING OFF!
18

A FACT EVEN LORD VISIS, IN THE SECURITY OF HIS STRONGHOLD--
--PREOCCUPIED WITH THE SETTLING OF SCORES--
--AND THE SALVAGING OF AMBITIONS--

--CANNOT TOTALLY IGNORE!
VA-KOOOM!
NOR, UNFORTUNATELY, CAN OTHERS--

--OTHERS SUCH AS THE FAIR JARELLA.
NO, MY LOVE... NO!
IT CANNOT BE HAPPENING AGAIN--
I MUST NOT BE LOSING YOU AS BEFORE!
PLEASE, O QUEEN... HAVE CARE! 'TIS BEYOND OUR HELPING--
AND HE GROWS WITH SUCH ERRATIC FORCE--

19.

SO YOU COME ONCE MORE TO EARTH, HULK, THE SLATE OF YOUR MEMORY WIPED CLEAN...SAVE PERHAPS, FOR A DIMLY PERCEIVED SENSE OF LOSS--

202
AUG

25¢
CC

MARVEL COMICS GROUP™

APPROVED BY THE COMICS CODE AUTHORITY

THE INCREDIBLE HULK

™

BECAUSE YOU DEMANDED IT! THE RETURN OF JARELLA! THE WOMAN THE MAN-BRUTE LOVES!

HAVOC
AT THE HEART OF THE ATOM!!

Caught in the heart of a ***Nuclear Explosion,*** victim of ***Gamma-Radiation*** gone wild, ***Doctor Robert Bruce Banner*** now finds himself transformed in times of stress into seven feet, one thousand pounds of unfettered ***Fury***—the most powerful creature to ever walk the earth—

Stan Lee PRESENTS: **THE INCREDIBLE HULK!** TM

LEN WEIN WRITER/EDITOR ✱ SAL BUSCEMA & JOE STATON ILLUSTRATORS ✱ GLYNIS WEIN COLORIST ✱ I. WATANABE LETTERER ✱ MARV WOLFMAN BIG KAHUNA

LIKE SOME OBSCENE BILLIARD BALL, THE EMERALD MAN-BRUTE CAROMS PAST THE MYRIAD MOLECULES THAT COMPOSE THIS SUB-ATOMIC UNIVERSE--

--HIS DENSE, BECLOUDED MIND FAIRLY ROILING IN CONFUSION!
WHERE IS HULK?
HOW DID HULK GET TO THIS STRANGE PLACE?

NATURALLY, HE DOES NOT RECALL THAT MERE MINUTES--OR WAS IT CENTURIES--BEFORE, HE HAD UNWITTINGLY HELPED THE PRIMITIVE PEOPLE OF TERRAGONIA OVERTHROW THE DESPOTIC RULE OF ONE KRONAK THE BARBARIAN*--
--NOR DOES IT TRULY MATTER NOW!
*AS DETAILED LAST ISH--LEN.

AT THE MOMENT, ALL THAT CONCERNS THE MIGHTILY-BEWILDERED HULK IS HIS AS-YET-UNKNOWN DESTINATION--

--A QUESTION WHOSE ANSWER RATHER ABRUPTLY BECOMES APPARENT!
WHUMP!

AT LAST! HULK HAS LANDED!
BUT WHERE IS HULK NOW?
LOOKS LIKE FOREST!
GOOD! HULK LIKES FOREST! FOREST IS PLACE WHERE HULK CAN BE ALONE!

RONNKK! RRONNK!
HUH? THAT SOUND--!
LIKE SNARLING OF A DOG--OR GRUNTING OF A PIG--!

HAH! NOW HULK KNOWS WHERE HULK IS! HULK HAS BEEN HERE BEFORE! *
RONNKK!
RRONKK!
HULK IS IN FOREST OF PIG-DOGS!
GIANT ANIMALS CALLED WO... WAR...WARTHOS!
*BACK IN HULK #140 & 156.--LEN.

LAST TIME HULK WAS HERE, WARTHOS ATTACKED HULK-- TRIED TO EAT HULK--
--BUT THIS TIME, HULK WILL STRIKE FIRST!

THERE! HULK WAS FASTER THAN WARTHO!
NOW YOUR MOUTH CANNOT EAT HULK--YOUR HORNS CANNOT STAB HULK--

--BUT THERE IS MUCH HULK CAN DO TO YOU!!

PUNY WARTHO--HULK WAS TOO SMART FOR YOU! WARTHO CANNOT EAT HULK IF ITS HEAD IS STUCK IN GROUND!
NOTHING CAN EAT HULK SO LONG AS HULK IS...

UUMPPHH!!
GLOMP!

BAH! STUPID WARTHO!
KRROONK?
HULK SAID NOTHING COULD EAT HULK--

--AND HULK MEANT IT!!
WHAM!

HULK DID NOT COME TO THIS FOREST TO FIGHT UGLY PIG-DOGS!
HULK CAME HERE TO BE ALONE!

HULK WANTS TO BE LEFT ALONE MORE THAN ANYTHING ELSE, WARTHOS--

--AND WHAT HULK WANTS, HULK GETS!!

STILL SNARLING, THE MASSIVE MAN-BRUTE WATCHES THE TWO HUGE TWISTED FORMS DISAPPEAR INTO THE DISTANCE--
--AND HE GRUNTS IN SATISFACTION WHEN AT LAST THE GROUND TREMBLES SLIGHTLY BENEATH HIS FEET.

THEN, HIS DARK EYES NARROWING, THE GREEN GOLIATH LUMBERS AWAY INTO THE UNDERBRUSH--
--AND IS SWIFTLY SWALLOWED BY THE DEEPENING SHADOWS!

GAMMA BASE, DEEP IN THE NEW MEXICAN DESERT: A SECLUDED INSTALLATION COUNTLESS WORLDS AWAY FROM THE CURRENTLY-INFINITESIMAL HULK--
--YET FAR CLOSER TO THE MAN-BRUTE THAN ONE COULD EVER IMAGINE!

CONFUSED, FAITHFUL ONE? WELL, YOU'RE NOT ALONE. JUST LISTEN TO THE QUIET CONVERSATION TRANSPIRING BETWEEN A RECENTLY-REVIVED MAJOR GLENN TALBOT AND HIS WORRIED WIFE BETTY--
--AND PERHAPS YOU'LL UNDERSTAND WHAT WE MEAN!

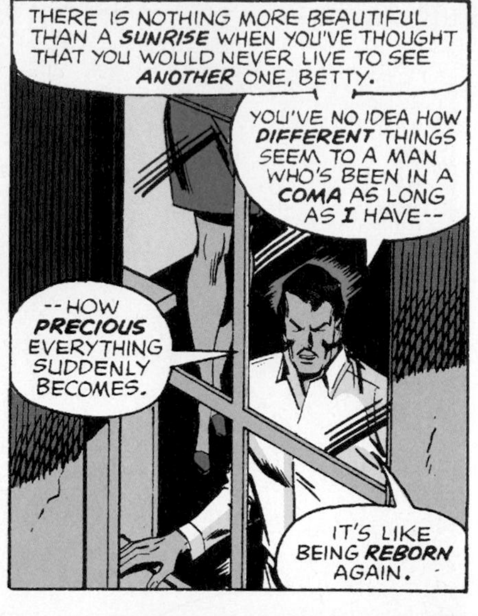
THERE IS NOTHING MORE BEAUTIFUL THAN A SUNRISE WHEN YOU'VE THOUGHT THAT YOU WOULD NEVER LIVE TO SEE ANOTHER ONE, BETTY.
YOU'VE NO IDEA HOW DIFFERENT THINGS SEEM TO A MAN WHO'S BEEN IN A COMA AS LONG AS I HAVE--
--HOW PRECIOUS EVERYTHING SUDDENLY BECOMES.
IT'S LIKE BEING REBORN AGAIN.

THEN WHY RISK LOSING IT ALL OVER AGAIN, DARLING?
LEN SAMSON HAS CURED YOU, GLENN. I BEG YOU--LEAVE WELL ENOUGH ALONE!
DON'T YOU UNDERSTAND, BETTY? I HAVE NO CHOICE!

DOC SAMSON MAY HAVE REDUCED THE HULK TO PREVENT THE MONSTER FROM EXPLODING MY BRAIN FROM WITHIN*--
--BUT SUB-MICROSCOPIC SIZE OR NOT, THE HULK IS STILL INSIDE MY SKULL--AND HE HAS TO BE GOTTEN OUT!
BUT, DARLING, I...
*AS EXPLAINED IN GREAT DETAIL BACK IN ISH #200, RIGHT?--LEN.

TALBOT, THEY'RE READY FOR US DOWN IN MICRO-SURGERY, SO I THOUGHT I'D...
OH, SORRY. HOPE I'M NOT INTERRUPTING ANYTHING, FOLKS.

NO, LEN... NOTHING AT ALL.
BETTY, PLEASE--THIS IS SOMETHING I MUST DO--
--FOR BOTH OF US!

DEAR LORD, IF YOU HAVE ANY MERCY--LET HIM COME BACK TO ME!
I COULDN'T BEAR TO LOSE HIM A SECOND TIME!
DON'T WORRY, BETTY. WE'LL BE BACK SOON.

THE JUNGLE AIR IS FILLED WITH THE HAPPY **CHIRPING** OF BIRDS HIGH IN THE TREES, WITH THE **GROWL** OF CREATURES PROWLING THRU THE BUSH--

--AND WITH SOMETHING **ELSE**!

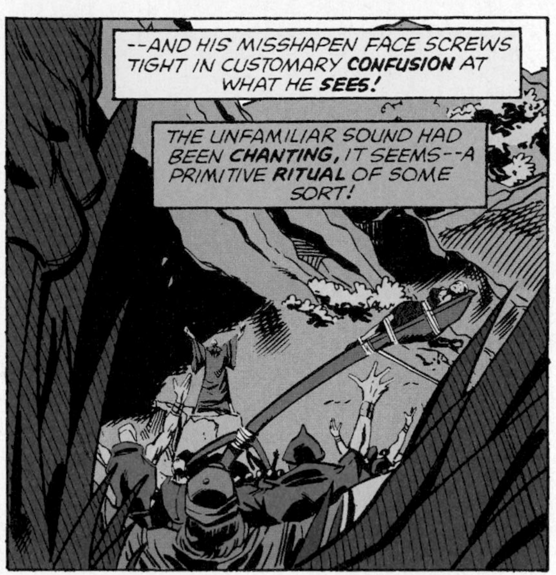

BUT EVEN AS THE GREEN GOLIATH SHOUTS HER NAME, THE HOODED HEADSMAN'S GLEAMING AXE SEVERS JARELLA'S FLIMSY LIFELINE--
CHOK!

--AND THE SEMI-CONSCIOUS WOMAN HURTLES SKYWARD, TOWARDS AN INEVITABLE RENDEZVOUS WITH DEATH!
WHUNNGG!

ER--AH--DID WE--AH--SAY INEVITABLE?
NO! HULK CAN-NOT HAVE FOUND JARELLA AGAIN--
--ONLY TO LOSE HER FOREVER!

HULK WILL SAVE JARELLA!
HULK MUST SAVE JARELLA--HULK MUST!!
CRUDE THOUGH IT WAS, THE WOODEN CATAPULT PRO-PELLED THE WOMAN AT DIZZYING SPEED TOWARD THE SHEER CLIFF WALL--

--BUT THE MOST POWER-FUL LEG MUSCLES EVER KNOWN PROPEL THE MAN-BRUTE FASTER!
HAH! HULK DID IT!
NO! IT ISN'T POSSIBLE! I MUST BE DREAMING--OR DEAD!
YOU CAN'T BE HERE--YOU CAN'T!!

AND THE EMERALD-SKINNED PEOPLE FAR BELOW SHARE JARELLA'S INCREDULITY--IF NOT HER RELIEF!
NO! THE BRUTISH ONE HAS STOLEN THE SACRIFICE!
THE GOD OF THE MOUNTAIN WILL SUFFER HIS WRATH UPON US UNLESS SHE IS SLAIN!

BAH! KEEP AWAY, LITTLE MEN!
IF ANY OF YOU TRIES TO HURT HULK'S JARELLA--
--HULK WILL SMASH!!
FOR YOUR OWN SAKES, PLEASE--STAY BACK!

YOU ARE NO LONGER OUR QUEEN, JARELLA--WE WILL NOT OBEY YOU!
FORGIVE US, JARELLA--BUT THE GOD OF THE MOUNTAIN WILL DESTROY US UNLESS WE DESTROY YOU!
HULK WARNED YOU, LITTLE MEN!
HULK DOES NOT WANT TO FIGHT YOU, BUT HULK TOLD YOU TO LEAVE JARELLA ALONE--

--AND HULK MEANS WHAT HULK SAYS!!
THOOM!

THE SHOCK-WAVE IS IMPRESSIVE, AS ALWAYS.
THE WOULD-BE ATTACKERS ARE SNAPPED INTO THE AIR LIKE TWISTED RAG DOLLS--AND WHIPLASH ABOUNDS.

BUT UNLIKE ALWAYS, THE REVERBERATIONS OF THE MAN-BRUTE'S MIGHTY BLOW NEVER SEEM TO CEASE!
WH-WHAT IS HAPPENING? HULK DID NOT SMASH GROUND THAT HARD!
IT IS NOT YOUR BLOW THAT CAUSES THIS, MY LOVE.

RATHER IT IS THE DREADFUL CURSE THAT HAS PLAGUED US SINCE LAST YOU LEFT OUR WORLD--

--A PLAGUE OF--EARTHQUAKES!

COME, JARELLA--WE WILL GO AWAY FROM HERE BEFORE YOU ARE HURT!
BUT WHAT ABOUT MY POOR PEOPLE, MY LOVE? WE CAN'T JUST LEAVE THEM HERE TO DIE!
HUH?

PLEASE, BELOVED--YOU MUST DO SOMETHING TO HELP THEM!
LITTLE MEN TRY TO KILL JARELLA--AND STILL JARELLA WANTS TO SAVE THEM?
HULK DOES NOT UNDER-STAND--

--BUT IF JARELLA WANTS HULK TO CLOSE UGLY HOLE IN GROUND--

--THEN THAT IS WHAT HULK WILL DO!

BY THE SEVEN-SIDED CIRCLE! THE BEHEMOTH PULLED SHUT THE FISSURE THAT THREATENED TO DEVOUR US--!
AND HE D-DID IT WITH HIS BARE HANDS!

BAH! HULK'S HANDS WILL CRUSH YOU, LITTLE MEN--IF YOU TRY TO TOUCH JARELLA AGAIN!
NO, DARLING --PLEASE! THEY'RE MY PEOPLE!
THEY'RE... YOUR PEOPLE!

NO! MAYBE LITTLE MEN HAVE GREEN SKIN LIKE HULK-- BUT THEY ARE NOT HULK'S FRIENDS!
ONLY JARELLA IS HULK'S FRIEND--
--SO HULK WILL TAKE JARELLA WHERE SHE CAN BE SAFE!

SHORTLY THEREAFTER, SOME DISTANCE AWAY...
IT IS TRULY A MIRACLE, MY LOVE-- YOUR RETURNING TO US THUS, IN OUR TIME OF MOST DIRE NEED.
I THOUGHT I HAD LOST YOU FOREVER--BUT FOR ONCE THE GODS HAVE BEEN KIND.

THEY'VE BROUGHT YOU BACK FROM THE WORLD OF PINK-SKINNED MEN AND TAUGHT YOU OUR LANGUAGE ONCE MORE, AFTER I'D STOLEN THAT KNOWLEDGE FROM YOU TO SAVE YOUR VERY LIFE.
AND THAT, GENTLE HULK, IS PERHAPS THE GREATEST GIFT OF ALL!
*AGAIN, BACK IN ISH #156.--LEN.

FOR NOW PERHAPS YOU CAN UNDERSTAND WHAT I WANT SO MUCH TO SAY--

--AND YOU CAN KNOW HOW MUCH I--
...LOVE...
...YOU...

MERE WORDS WOULD BE WHOLLY INADEQUATE TO DESCRIBE JARELLA'S REACTION TO THE MAN-BRUTE'S CHILD-LIKE GESTURE--
--BUT HER TEAR-TOUCHED EXPRESSION SPEAKS WITH OBVIOUS ELOQUENCE.

WILLIAM WORDSWORTH SAID: "THE CHILD IS FATHER OF THE MAN."

WILLIAM SHAKESPEARE SAID: "LOVE DOTH MAKE CHILDREN OF US ALL."

NEED WE SAY MORE?

BUT, ALAS, LOVE'S LABOURS SELDOM LAST...
HUHNN??
GROUND IS SHAKING AGAIN--?!?
DO NOT WORRY, BELOVED. IT IS ONLY A MILD TREMOR. IT WILL QUICKLY PASS.

HULK IS NOT WORRIED, JARELLA. HULK ONLY WANTS TO KNOW WHERE SHAKING COMES FROM!
THERE ARE THOSE WHO SAY THAT I BROUGHT THIS FATE UPON US, MY LOVE--BY DARING TO LOVE AN OUT-WORLDER SUCH AS YOU!
THOSE SAME FRIGHTENED ZEALOTS WERE TRYING TO SACRIFICE ME TO HE WHO DWELLS ABOVE THE CLOUDS WHEN YOU APPEARED TO SAVE ME!
HE...WHO... DWELLS...?

A GREAT DEITY OF ANCIENT LEGEND, HULK --GENTLE IN HIS GENEROSITY AND AWESOME IN HIS WRATH!
HE IS CALLED --THE GOD OF THE MOUNTAIN!

BAH! IF PUNY GOD IS ALL THAT MAKES GROUND SHAKE, HULK WILL CLIMB TO TOP OF MOUNTAIN--
--AND MAKE GOD STOP!!

WAIT HERE, JARELLA. HULK WILL COME BACK TO YOU SOON!
NO, MY LOVE--I AM COMING WITH YOU! WHATEVER THE DANGER, I WILL FACE IT AT YOUR SIDE!
I OWE MY PEOPLE THAT MUCH AT LEAST.

OTHER MEN MIGHT OBJECT TO JARELLA'S DETERMINATION, BUT THE THOUGHT NEVER EVEN OCCURS TO THE THICK-HEADED HULK--AT LEAST NOT UNTIL...
JARELLA DID NOT HAVE TO COME WITH HULK.
HULK CAN SMASH MOUNTAIN GOD ALL ALONE!
I WAS ONCE QUEEN OF THIS LAND, MY LOVE. I CANNOT SHIRK MY DUTY.

UHHMM--BUT IF CLIMBING MAKES YOU TIRED, JARELLA--TELL HULK AND HULK WILL...
NO--! I LOST MY GRIP--!
I'M FALLING--!!

THE MOVEMENT OF THE BRAWNY EMERALD HAND IS ALMOST TOO SWIFT TO BE SEEN...

NOW HOLD ON TIGHT, JARELLA-- AND LET HULK DO THE CLIMBING FOR YOU!
CLINGING TO YOU, MY LOVE, IS A TASK I COULD EASILY BECOME ACCUSTOMED TO.

THE HULK GRUNTS SOFTLY IN REPLY--
--THEN, HIS JACKHAMMER FINGERS DIGGING HANDHOLDS INTO THE OBSTINATE ROCK, THE MAN-BRUTE AND HIS PRECIOUS BURDEN ARE SOON CONSUMED BY THE SWIRLING MISTS THAT CROWN THE MOUNTAIN'S PINNACLE--

--MISTS THAT ABRUPTLY PART, TO REVEAL...
THERE, HULK--DO YOU SEE? THE LEGENDS ARE ALL TRUE!
BEFORE US STANDS THE CASTLE OF THE MOUNTAIN GOD!
BAH! LOOKS LIKE BIG ROCK WITH WINDOWS TO HULK!
BUT IF THAT IS WHERE HULK WILL FIND MOUNTAIN GOD, THEN THAT IS WHERE HULK WILL GO!

UUHMM --DOOR IS BIG!
TOO HIGH FOR HULK TO REACH HANDLE!
IT WILL BE FAR SIMPLER FOR US TO ENTER THRU THE OPENING UNDER THE DOOR, BELOVED.

BUT IF THE CASTLE DOOR IS THIS HUGE, HULK--CAN YOU IMAGINE THE SIZE OF THE MOUNTAIN GOD HIMSELF?
SIZE DOES NOT MATTER TO HULK!
BIG...SMALL... HULK WILL SMASH ANYTHING THAT GETS IN HULK'S WAY!

BLOOD IN RIVERS RUNNING DEEP--**WHO DARES INVADE MY CASTLE KEEP?**

HUH?

IT IS-- **GIANT!**

SO! LITTLE **GNATS** COME TO BOTHER ME, AY?

THEN TONIGHT THE GOD OF THE MOUNTAIN WILL **FEAST!**

THOUGH I DOUBT EITHER OF YOU WILL PROVIDE ME WITH MORE THAN A MOUTHFUL!
CHOOM!

STAY BACK, JARELLA --WHERE IT IS SAFE! LEAVE THE FIGHTING TO HULK!
FIGHTING IS WHAT HULK DOES BEST!
DARLING-- DON'T--!
NO! MOUNTAIN GOD SHOOK THE GROUND TO HURT JARELLA'S PEOPLE!
MOUNTAIN GOD TRIED TO CHOP HULK AND JARELLA UP WITH AXE--

--AND, MOUNTAIN GOD--THAT MAKES HULK MAD!
POW!

INCONSEQUENTIAL GNAT! DO YOU TRULY THINK YOU ARE STRONG ENOUGH TO CONQUER THE GOD OF THE MOUNTAIN?
WHAK!

HULK IS STRONGER THAN ANYONE, GIANT--
UUNNGGHH!!
--AND WHEN HULK GETS UP, HULK WILL PROVE IT!
THWAMM!

YOU WILL DO NOTHING, HULK-GNAT-- EXCEPT DIE!
I'LL GRIND YOUR BONES TO MAKE MY BREAD!
NO!

HULK WILL NOT BE FOOD FOR UGLY GIANT!

WHEREVER HULK GOES IN THIS STRANGE LAND, SOMETHING TRIES TO EAT HULK--
EH?

--AND HULK IS SICK AND TIRED OF IT!!
WOOM! THOOM!
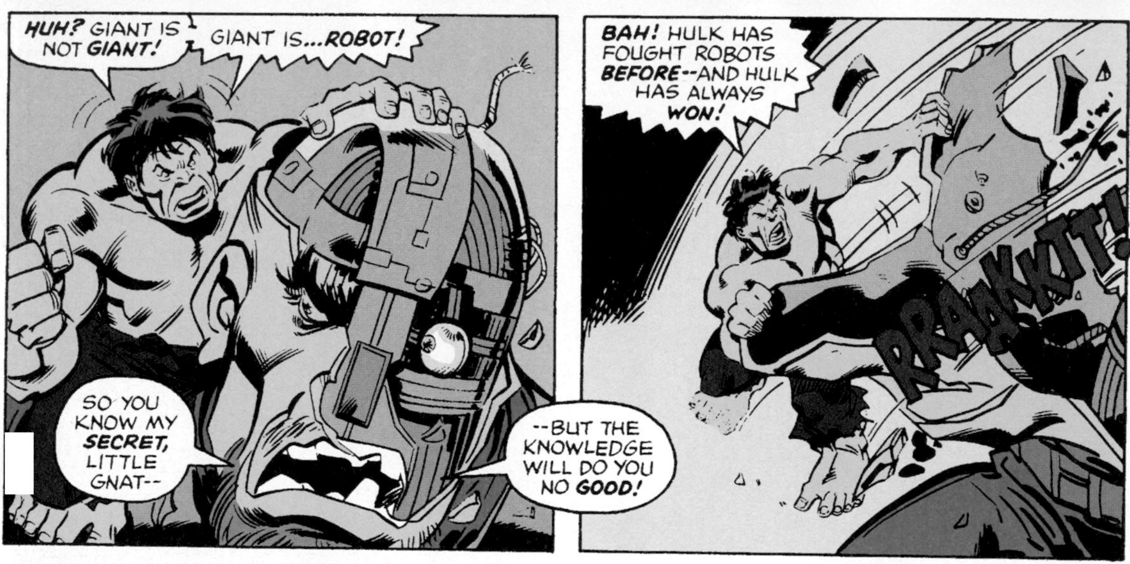
HUH? GIANT IS NOT GIANT!
GIANT IS...ROBOT!
SO YOU KNOW MY SECRET, LITTLE GNAT--
--BUT THE KNOWLEDGE WILL DO YOU NO GOOD!
BAH! HULK HAS FOUGHT ROBOTS BEFORE--AND HULK HAS ALWAYS WON!
RRAAKKIT!

PERHAPS, HULK-GNAT-- BUT YOU HAVE NEVER BATTLED A ROBOT WHO WAS ALSO A GOD!
A GOD CANNOT DIE!
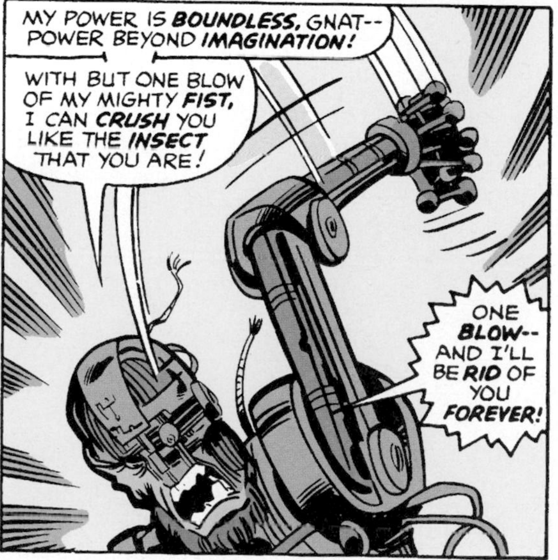
MY POWER IS BOUNDLESS, GNAT-- POWER BEYOND IMAGINATION!
WITH BUT ONE BLOW OF MY MIGHTY FIST, I CAN CRUSH YOU LIKE THE INSECT THAT YOU ARE!
ONE BLOW-- AND I'LL BE RID OF YOU FOREVER!

BAH!

NO! NOOOO!!
ROBOT TALKS TOO MUCH--LIKE PUNY HUMAN!
AND HULK HAS HEARD ENOUGH!

THE MECHANOID'S ARM IS SEVERED FROM ITS SHOULDER WITH AN UNNERVING SQUEAL OF TWISTING METAL, A SOUND SUDDENLY SMOTHERED BY THE CRASH OF ERUPTING GRANITE--
GODS CANNOT DIEEEEEEEEE
--AND THE ROBOT'S DEATH-CRY COMES TO A SHATTERING END, HALFWAY DOWN THE MOUNTAINSIDE!
WHILE, BACK INSIDE THE CRAGGY CASTLE...
ROBOT THOUGHT IT WAS STRONGER THAN HULK--BUT ROBOT WAS WRONG!
HULK IS THE STRONGEST ONE THERE IS!
KKRRUUNNCCHH!!

A-ARE YOU ALL RIGHT, MY LOVE? I WAS SO WORRIED!
DUST, JARELLA.
IS THERE ANYTHING LEFT OF THE MONSTER, HULK?
ONLY DUST IS LEFT.

MOUNTAIN GOD IS GONE, JARELLA. THE GROUND WILL SHAKE NO MORE.
NOW COME! HULK WILL TAKE YOU AWAY FROM HERE.
DARLING--WAIT! WE STILL DO NOT KNOW WHO BUILT THAT METALLIC MONSTROSITY.
AND HULK DOES NOT CARE! HULK SMASHED STUPID ROBOT, AND THAT IS ENOUGH FOR...

H-HE LIES SO SOLEMN--SO STILL! BY THE ALL THE GODS, I CANNOT HAVE FOUND MY ONE TRUE LOVE AGAIN, ONLY TO HAVE LED HIM TO HIS DEATH!

HULK? HULK?? I BEG YOU, MY LOVE--PLEASE SPEAK TO ME!

YOU ARE WASTING YOUR BREATH, WOMAN, THE MAN-BRUTE CANNOT HEAR YOU--WHICH IS, IN IT'S FASHION, A PITY!

YOU WANTED TO KNOW WHO CONSTRUCTED THE GOD OF THE MOUNTAIN, AND NOW YOU HAVE YOUR ANSWER--BUT IT WILL AVAIL YOU NOTHING!

FOR NOTHING THAT LIVES CAN HOPE TO STAND BEFORE THE POWER OF--PSYKLOP!

NEXT ISSUE: MORE MIND-BENDING MAYHEM THAN YOU CAN SHAKE A GAMMA-IRRADIATED STICK AT--PLUS (WE HOPE) A SURPRISE OR TWO! BE HERE FOR...

THE TOWER THAT TORE THE SKY!

INCREDIBLE HULK

MARVEL COMICS GROUP™

APPROVED BY THE COMICS CODE AUTHORITY

30¢ 203 SEPT 02456

THE INCREDIBLE HULK®

IF *ONE* PSYKLOP IS MORE THAN A *MATCH* FOR YOU, MAN-BRUTE--

ROMITA

--WHAT CHANCE DO YOU STAND AGAINST AN *ARMY* OF US!!

ASSAULT ON PSYKLOP!

Caught in the heart of a ***Nuclear Explosion,*** victim of ***Gamma-Radiation*** gone wild, ***Doctor Robert Bruce Banner*** now finds himself transformed in times of stress into seven feet, one thousand pounds of unfettered ***Fury***—the most powerful creature to ever walk the earth—

Stan Lee PRESENTS: **THE INCREDIBLE HULK!**™

LEN WEIN WRITER / EDITOR / SAL BUSCEMA & JOE STATON ARTISTS / ILLUSTRATORS / GLYNIS WEIN COLORIST / IRV WATANABE LETTERER

OF COURSE, I MIGHT BE PERSUADED TO MAKE YOUR DEATH A MORE PLEASANT ONE, JARELLA--AS BEFITS A FORMER QUEEN!
PLEASE--DON'T TOUCH ME!

LEAVE JARELLA ALONE, ONE-EYE--OR HULK WILL SMASH!
YOU'LL DO NOTHING, MAN-BRUTE! YOUR BONDS ARE FORGED OF DIMUNDIUM STEEL--UTTERLY UNBREAKABLE!
YOU ARE MY PRISONER, HULK--AND SOON YOU SHALL BE MY VICTIM!

NO! HULK WILL BE NO ONE'S VICTIM!
HULK WILL BE NO ONE'S PRISONER!

HULK WILL BE WHAT HULK WANTS TO BE--
--AND HULK WANTS TO BE FREE!!
KAR-ROOMM!

NOW GIVE JARELLA BACK TO HULK, ONE-EYE--
--OR HULK WILL CRUSH YOU LIKE A BUG!

YOU THINK TO INSULT ME, MONSTER--BUT YOU'VE NO IDEA HOW TRULY YOU SPEAK!
MY RACE DID INDEED EVOLVE FROM THE LOWLY INSECT--TO BECOME THE RULERS OF ANCIENT EARTH!
KLIK!
OUR SCIENTIFIC PROWESS WAS UNPARALLELED--

--AND WE HAD WEAPONS UNDREAMED OF AT OUR FINGERTIPS!
ZZAKK!
BAH! PUNY RAYS CANNOT HURT HULK!

INCREDIBLE! THOSE SPASM-RAYS SHOULD HAVE DISRUPTED YOUR ENTIRE NERVOUS SYSTEM!
AND NOT EVEN A SONIC DISPLACER HAS ANY EFFECT ON YOUR GAMMA-IRRADIATED FORM!
NOTHING WILL STOP HULK, ONE-EYE--UNTIL HULK HAS STOPPED YOU!

I'M WARNING YOU, BRUTE--STAY BACK! THE CONSEQUENCES ARE DIRE FOR ANYONE WHO DARES ATTACK IMMORTAL PSYKLOP!
HAH! ONE-EYE WANTED TO KILL HULK!
WHAT IS WORSE THAN DEATH?

LIFE, MONSTER--LIFE WITHOUT CONSCIOUS THOUGHT OR VOLUNTARY DEED!
LIFE AS AN UNWILLING SLAVE OF MY HYPNOTIC POWER!

THE BEHEMOTH STOPS SHORT, AS IF STRUCK A MORTAL BLOW. FOR AN INSTANT, HIS MASSIVE FORM TOTTERS FROM SIDE-TO-SIDE--
--THEN HIS DULLISH EYES ROLL BACK INTO HIS HEAD--

--AND HE TOPPLES LIKE A FELLED SEQUOIA TREE!
DO YOU SEE, HULK--YOUR SAVAGE POWER PALES BEFORE MINE!
NO! WHAT HAVE YOU DONE TO HIM! WHAT HAVE YOU DONE TO MY BELOVED?
WHUMP!

I'VE NEUTRALIZED THE MAN-BRUTE'S THREAT TO ME, WOMAN--
--AS I SHOULD HAVE DONE WHEN FIRST HE AND I MET, THOSE MANY LONG MONTHS AGO!
IS THAT IT? IS IT REVENGE YOU SEEK? IS THAT WHY YOU'VE DEVASTATED MY WORLD?
THERE IS A GREAT DEAL MORE TO THINGS THAN THAT, JARELLA...
... BUT PERHAPS I'D BEST START FROM THE BEGINNING...

"...FOR, IN A WAY, THE ACCURSED AVENGERS ARE RESPONSIBLE FOR ALL THIS--
"--BY DARING TO ATTACK ME IN MY HIDDEN LAIR AS I EXPERIMENTED UPON THE UNCONSCIOUS HULK!

"SHRUNK WILDLY OUT OF CONTROL, THE MAN-BRUTE EVENTUALLY FOUND HIMSELF ON YOUR SUB-MICROSCOPIC WORLD--
"--WHERE HE WAS SOON WORSHIPPED AS THE CHAMPION OF YOUR PEOPLE!

"IN TRUTH, HE MIGHT HAVE REMAINED UPON K'AI FOREVER--
"--HAD I NOT FINALLY LOCATED THE HULK AND RECAPTURED HIM!

"FOR I HAD NEED OF THE MAN-MONSTER'S POWER TO FEED THE DARK GODS THAT I SERVED--
"--SO THAT THEY WOULD AWAKEN MY PEOPLE FROM THEIR EONS-LONG SLEEP.

"BUT WHEN WE RETURNED TO MY UNDERGROUND EYRIE, THE HULK WENT BERSERK, DESTROYING MY IRREPLACABLE MECHANISMS IN HIS MINDLESS RAGE--

"--LEAVING ME ALONE TO FACE THE HORRIBLE WRATH OF THE DARK GODS, WHEN THEY LEARNED THAT I HAD FAILED THEM!"*
*THE PRECEDING FLASHBACKS WILL BECOME CLEAR TO YOU IF YOU READ AVENGERS #88 AND HULK #140. --KNOW-IT-ALL LEN.

BUT IF YOU MET YOUR DEFEAT ON THE WORLD OF PINK-SKINNED MEN, WHAT HAS ALL THIS TO DO WITH US?
WHY HAVE YOU RETURNED TO K'AI?
I ASSURE YOU, JARELLA--IT WAS NOT MY OWN IDEA!
THE DARK GODS EXILED ME HERE THINKING IT A FITTING PUNISHMENT FOR MY FAILURE!

"FOR MONTHS, I REMAINED ALONE IN THIS MOUNTAIN RETREAT, UTILIZING MY INCOMPARABLE SCIENTIFIC KNOWLEDGE TO CONSTRUCT MACHINES TO ASSURE MY COMFORT--
"--BUILDING THE GIANT MECHANICAL MOUNTAIN GOD* TO ASSURE MY PRIVACY--
"--USING THE TIME TO THINK, TO ASSURE MY REVENGE!
*SEE LAST ISSUE.--LEN AGAIN.

"ON MY PLANET-SPANNING VIEW-SCANNERS, I WATCHED AS THE HULK RETURNED TO K'AI--TO FREE ITS PEOPLE FROM THE EVIL LORD VISIS*--
*ISSUE #156.--LIVELY YOU-KNOW-WHO.

"--AND I WATCHED AS HE GREW TOO HUGE FOR YOUR WORLD TO CONTAIN HIM--
"--AND, WITH A SINGLE THRUST OF HIS GIGANTIC FOOT, ACCIDENTALLY KICKED THE WORLD OF K'AI FROM ITS ORBIT!"

IT IS THAT WHICH IS ACTUALLY RESPONSIBLE FOR THE EARTHQUAKES WHICH HAVE PLAGUED THIS PLANET SINCE THAT DAY--
--THOUGH YOUR SIMPLE-MINDED SUBJECTS CHOSE TO BELIEVE IT WAS THE ANGER OF THEIR LEGENDARY MOUNTAIN GOD!

FOR MY OWN PURPOSES, I ALLOWED THEM TO CONTINUE IN THAT BELIEF, AND WHEN THE QUAKES BEGAN TO ABATE...
WELL, I TOOK STEPS TO INSURE THAT WILL NEVER HAPPEN!
BY THE SEVEN-SIDED CIRCLE! IT --IT ISN'T POSSIBLE--!

ANYTHING IS POSSIBLE, WOMAN--
--WHEN ONE POSSESSES THE INCOMPARABLE PROWESS OF PSYKLOP!

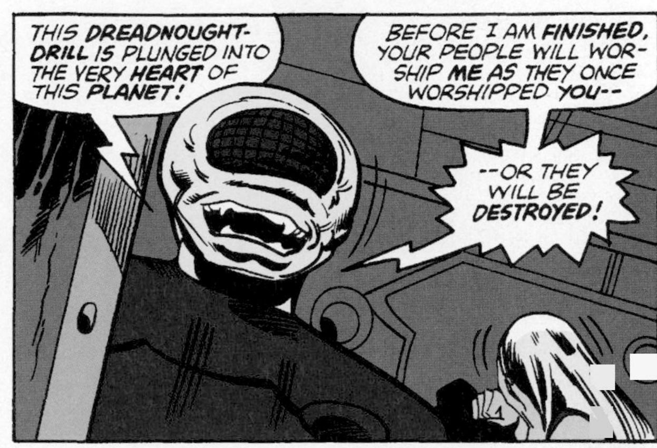

--LET US WHIRL MYRIAD WORLDS AWAY, TO THE SECLUDED NEW MEXICAN RESEARCH INSTALLATION CODE-NAMED GAMMA BASE--

--SO WE CAN WITNESS A MOST IMPORTANT CONVERSATION BETWEEN MAJOR GLENN TALBOT AND THE EMERALD-TRESSED DOC SAMSON!
YOU CAN GET UP NOW, TALBOT.
YOU MEAN IT'S OVER? THAT'S IT? I DIDN'T FEEL A THING--
--EXCEPT FOR A PIN-PRICK THAT MADE MY EYES SPIN FOR A SECOND.
THE MIRACLES OF MICRO-SURGERY, MAJOR. THAT'S ALL IT TOOK FOR US TO GET WHAT WE WERE AFTER INSIDE YOUR HEAD.

WE'VE EXTRACTED THE ATOM THAT CONTAINS THE SUB-MICROSCOPIC HULK FROM YOUR BRAIN--AND TRANSFERED IT TO THIS SLIDE.

NOW ALL WE HAVE TO DO IS PLACE THE SLIDE UNDER THE MICRON-CANNON AND TRY TO REVERSE THE PROCEDURE THAT...
EVERYTHING GOING ALL RIGHT, GENTLEMEN?
RIGHT ON THE NUMBERS, GENERAL ROSS.

OUR RECALIBRATED SCANNERS FINALLY DETECTED THE HULK'S GAMMA RADIATION INSIDE YOUR MAJOR'S SKULL, GENERAL--
--AND NOW THAT WE'VE REMOVED THE OFFENDING ATOMS FROM SAID ORGANISM--

--WE'RE GOING TO ATTEMPT TO RESTORE JADE-JAWS TO HIS FORMER STATURE, ALL ONE THOUSAND ADORABLE POUNDS OF HIM!
AND ONCE YOU BRING HIM BACK TO US, SAMSON? WHAT THEN?

IF I BRING HIM BACK, GENERAL--HE'S OUR RESPONSIBILITY AGAIN...
...JUST AS HE'S ALWAYS BEEN.

WHILE, ON K'AI...
HE MAKES A MOST EFFICIENT SERVANT, DOES HE NOT?
THE HULK'S SHEER BRUTE STRENGTH CAN ACCOMPLISH IN MINUTES WHAT MY AUTOMATED MECHANISMS REQUIRED HOURS TO PERFORM.
A PITY I DID NOT HAVE HIS SERVICES WHEN I BEGAN MY MASTER PLAN!

THEN WHAT I'VE FEARED IS TRUE! THERE IS MORE TO ALL OF THIS THAN A SIMPLE THIRST FOR VENGEANCE, ISN'T THERE?
BUT WHAT? WHAT??

THE ANSWER TO THAT IS RATHER DIFFICULT TO EXPLAIN TO ONE OF YOUR LIMITED INTELLIGENCE. PERHAPS IT WOULD BE BEST IF I SHOWED YOU.
IF YOU WOULD ACCOMPANY ME, MY GOOD EX-QUEEN--?
HAVE I ANY CHOICE?

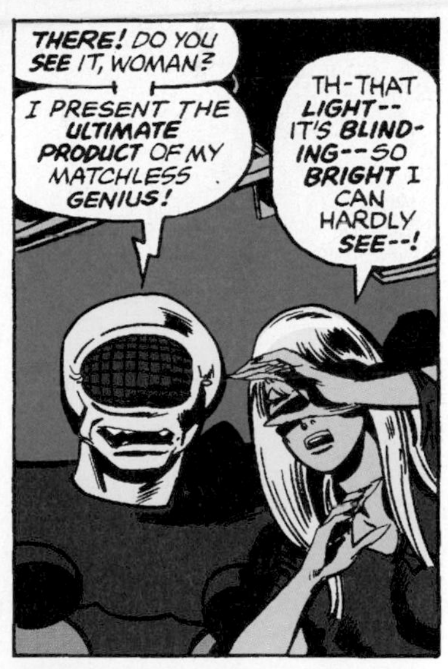
THERE! DO YOU SEE IT, WOMAN?
I PRESENT THE ULTIMATE PRODUCT OF MY MATCHLESS GENIUS!
TH-THAT LIGHT-- IT'S BLINDING--SO BRIGHT I CAN HARDLY SEE--!

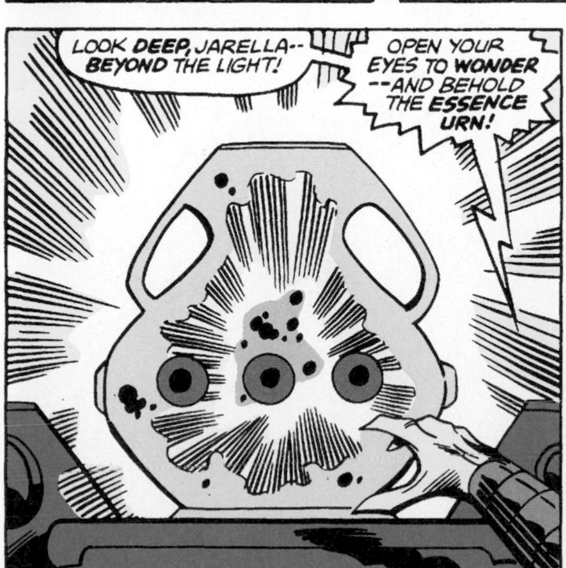
LOOK DEEP, JARELLA-- BEYOND THE LIGHT!
OPEN YOUR EYES TO WONDER --AND BEHOLD THE ESSENCE URN!

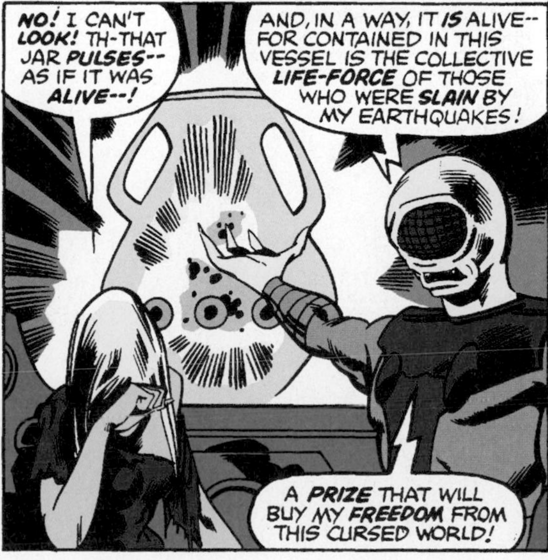
NO! I CAN'T LOOK! TH-THAT JAR PULSES-- AS IF IT WAS ALIVE--!
AND, IN A WAY, IT IS ALIVE-- FOR CONTAINED IN THIS VESSEL IS THE COLLECTIVE LIFE-FORCE OF THOSE WHO WERE SLAIN BY MY EARTHQUAKES!
A PRIZE THAT WILL BUY MY FREEDOM FROM THIS CURSED WORLD!

SHORTLY, THE MULTI-UNIVERSAL ENERGIES WILL AT LAST BE IN PERFECT CONJUNCTION--
--AND I SHALL OFFER UP THOSE STOLEN LIFE-FORCES TO FEED THE DREAD DARK GODS!
YOU UNHOLY GHOUL--!

GHOUL? YES, I AM ALL THAT AND MORE--
--FOR I WILL STOP AT NOTHING TO GAIN THE GRATITUDE OF THE GODS AND THUS EARN MY FREEDOM!

YOUR PEOPLE ARE MERELY UN-FORTUNATE PAWNS WHO MUST BE SACRIFICED TO ACCOMPLISH MY...
EH? THE SECURITY ALARM--!
PING! PING! PING!

SO! IT APPEARS YOUR SUBJECTS ARE STILL LOYAL TO YOU, JARELLA--DESPITE THEIR FEAR OF THE MOUNTAIN GOD'S WRATH!*
*AS EXPLAINED LAST ISH.--LEN.

THEY HAVE SCALED THIS PINNACLE SEARCHING FOR THEIR QUEEN--
--BUT ALL THEY WILL FIND IS--DEATH!

NO! WHAT ARE YOU DOING TO MY DARLING?
MERELY EM-PLOYING A SIMPLE POST-HYPNOTIC PROCEDURE, WOMAN.
SOMEWHERE DEEP IN THE MAN-BRUTE'S MINISCULE MIND, THERE IS NO ONE HE HATES RIGHT NOW MORE THAN PSYKLOP!
HE NOW HAS MY PERMISSION TO GAIN HIS REVENGE!

GO, HULK! SEEK OUT THE ONE YOU HATE--
--AND KILL HIM!!

OUTSIDE PSYKLOP'S STRONGHOLD, THE PEOPLE OF K'AI--LED BY TORLA AND THE PANTHEON OF SORCERERS--PRESS CAUTIOUSLY FORWARD...
...PREPARED FOR ALMOST ANYTHING...

...EXCEPT THE SUDDEN, UNEXPECTED APPEARANCE OF A RAMPAGING HULK!
SHOW YOURSELF, ONE-EYE--AND HULK WILL SMASH!
WHERE IS PSYKLOP?

HESITANTLY, UNCERTAINLY, THE MAKESHIFT WARRIORS APPROACH THE BRUTISH BEHEMOTH WHO ONE HAD BEEN THEIR ALLY--

--BUT THE FURIOUS HULK'S HYPNOTICALLY-TWISTED MIND SEES NOT THE GENTLE PRIMITIVES HE HAD KNOWN COMING CLOSER--

--BUT RATHER WHAT APPEARS TO BE A BLOOD-THIRSTY HORDE OF THE ALIEN CALLED--
--PSYKLOP!

SO! NOW MANY PSYKLOPS TRY TO ATTACK HULK--
--BUT HULK WILL STRIKE FIRST!

AND HULK WILL STRIKE HARDEST!
FLEE FOR YOUR LIVES! THE HULK HAS GONE MAD!

MAD? YES, ONE-EYE --HULK IS MAD!
HULK IS MAD THAT YOU TRIED TO HURT JARELLA!
HULK IS MAD THAT YOU TRIED TO TRICK HULK'S EYES!

BUT NOW HULK SEES YOU FOR WHAT YOU REALLY ARE!
POW!

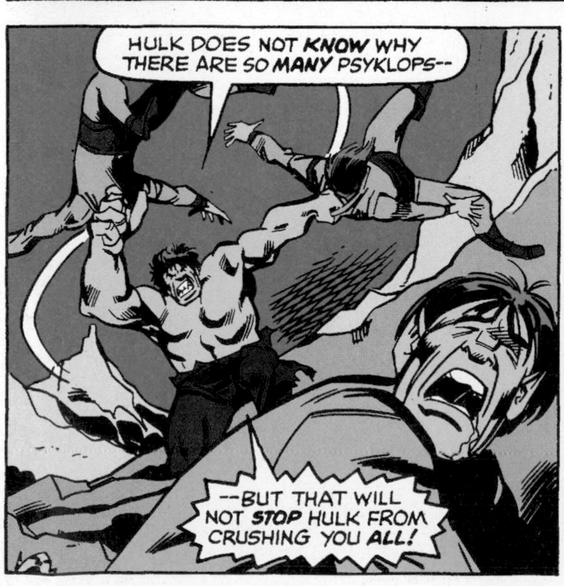
HULK DOES NOT KNOW WHY THERE ARE SO MANY PSYKLOPS--
--BUT THAT WILL NOT STOP HULK FROM CRUSHING YOU ALL!

HOLI! MOLI! DO YOU HEAR THE MAN-MONSTER'S WORDS?
IT IS NOT OUR POOR BATTERED COMRADES HE IS FIGHTING!
SOMEHOW, HE BELIEVES HE DOES BATTLE WITH THE ONE-EYED DEMON WE CAME HERE TO CONFRONT!

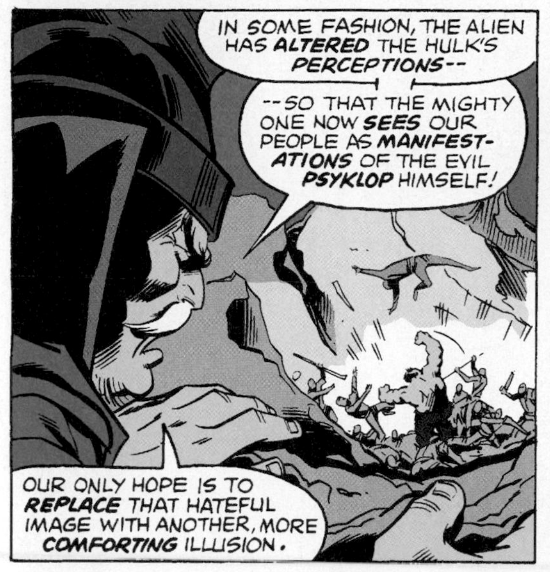
IN SOME FASHION, THE ALIEN HAS ALTERED THE HULK'S PERCEPTIONS--
--SO THAT THE MIGHTY ONE NOW SEES OUR PEOPLE AS MANIFESTATIONS OF THE EVIL PSYKLOP HIMSELF!
OUR ONLY HOPE IS TO REPLACE THAT HATEFUL IMAGE WITH ANOTHER, MORE COMFORTING ILLUSION.

THUS LET THE PANTHEON OF SORCERERS NOW FORM THE MYSTIC TRIAD! LET US BEGIN THE ANCIENT CHANTS--
--AND, IF THE POWERS BE WILLING, LET US PREVAIL!

THE HULK, MEANWHILE, CONTINUES HIS MINDLESS RAMPAGE, SAVAGELY TOSSING THE ERSTWHILE EMERALD INVADERS ABOUT LIKE SO MANY SACKS OF WHEAT--

--UNTIL A BOLT OF MENTAL ENERGY FROM THE THREE GATHERED SORCERERS ABRUPTLY ROOTS THE MAN-BRUTE TO THE SPOT--
--AND THINGS SLOWLY BEGIN TO--CHANGE!

THE HULK BLINKS--AND THE COUNTLESS IMAGES OF PSYKLOP FALLEN AT HIS FEET--

--BEGIN TO SHIMMER LIKE SMOKE BEFORE HIS STARTLED EYES--

--THEN SUDDENLY ASSUME A FAR MORE APPEALING GUISE!

JARELLA?

IMPOSSIBLE! SOMEHOW THOSE SAVAGES HAVE BROKEN MY HYPNOTIC SPELL!
I MUST GET TO THE HULK SWIFTLY --BEFORE MY INFLUENCE WEARS OFF!

I ORDER YOU, HULK--RENEW YOUR ASSAULT!
THE ONE YOU HATE STANDS BEFORE YOU!
LASH OUT --AND DESTROY HIM!

NO! THE ONE HULK HATES STANDS BEHIND HULK-- THE ONE WHO TRIED TO TWIST HULK'S MIND!
YOU!

YOU ARE THE ONE HULK HATES, ONE-EYE!
YOU ARE THE ONE HULK WILL DESTROY!

NO! STAY BACK, BRUTE!
STAY BACK-- IF YOU VALUE YOUR WOMAN'S LIFE!
PLEASE--! LET ME GO, PSYKLOP--BEFORE IT'S TOO LATE!

IT IS ALREADY TOO LATE, JARELLA! ONE-EYE DARED TO HURT YOU--
--AND FOR THAT, HULK WILL CRUSH ONE-EYE TO PULP!
FOOL! MY HYPNOTIC POWERS SUBDUED YOU ONCE, BUT THIS TIME THEY WILL...
NO! IT CAN'T BE! MY POWERS HAVE NO EFFECT ON HIM!
WHEN HE GETS THIS ANGRY, THERE IS NOTHING THAT CAN AFFECT HIM, PSYKLOP!
I BEG YOU--SURRENDER WHILE YOU STILL CAN!

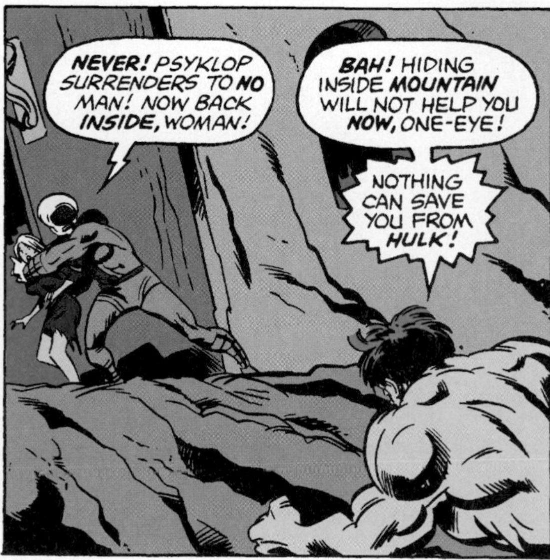
NEVER! PSYKLOP SURRENDERS TO NO MAN! NOW BACK INSIDE, WOMAN!
BAH! HIDING INSIDE MOUNTAIN WILL NOT HELP YOU NOW, ONE-EYE!
NOTHING CAN SAVE YOU FROM HULK!

DARLING, PLEASE --BE CAREFUL! PSYKLOP HAS GONE INSANE!
DIE! DIE! CURSE YOU, MONSTER--WHY WON'T YOU DIE?

FIRST YOU WILL RELEASE HULK'S JARELLA, ONE-EYE--
--AND THEN WE WILL SEE WHO DIES!
THOOM!

NO! THE HULK'S BLOW BUCKLES THE VERY FLOOR--! CAN'T KEEP MY FOOTING--!
THEN AT LAST, PSYKLOP-- IT'S OVER!

ALL MY EFFORTS--ALL MY SUBTLE CALCULATIONS--THEY CANNOT HAVE BEEN IN VAIN!
THE TIME OF COSMIC CONJUNCTION WILL BE UPON US IN MOMENTS--BUT SO LONG AS I POSSESS THE ESSENCE URN, I CAN STILL TRIUMPH!

THEN HULK WILL SMASH GLOWING JAR--BEFORE HULK SMASHES ONE-EYE!
PLEASE, HULK-- YOU CAN'T YOU'VE NO IDEA WHAT IS AT STAKE HERE!
BAH! HULK DOES NOT KNOW --AND HULK DOES NOT CARE!

AND ONCE HULK CRUSHES ONE-EYE, IT WILL MAKE NO DIFFERENCE--!
NO, MY LOVE-- THERE IS NO NEED FOR FURTHER VIOLENCE! THE BATTLE IS OVER, HULK--AND YOU HAVE WON.
HUH?

BY THE DARK GODS-- NO!
THE MAN-BRUTE'S SHOCK-WAVE HAS CRACKED THE ESSENCE URN!
I'VE GOT TO RESEAL IT BEFORE...

PSYKLOP'S FINAL AGONIZED SCREAM IS CUT IMPOSSIBLY SHORT, AS THE SINGLE-ORBED ALIEN IS ABRUPTLY ENVELOPED BY THE ETHEREAL FORCES THAT EXPLODE FROM THE RUPTURED ESSENCE URN!
FOR A TIMELESS INSTANT, THE AIR SEEMS FILLED WITH THE TORMENTED MOANING OF LOST SOULS--
--THEN THE SOUND BECOMES A SPINE-CHILLING SIGH OF SATISFACTION--
--AND FADES!

HUH? ONE-EYE IS... GONE!
BUT WHERE DID HE GO, JARELLA? WHERE?
PSYKLOP WAS CONSUMED, MY LOVE--BY THE VERY SPIRITS OF THOSE HE HAD SLAIN.

A MOST IRONIC FATE, MY LADY--BUT A JUST ONE.
NOW K'AI IS FREE ONCE MORE--AND THE EARTHQUAKES WILL BOTHER US NO LONGER!
IN TRUTH, THIS IS A DAY FOR GREAT REJOICING!

THEN LET US MAKE IT A DAY FOR CELEBRATION AS WELL, GOOD TORLA--FOR, IF THE HULK WILL HAVE ME, TODAY I WOULD BE HIS BRIDE!
JARELLA WANTS TO ... MARRY HULK?
YES, JARELLA--YES!!

AT FIRST, THERE IS SILENCE--THEN THE VOICES OF THE GATHERED THRONG ARE RAISED AS ONE--
HAIL HULK! HAIL!
HAIL JARELLA!
HAIL!
HAIL!
--AND THE SHOUTS OF JUBILATION ECHO OUT ACROSS THE LAND!

BUT, AS ALWAYS, THE MAN-BRUTE'S HAPPINESS IS TERRIBLY SHORT-LIVED!
HUH? NOW RAY HITS HULK!
F-FEEL SO STRANGE--! DARLING, WHAT'S HAPPENING TO US?

WE ARE GROWING BIGGER, JARELLA--TURNING INTO GIANTS!
BUT WHY? WHY? HULK DOES NOT UNDERSTAND!
BY THE SEVEN-SIDED CIRCLE!

NOW, WE ARE SO BIG, EVEN MOUNTAIN CANNOT HOLD US!
BUT DO NOT WORRY, JARELLA. HULK WILL NOT LET NOTHING HURT YOU!
KRUMPP!

GODS OF K'AI! THEY HAVE GROWN SO HUGE THAT THEY HAVE VANISHED FROM OUR SIGHT!
IT IS THE SAME CURSE THAT HAS STOLEN THE HULK FROM US TWICE BEFORE--
--BUT THIS TIME IT HAS TAKEN OUR BELOVED QUEEN AS WELL!

BY NOW, THE HULK HAS GROWN ACCUSTOMED TO THE STRANGE SENSATION OF PASSAGE--BUT STILL HE MUST COMFORT HIS TENDER CHANGE...
DO NOT BE FRIGHTENED, JARELLA. HULK WILL PROTECT YOU.
I COULD NEVER BE FRIGHTENED, BELOVED--SO LONG AS I'M WITH YOU!

IN A TOP SECRET RESEARCH LAB DEEP BELOW GAMMA BASE, A SIMPLE GLASS SLIDE BEGINS TO GLOW WITH AN UNNATURAL LIGHT--

--AND THOSE GATHERED IN THE PRESENCE OF THIS MIRACLE BASK TRIUMPHANTLY IN ITS BRILLIANCE...
IT WORKED, GENERAL! SOMETHING IS MATERIALIZING ON THE SLIDE!
YOU'VE BROUGHT BACK THE HULK ALL RIGHT, SAMSON--

NEXT ISSUE: MRS. BRUCE BANNER? THE DEATH OF RICK JONES? THE TIME-TWISTING MENACE OF KRONUS, THE TEMPORAL MAN? YEP, ALL THIS AND MORE, IN THE SHOCKER WE CALL... VICIOUS CIRCLE! BE HERE!

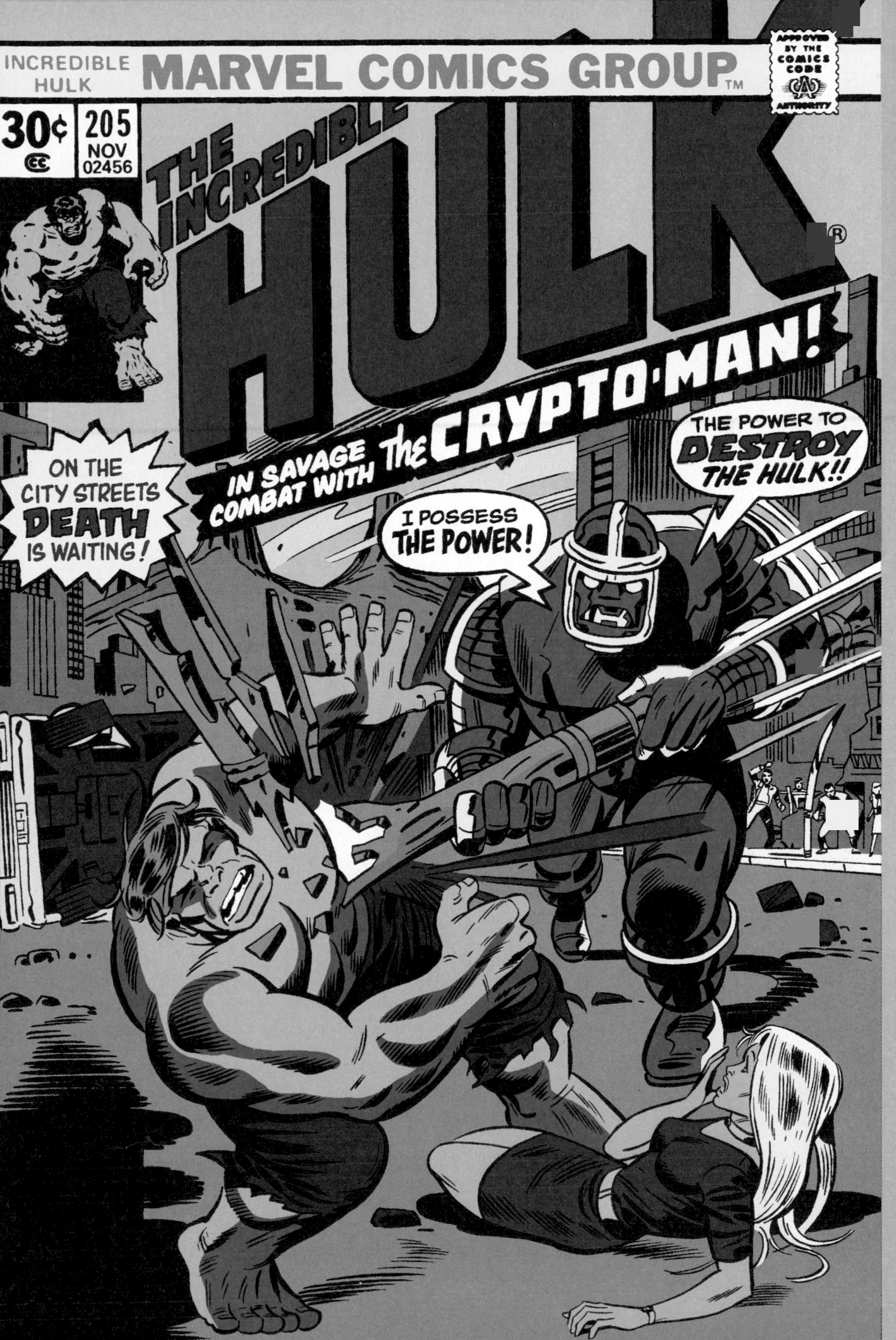
INCREDIBLE HULK
MARVEL COMICS GROUP
30¢
205
NOV
02456
THE INCREDIBLE HULK
IN SAVAGE COMBAT WITH The CRYPTO-MAN!
ON THE CITY STREETS DEATH IS WAITING!
I POSSESS THE POWER!
THE POWER TO DESTROY THE HULK!!

Caught in the heart of a ***Nuclear Explosion,*** victim of ***Gamma-Radiation*** gone wild, ***Doctor Robert Bruce Banner*** now finds himself transformed in times of stress into seven feet, one thousand pounds of unfettered ***Fury***—the most powerful creature to ever walk the earth—

STAN LEE PRESENTS: THE INCREDIBLE HULK!™

LEN WEIN WRITER/EDITOR * SAL BUSCEMA & JOE STATON ILLUSTRATORS * GLYNIS WEIN COLORIST * JOHN COSTANZA LETTERER

WELL, JARELLA-- HOW DOES EARTH COMPARE TO THE MICRO-WORLD OF K'AI?
MY HOMEWORLD SEEMS SO... SO PRIMITIVE BESIDE YOURS, BELOVED.
EACH NEW DISCOVERY I MAKE HERE IS MORE AMAZING THAN THE LAST.

ACTUALLY, IT'S ONLY OUR TECHNOLOGY THAT'S ALL THAT DIFFERENT, SWEET-HEART.
IN MANY WAYS, OUR PEOPLE ARE VERY MUCH ALIKE!
HEY, WILL YA TAKE A LOOK AT THAT LIVING DOLL?
MAN, TALK ABOUT TOO MUCH MAKE-UP! HER WHOLE FACE LOOKS GREEN.

BUT WHAT THE HECK? VARIETY IS THE SPICE OF LIFE, RIGHT?
HEY, SUGAR--WHAT SAY YA DITCH THE CREEP, AN' HOOK UP WITH A REAL MAN?
OKAY, THAT'S ENOUGH! WHY DON'T YOU FELLAS JUST LAY OFF-- BEFORE SOMEBODY GETS HURT!
WELL, WHATTYA KNOW-- A TOUGH GUY!

LOOK, I'M WARNING YOU! FOR YOUR OWN SAKES, DON'T MAKE ME MAD--
--OR THEY'LL HAVE TO SCRAPE YOU ALL OFF THE SIDEWALK WITH A TROWEL!

I'VE GONE THRU ENOUGH GARBAGE LATELY, WITHOUT HAVING TO PUT UP WITH... WITH...
BELOVED, PLEASE-- CALM YOURSELF! YOU KNOW WHAT MIGHT HAPPEN IF YOU BECOME ANGRY!
PLEASE--THOSE MEN SIMPLY ARE NOT WORTH THAT!

YES... OF COURSE... Y-YOU'RE RIGHT. I'M... CALM NOW.
IT JUST BECOMES SO EASY SOMETIMES TO WANT TO GIVE IN TO THE IMPULSE --AND LET HIM TAKE OVER!
D-DARLING...?

NEVER MIND, JARELLA. LET'S JUST GET AWAY FROM HERE--
--BEFORE I CHANGE MY MIND!
G'WAN, YA CRAZY LUNATIC-- TAKE A WALK!
YOU AN' THAT PASTY-FACED CHICK OF YOURS DESERVE EACH OTHER!

HE'S RIGHT! WE DO DESERVE EACH OTHER--A SKINNY SCIENTIST WITH A HALF-TON MONSTER ON HIS BACK, AND A QUEEN WHO'S LOST HER KINGDOM!
WE MAKE QUITE A PAIR, DON'T WE?
BUT I WOULD HAVE IT NO OTHER WAY, MY LOVE.

YOU ARE ALL I HAVE LEFT NOW THAT MY NATIVE WORLD IS FOREVER LOST TO ME--AND BEFORE I WOULD LOSE YOU AS WELL, I WOULD...
GODS OF K'AI! NEVER BEFORE HAVE I SEEN SUCH... SUCH REVEALING CLOTHING.
YEAH. I GUESS MY WORLD DOES HAVE SOME GOOD POINTS AT THAT.

AND RIGHT HERE WE HAVE ONE OF THE BEST!
YOU, MY FAIR-HAIRED BEAUTY, ARE ABOUT TO PARTAKE OF A CONFECTION THAT WOULD MAKE THOSE FABLED GODS OF YOURS DROOL!
ICE CREAM PARLOR
FLAVORS
WH-WHAT DO YOU MEAN, BRUCE?

IN ALL THE TIME THAT I HAVE KNOWN YOU, BELOVED-- NEVER HAVE I SEEN YOU GLOW WITH SUCH ENTHUSIASM!
THAT'S BECAUSE YOU'VE NEVER TASTED THE SINGLE MOST PRECIOUS TREASURE MY WORLD HAS TO OFFER!
JARELLA, I AM ABOUT TO INTRODUCE YOU TO-- TA-DAH-- THE TWO-TONE CHOCOLATE MILK SHAKE!
YOU CAN SAVE THE APPLAUSE TILL LATER.

IN ALL ACTUALITY, THEY'RE REALLY NOT SO UNUSUAL, THESE TWO STAR-CROSSED WAYFARERS ON THE CHURNING SEA OF LIFE. THEY'RE YOUNG, THEY'RE IN LOVE--
--AND IT SEEMS LOVE IS THE SAME NO MATTER WHERE YOU GO!

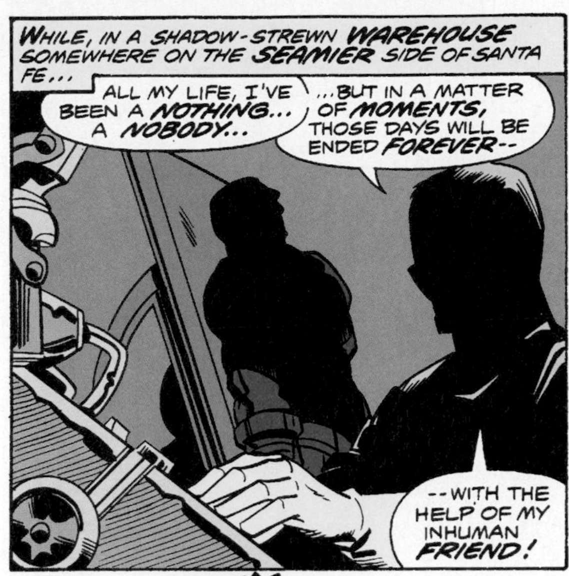
WHILE, IN A SHADOW-STREWN WAREHOUSE SOMEWHERE ON THE SEAMIER SIDE OF SANTA FE...
ALL MY LIFE, I'VE BEEN A NOTHING... A NOBODY...
...BUT IN A MATTER OF MOMENTS, THOSE DAYS WILL BE ENDED FOREVER--
--WITH THE HELP OF MY INHUMAN FRIEND!

EVER SINCE I FIRST FOUND JASPER WHYTE'S ALL-POWERFUL ANDROID, I'VE DEVOTED MYSELF TO RESTORING HIS REMARKABLE CREATION!
...A CREATURE WHO ONCE POSSESSED FULLY HALF THE INCOMPARABLE STRENGTH OF THE MIGHTY THOR HIMSELF! *
* CHECK OUT THOR #174 FOR ALL THE DRAMATIC DETAILS, PILGRIM. --LEN.

CLIK!
BUT NOW, THRU TRIAL AND ERROR AND UNSTINTING EFFORT, I HAVE ACTUALLY DOUBLED THE ANDROID'S POWER!
ALL I NEED DO IS ACTIVATE THE SPECIAL ENERGY-DYNAMO I CONSTRUCTED BASED ON WHYTE'S OWN DESIGNS--
--AND MY DAYS OF ANONYMITY WILL BE OVER!

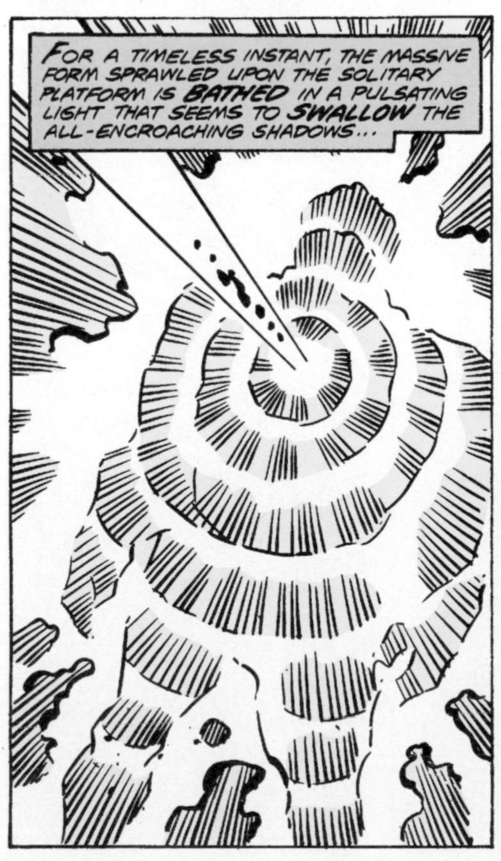
FOR A TIMELESS INSTANT, THE MASSIVE FORM SPRAWLED UPON THE SOLITARY PLATFORM IS BATHED IN A PULSATING LIGHT THAT SEEMS TO SWALLOW THE ALL-ENCROACHING SHADOWS...

AND THEN, SUDDENLY...
I... POSSESS... POWER!
BY HEAVEN, I'VE DONE IT!
THE CRYPTO-MAN LIVES AGAIN!!

AND WHILE ONE LIFE (OF SORTS) BEGINS ANEW, SEVERAL HUNDRED MILES AWAY, AT THE SECLUDED PARA-MILITARY INSTALLATION CODE-NAMED GAMMA BASE, ANOTHER LIFE HAS GROUND TO A VIRTUAL STANDSTILL--

--SPECIFICALLY, THE MUCH-TORMENTED LIFE OF MAJOR GLENN TALBOT!
HE REALLY IS QUITE A FELLA, ISN'T HE?
I COULDN'T BLAME ANY WOMAN FOR FALLING FOR HIM--
--NOT EVEN BETTY!

I MEAN, LOOK AT HIM-- JUGGLING TWO-TON MACHINES AROUND LIKE THEY WERE THE PROVERBIAL TINKER-TOYS!
FACE IT, TALBOT-- DOC SAMSON IS ALL MAN!

AND WHAT ABOUT YOU, GLENN-- WHAT ARE YOU?
WHO--?!?

OH. BETTY. I DIDN'T HEAR YOU COMING, DARLING.
AND IF YOU HAD, GLENN? WHAT WOULD YOU HAVE DONE THEN?

WOULD YOU HAVE PUT ON A HAPPY FACE AND PRETENDED EVERYTHING WAS ALL SWEET-NESS AND LIGHT?
WOULD YOU REALLY HAVE LIED TO ME LIKE THAT, GLENN?
BUT IT'S FOR YOUR OWN GOOD, DARLING. DON'T YOU UNDER-STAND--?

WHEN I MARRIED YOU, I PROMISED TO TAKE YOU AWAY FROM ALL THE GRIEF YOU KNEW WHEN YOU LOVED BRUCE BANNER--
--BUT IT SEEMS ALL I'VE GIVEN YOU IS A WHOLE NEW KIND OF HEARTBREAK!
BETTY, I LOVE YOU. I JUST WANT TO SPARE YOU ANY MORE SORROW.

SPARE ME? SWEET LORD, GLENN-- I'M NOT SOME FRAGILE DRESDEN DOLL TO BE PROTECTED FOR FEAR SHE'LL BREAK!
I'M YOUR WIFE, GLENN...

...AND WHATEVER BRINGS YOU HAPPINESS... OR WHATEVER BRINGS YOU PAIN...
...I WANT TO SHARE!

AND, BACK IN SANTA FE...
DID YOU SEE THE EXPRESSION ON THAT SALESWOMAN'S FACE WHEN SHE REALIZED YOU WEREN'T WEARING MAKE-UP?
I ADMIT IT WAS A TRIFLE DISCONCERTING AT FIRST, BELOVED--
--BUT I SUPPOSE IT CAN BECOME QUITE AMUSING AFTER AWHILE.

WHILE, SEVERAL BLOCKS AWAY...
STAND... ASIDE... HUMANS!
I... POSSESS... POWER!
SKRASHH!
HOLY CATFISH! IT'S SOME KIND'A ROBOT!

WELL, WHATEVER IT IS--IT'S NOT COMING ANY CLOSER!
AT LEAST, NOT IN ONE PIECE!
BLAM! BLAM! SPOW!
KEEP FIRING! THESE HEAVY STEEL SLUGS AREN'T EVEN SLOWING HIM DOWN!

OUT... OF... MY... WAY... HUMANS!
SWAKK!
NOTHING... CAN... STOP... THE... CRYPTO-MAN!

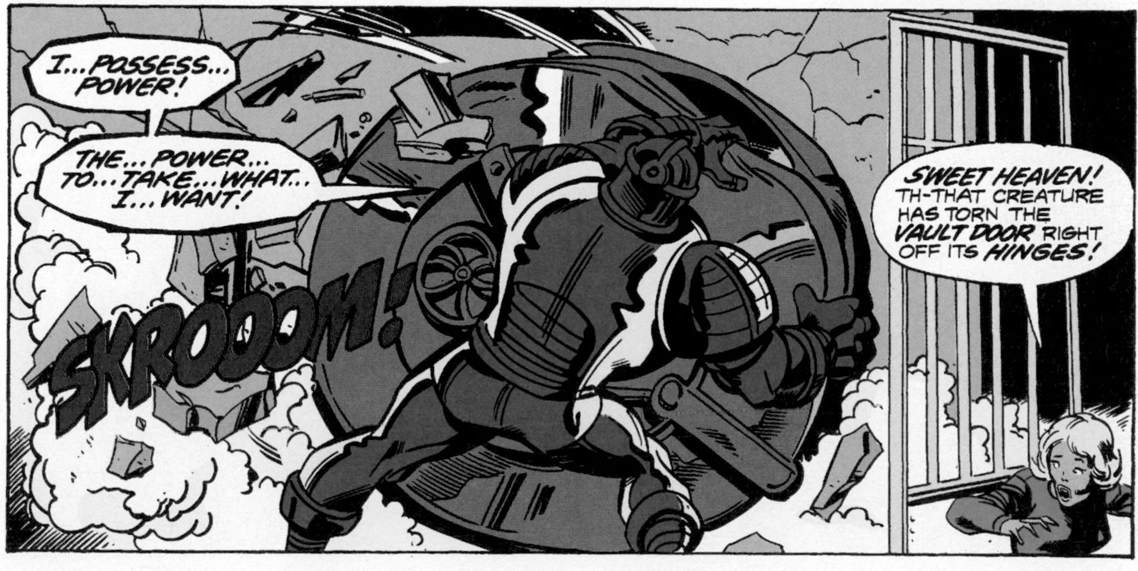
I... POSSESS... POWER!
THE... POWER... TO... TAKE... WHAT... I... WANT!
SKROOOM!
SWEET HEAVEN! TH-THAT CREATURE HAS TORN THE VAULT DOOR RIGHT OFF ITS HINGES!

I'LL TELL YOU, HONEY-- I REALLY NEEDED THIS BREAK.
I KNOW, MY LOVE. SOMEHOW, GAMMA BASE SEEMS FAR MORE HECTIC THAN THIS GREAT CITY.
WANNA BET?
KROOM!
BY THE SEVEN-SIDED CIRCLE! WHAT MANNER OF CREATURE IS THIS?
SOME SORT OF ROBOT-- AND IT'S ON A RAMPAGE!
OUT... OF... MY... WAY... HUMANS... OR... DIE!

WHY, BLAST IT? WHY DOES TROUBLE FOLLOW ME WHEREVER I GO? WHY CAN'T I JUST BE LEFT IN PEACE?
CALM YOURSELF, BELOVED! THOSE IN AUTHORITY WILL DEAL WITH THE CREATURE!

CLEAR...THE... PATH...BEFORE... ME...HUMANS!
WRUNCH!
THE...CRYPTO-MAN...IS...POWER ...PERSONIFIED!

STAND... ASIDE...OR...I... WILL...CRUSH...YOU... ALL...LIKE... EH?
THAT...WOMAN! HER...SKIN... IS... GREEN... LIKE...THAT... OF... THE...MONSTROUS... HULK...WHO...PROWLS... THIS... REGION!
OH... NO.

AND IF HER STRENGTH IS ALSO LIKE THAT OF THE HULK, I MUST HAVE IT--
--TO SIPHON INTO MY CRYPTO-MAN!

"I NEED ONLY INITIATE THE PROPER PROGRAMMING AND..."
GET BEHIND ME, JARELLA! HE'S COMING AFTER YOU!

THERE IS NOWHERE FOR US TO RUN, BRUCE!
BUT WHATEVER HAPPENS NOW, MY LOVE-- I WILL FACE IT LIKE A QUEEN!

THE BLOOD OF ANCIENT ROYALTY FLOWS THRU MY VEINS AND I WILL NOT ALLOW MYSELF TO...
...TO...

NO! HE'S ALMOST UPON US!
HELP ME, BELOVED-- HELP ME!

DO NOT WORRY, JARELLA!
NOTHING WILL HURT YOU WHILE HULK IS HERE!
POW!
GODS OF K'AI!

INCREDIBLE! THE EMERALD MAN-BRUTE HIMSELF HAS SUDDENLY APPEARED UPON THE SCENE!
IF THE CRYPTO-MAN CAN DEFEAT HIM, MY REPUTATION IS ASSURED!
STAY BACK, ROBOT-- OR HULK WILL SMASH!

YOUR...THREATS...MEAN... NOTHING...TO...ME... MONSTER!
I...POSSESS... POWER!
BAH! HULK HAS POWER TOO, ROBOT-- POWER ENOUGH TO CRUSH YOU!

YOU... ARE... WELCOME... TO... COME... AHEAD... AND... TRY... BRUTE...
SKRAKK!
...BUT... NOTHING... THAT... LIVES... CAN... DEFY... THE... CRYPTO-MAN!

NOT... EVEN... YOU!
WHOM!

YOU ARE STRONG, CRYPTO-MAN-- BUT NOTHING CAN BEAT HULK!
THAT... REMAINS... TO... BE... SEEN!

JUST KEEP BACK OUT OF THEIR WAY, EVERYONE!
WE'LL HAVE TO LET THOSE TWO MONSTERS WORK THIS OUT BETWEEN THEMSELVES!
BUT NO MATTER WHICH ONE WINS-- THE CITY LOSES!

IT... IS... MY... DUTY... TO... DESTROY ... YOU... HULK...
...SO... THAT... THE... WHOLE... WORLD... CAN... KNOW... OF... MY... MASTER'S... BRILLIANCE!

HAH! HULK WAS TOO FAST FOR CRYPTO-MAN!
PUNY CAR FLEW OVER HULK'S HEAD!

THERE COMES AN INSTANT OF SHATTERING IMPACT--
SKRUMP!
--THEN A HASTILY-HURLED AUTOMOBILE BECOMES A CRUMPLED BALL OF SCRAP--

--AND A TOPPLING BRICK WALL BECOMES A VERY DEAD-LY WEAPON!
GODS OF K'AI! THAT FALLING RUBBLE--!

AN INNOCENT CHILD STANDS BENEATH IT--UNMINDFUL OF HIS DANGER!

ONLY ONE CHANCE TO SAVE HIM--IF THE GRACIOUS GODS WILL GRANT ME WINGS!
MAMA?

ON HER HOMEWORLD, THE WOMAN CALLED JARELLA HAD BEEN A QUEEN. THE LIVES OF COUNTLESS BEINGS WERE HER RESPONSIBILITY--AND HERS ALONE.
IT SEEMS THAT SOME HABITS ARE UNFORTUNATELY HARD TO BREAK!

THE CHILD FALLS CLEAR OF THE BATTLE-BORN AVALANCHE, A FRIGHTENED WHIMPER ON HIS LIPS--
--BUT THE JADE-SKINNED JAR-ELLA DOES NOT FARE NEARLY AS WELL!

NOW... HULK... I... WILL...
JARELLA?
JARELLA!!

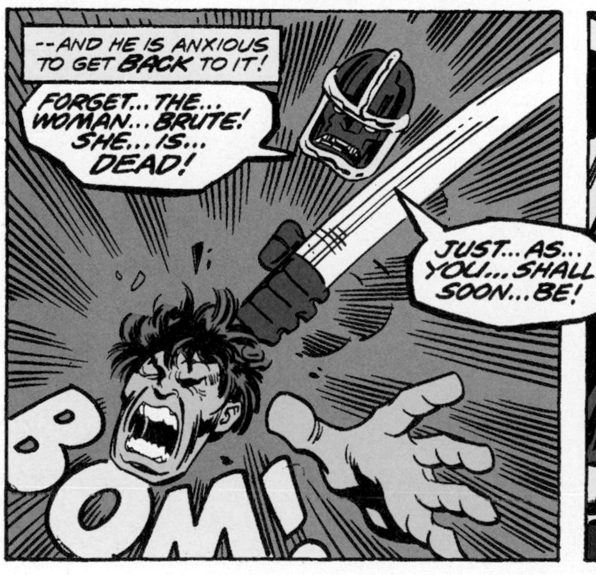

NO, CRYPTO-MAN-- YOU ARE WRONG! IT IS YOUR FAULT THAT HULK'S JARELLA IS HURT...

...AND IT IS YOU WHO ARE GOING TO DIE!

DEAR HEAVEN! THAT FACE--!
IT'S THE LIVING EMBODIMENT OF SHEER, UNADULTERATED HATRED!
YOU WANTED A FIGHT, CRYPTO-MAN--

--AND NOW YOU HAVE ONE!

FOR ALL HULK'S LIFE, HULK HAS BEEN ALONE!
BUT THEN HULK FOUND JARELLA-- AND HULK WAS HAPPY FOR THE FIRST TIME!

NOW YOU HAVE TAKEN JARELLA AWAY FROM HULK, CRYPTO-MAN! AND FOR THAT--
HULK WILL MAKE YOU PAY!!

NO! EVERYTHING HAS SUDDENLY GONE WRONG! I'VE GOT TO FEED THE CRYPTO-MAN MORE POWER--
--POWER ENOUGH TO DEVASTATE THIS PLANET IF NEED BE!
MY DREAMS OF GLORY WILL NOT BE STOLEN FROM ME NOW!

I...POSSESS... POWER!
BUT HULK HAS HATE, ROBOT--
--AND HATE IS ALL HULK NEEDS!

THEN...YOU...WILL... CARRY...THAT... HATRED...TO... THE...GRAVE... MONSTER!
FOR...WHEN...YOU... HAVE...BEEN...DESTROYED ...MY MASTER...WILL... AT...LAST...BE... FAMOUS!
WRAMM!

BAH!
STKOW!
IF CRYPTO-MAN'S MASTER WANTS HULK DESTROYED, WHY DOESN'T MASTER FIGHT HULK HIMSELF?

CHOK!
INSTEAD, PUNY MASTER SENDS BIG ROBOT TO FIGHT FOR HIM--

--BUT NO PUNY ROBOT IS A MATCH FOR HULK!
BROK!
NO! NO! I...POSSESS... POWER!

YOU ARE STRONG, CRYPTO-MAN--
BUT SO DOES HULK, CRYPTO-MAN-- POWER ENOUGH TO SMASH YOU!

KHA-DOOMM!
--BUT HULK IS THE STRONGEST ONE THERE IS!!
NO! IT'S NOT POSSIBLE--!
ZAKK!
DESPITE THE INCALCULABLE AMOUNT OF POWER I TRANSMITTED TO HIM, MY CRYPTO-MAN HAS BEEN DESTROYED!

AND NOW THE INCREDIBLE POWER-FEED-BACK IS DESTROYING MY EQUIPMENT AS WELL!
I'VE GOT TO BREAK THE CIRCUITS BEFORE...

BUT IT IS ALREADY FAR TOO LATE!
AND THE BLAST THAT STEALS HIS LIFE AWAY IS TRULY TERRIBLE TO HEAR!

OUTSIDE, A PASSERBY WHO WAS STARTLED BY THE EX-PLOSION EVEN NOW IS CALLING THE POLICE.
THE RUINED BODY THEY FIND HERE WILL BE BURIED AT THE CITY'S EXPENSE; ITS IDENTITY WILL NEVER BE KNOWN--
--AND SOMEWHERE, A TORTURED SOUL WILL SCREAM FOR ALL ETERNITY!

BUT, ALL THINGS CONSIDERED, THAT IS A VERY SPECIAL KIND OF JUSTICE!
JARELLA?
PLEASE, JARELLA--TELL HULK HOW TO MAKE YOU WELL AGAIN!
JUST... HOLD ME... BELOVED.

BUT...
MAYBE IT IS... BETTER THIS WAY, MY LOVE. I WAS NOT A... PART OF YOUR WORLD... I DID NOT BELONG HERE...
...BUT YOU MADE MY TIME HERE... A HAPPY ONE...
PLEASE... BE KIND TO YOUR-SELF... MY DARLING... UNTIL WE MEET AGAIN...

JARELLA?
DON'T LEAVE, JARELLA!
PLEASE... DON'T LEAVE HULK ALONE AGAIN.

NO... SHE DOES NOT ANSWER...
...BUT HULK WILL NOT LET JARELLA DIE!

SOME-WHERE...
SOME-HOW...
...HULK WILL FIND SOMEONE TO HELP HER!

AIMLESSLY, THE MAN-BRUTE BOUNDS ABOUT THE COUNTRYSIDE, UNTIL HE FINALLY STUMBLES UPON...
GAMMA BASE! THE ONE CALLED ROSS LIVES HERE!
ROSS WILL USE HIS BIG MACHINES TO MAKE JARELLA WELL AGAIN--
--OR HULK WILL SMASH!

ROSS! JARELLA IS HURT! HULK WANTS YOU TO FIX HER!
JUMPING JUPITER!
LORD, I WAS AFRAID OF SOMETHING LIKE THIS!

GENERAL, YOU'D BETTER GET YOUR TOP MEDICS UP HERE-- AND PRONTO!
IF THERE'S A SPARK OF LIFE STILL LEFT IN THIS GIRL, IT'S FADING FAST!

YOU'VE DONE ALL YOU CAN, HULK. WE'LL HANDLE THINGS FROM HERE ON!
JUST MAKE JARELLA WELL AGAIN, SAMSON...
...PLEASE.

PLEASE.

IT IS SEVERAL ETERNITIES LATER, WHEN THE DOORS OF THE OPERATING THEATRE HUSH OPEN ONCE MORE.
HOW IS JARELLA, SAMSON? IS SHE...?
I'M SORRY, HULK. WE WERE TOO LATE.
THERE WAS NOTHING WE COULD DO FOR HER.

HUH?
JARELLA IS... DEAD?
DEAD?

NEXT ISSUE: THE HULK HITS NEW YORK--AND, BOY, DO WE MEAN HITS! BE HERE TO WITNESS THE MOST SAVAGE HULK OF ALL IN...

A MAN-BRUTE BERSERK!

INCREDIBLE HULK

MARVEL COMICS GROUP™

APPROVED BY THE COMICS CODE AUTHORITY

30¢ 206 DEC 02456

THE INCREDIBLE HULK®

A MAN-BRUTE BERSERK!

NEW YORK STOCK EX

THIS IS IT!! THE HULK GOES ON A RAMPAGE-- MORE SAVAGE-- MORE BRUTAL-- THAN EVER BEFORE!!

COCKRUM

Caught in the heart of a ***Nuclear Explosion,*** victim of ***Gamma-Radiation*** gone wild, ***Doctor Robert Bruce Banner*** now finds himself transformed in times of stress into seven feet, one thousand pounds of unfettered ***Fury***—the most powerful creature to ever walk the earth—

Stan Lee PRESENTS: THE INCREDIBLE HULK!™

LEN WEIN WRITER/EDITOR * SAL BUSCEMA & JOE STATON ILLUSTRATORS * GLYNIS WEIN colorist * JOHN COSTANZA letterer

BUT DESPITE THE MAN-BRUTE'S PREOCCUPATION...
HUH? NOISE IN SKY BEHIND HULK--
--LIKE ROARING OF PLANES FLOWN BY PUNY HUMANS!

BAH! IT IS PLANES!
THAK-AK-AK!
THEY HAVE FOLLOWED HULK-- AND NOW THEY ARE SHOOTING AT HULK!

GO AWAY, PLANES! HULK DOES NOT HAVE TIME TO FIGHT WITH YOU NOW!
GO AWAY--OR HULK WILL SMASH!!
THP-IP-IP!

SO--PLANES HAVE TURNED AROUND TO ATTACK HULK AGAIN!
LITTLE MEN IN PLANES DIDN'T LISTEN TO HULK!
PUNY HUMANS NEVER LISTEN!

AND HULK IS TIRED OF WASTING HULK'S BREATH!!
KWA
ROOM!
HOLY HOPPIN' HANNAH!
THAT MONSTER OVERTOOK MY JET LIKE IT WAS STANDIN' STILL!

HAH! SECOND PLANE TRIED TO GET AWAY FROM HULK--
--BUT HULK WAS TOO FAST FOR IT!
GB-ONE TO GAMMA BASE! WE GOT US A PANIC SITUATION HERE! OVER?

HULK WARNED MEN IN PLANES TO LEAVE HULK ALONE, BUT YOU IGNORED HULK--
SKRAK!
--AND NOW HULK WILL MAKE YOU PAY!!
LORD-- NO! HE'S TORN MY CANOPY CLEAR OFF!
GOT TO EJECT-- WHILE I STILL CAN!

COME BACK, LITTLE MAN! DON'T RUN AWAY FROM HULK!
YOU WANTED TO FIGHT--NOW HULK IS GIVING YOU YOUR CHANCE!
COME BACK LITTLE MAN-- COME BACK!!

BAH! PUNY HUMAN WAS JUST LIKE ALL THE REST!
READY TO BATTLE HULK WITH BIG MACHINES ON HIS SIDE--BUT AFRAID OF HULK FACE-TO-FACE!
WHEREVER HULK GOES, PEOPLE ARE AFRAID OF HULK!
ALWAYS AFRAID!!

AND THE FURIOUS BEHEMOTH CONTINUES HIS RELENTLESS RANTING--
--ALL THE LONG WAY DOWN!
BWHOOM!

SEVERAL INTERMINABLE SECONDS PASS, FILLED WITH A SOLITARY SILENCE THAT IS BROKEN ONLY BY THE OCCASIONAL CLATTER OF FALLING METAL--
--OR THE FRAGILE CHICKLE OF A SPLINTERED SHARD OF GLASS--

--UNTIL, AT LAST, A VOICE LIKE CHURNING GRAVEL IS HEARD ONCE MORE!
HULK STILL LIVES!!

YOU TRIED, LITTLE MEN--
--BUT NOTHING CAN KILL HULK!
NOTHING!!

IF HULK HAD TIME, HULK WOULD STAY AND SMASH YOU BOTH--
--BUT NOW HULK HAS MORE IMPORTANT THINGS TO DO!

GB-TWO TO GAMMA BASE! DAMAGE REPORT, SIR--BOTH PLANES DESTROYED!
WE DID OUR BEST, GENERAL--
--BUT I'M AFRAID THE HULK STILL GOT AWAY!

YOU DID ALL YOU COULD DO, GB-TWO!
WE'LL DISPATCH A RETRIEVAL-CRAFT IMMEDIATELY TO PICK YOU BOTH UP!
AND THEN WHAT, GENERAL ROSS?
WILL YOU SEND OUT ANOTHER TEAM TO CAPTURE THE HULK? WILL YOU SEND OUT A THOUSAND OTHER TEAMS?
AND AFTER THEY CAPTURE HIM, WHAT THEN? WHAT HAPPENS WHEN HE ESCAPES ONCE MORE?
HOW MANY TIMES MUST THIS CAT-AND-MOUSE GAME BE REPLAYED BEFORE YOU'RE THRU?

WHAT ARE YOU JABBERING ABOUT, SAMSON? I'M ONLY DOING MY JOB!
I'VE BEEN AROUND HERE LONG ENOUGH TO KNOW THIS IS NO LONGER MERELY A JOB TO YOU, GENERAL--
--IT'S AN OBSESSION!

WHY DON'T YOU LEAVE BRUCE BANNER ALONE FOR A WHILE? LET HIM WORK OUT THIS HULK PROBLEM FOR HIMSELF?
LORD KNOWS HE HAS ENOUGH ON HIS SHOULDERS WITHOUT US ADDING TO HIS GRIEF!
BUT I... I...

NO. MAYBE YOU'RE RIGHT, SAMSON--MAYBE YOU'RE RIGHT!
I JUST WISH TO GOD I KNEW FOR SURE!

SEVERAL HOURS--AND SEVERAL HUNDRED MONUMENTAL LEAPS--HAVE FINALLY CARRIED THE ANGRY HULK TO THE MARSHY NEW JERSEY SHORE...
HUH?

...WITHIN CLEAR VIEW OF A VERY SPECIAL LADY!
IS STATUE!
HULK REMEMBERS STATUE!
HULK SPENT TIME HERE ONCE BEFORE! *
* BACK IN HULK #142, LIBERTY-LOVERS. --LEN.

AND RIGHT NOW, STATUE IS JUST WHAT HULK NEEDS!
STATUE IS HIGH! IT OVERLOOKS BIG CITY!

MAYBE FROM HERE, HULK CAN SEE HOUSE OF HULK'S FRIEND--
--HOUSE OF THE MAGICIAN CALLED STRANGE!

HULK NEEDS MAGICIAN'S HELP IF JARELLA IS GOING TO BE WELL AGAIN-- AND JARELLA MUST BE WELL!
JARELLA IS THE ONLY ONE WHO EVER CARED FOR HULK... WHO EVER LOVED HULK FOR WHAT HULK IS!
HULK NEEDS JARELLA TO HELP HULK UNDERSTAND WHAT...

HUH?
LIGHTS FROM SKY--PINNING HULK TO SPOTLIGHT--!
WHO DARES TO BOTHER HULK NOW?

BAH! MORE PUNY HUMANS-- IN HELICOPTERS!
GO AWAY, PUNY LITTLE MEN! LEAVE HULK ALONE-- SO HULK CAN THINK!
NO CHANCE, UGLY! THAT'S A NATIONAL MONUMENT YOU'RE STANDIN' ON--
--AND WE'RE BRINGIN' YOU DOWN BEFORE YOU HAVE TIME TO DAMAGE IT!
NYPD

ARGHH! NOW MEN AND HELICOPTERS HAVE COVERED HULK WITH HEAVY METAL NET!
BUT IF THEY THINK PUNY NET CAN HOLD HULK--

--THEY ARE WRONG!!
SKRAKT!

LOOKS LIKE WE'RE GONNA HAVE TO DO THIS THE HARD WAY, CHARLIE!
PREPARE TO FIRE GAS GRENADES--
--NOW!!

HAH! PUNY HUMANS ARE SHOOTING BOMBS AT HULK--!
TRYING TO BEAT HULK AGAIN WITH THE GAS THAT MAKES HULK SLEEP--!
WHUMP! WHUMP!

BUT THIS TIME, HULK IS TOO SMART FOR THEM!
THIS TIME, HULK WILL USE ARMS TO BLOW GAS AWAY!
WITHIN INSTANTS, THE NOXIOUS FUMES ARE GONE-- BUT THE MAN-BRUTE'S RAGE IS STILL GOING STRONG!
HULK ONLY WANTED TO BE LEFT ALONE-- TO FIND MAGICIAN'S HOUSE IN PEACE--
RRUNCH!
--BUT PUNY HUMANS KEEP ON HOUNDING HULK--
--AND HULK IS SICK AND TIRED OF IT!!

BUT EVEN AS CHARLIE SHRUGS HIS SHOULDERS HELPLESSLY AND THE TWO THOROUGHLY-SOAKED FIGURES MOROSELY STROKE TOWARDS SHORE...
BAH! HOW WILL HULK FIND MAGICIAN'S HOUSE NOW?
HEY!?! WH-WHUT'S GOIN' ON?
THOOM!
THIS AN EART'QUAKE OR SOMETHIN'?

OH... HIYA, PAL. D-DIDN'T SEE YA STANDIN' THERE!
CARE TA JOIN ME IN A LI'L DRINKY-POO?
IT'SA FINEST HOOCH 85 CENTS KIN BUY.

HUH? LITTLE MAN IN DIRTY CLOTHES OFFERS HULK A DRINK?
HULK DOESN'T TRUST PUNY HUMANS...
...BUT HULK IS... THIRSTY...

YES, LITTLE MAN--HULK WILL TAKE A DRINK!
AND THEN HULK WILL...

PFAUGH!!

SO! HULK WAS RIGHT NOT TO TRUST LITTLE MAN!
PUNY HUMAN TRIED TO POISON HULK--

--AND FOR THAT, HULK WILL SMASH!!
KKRRIIPP
HEY, NO--DON'T-!

LEMME OUTTA HERE! EVER'BODY IN THIS WHOLE BLAMED TOWN IS CRAZY!
BAH! CLOTHES ARE SO RAGGED, LITTLE MAN GOT AWAY FROM HULK!

LITTLE MAN HAS RUN AWAY-- BUT HULK'S ANGER STILL REMAINS!
WHY DO PUNY HUMANS TRY TO TRICK HULK--TRY TO HURT HULK--WHEREVER HULK GOES?

WHY?
WHY??
WHY??

WHY??
WH-WHAT--?!?
OH... TH-THANK GOD. IT WAS A DREAM-- ONLY A DREAM!
IT SOUNDED MORE LIKE A NIGHTMARE, GLENN DARLING.
WHAT FRIGHTENED YOU SO?

I--I WAS BACK IN RUSSIA, BETTY-- A PRISONER OF THAT LITTLE MONSTER CALLED THE GREMLIN...
...AND HE WAS ABOUT TO DESTROY MY MIND AGAIN! *
LORD, MY SPINE TURNS TO ICE JUST THINKING ABOUT IT!
*AS HE DID BACK IN HULK #188.--LEN.

I'M SORRY I WOKE YOU UP TOO, BETTY. GO BACK TO SLEEP.
AND LEAVE YOU TIED UP IN KNOTS LIKE THIS?
YOU SHOULD KNOW ME BETTER THAN THAT, GLENN. WHAT CAN I DO TO HELP YOU?
I WISH I KNEW, BETTY.

HONEST TO GOD, I WISH I KNEW.
GLENN, PLEASE-- NO MAN CAN GO THROUGH WHAT YOU'VE BEEN THROUGH WITHOUT SUFFERING SOME PSYCHOLOGICAL SCARS!
BUT YOU'VE GOT TO UNWIND, DARLING-- TRY TO FORGET!
DON'T LET THE PAST DESTROY OUR FUTURE TOGETHER.

THAT'S JUST WHAT WORRIES ME, BETTY...
DO WE EVEN HAVE A FUTURE TOGETHER?

IN HER OWN FASHION, BETTY ROSS TALBOT ECHOES HER HUSBAND'S THOUGHTS.

AND THUS THEY PASS THE NIGHT IN SILENT SOLITUDE; TWO PEOPLE BOUND TOGETHER BY THE HOLY STATE OF MATRIMONY--
--AND VERY LITTLE ELSE!

FOR SEVERAL HOURS, THE GREEN GOLIATH HAS WANDERED AIMLESSLY THRU THE SHADOW-STREWN ALLEYWAYS OF MANHATTAN, IN SEARCH OF A MOST UNIQUE EDIFICE...
HAH! AT LAST!

...THE GREENWICH VILLAGE SANCTUM SANCTORUM OF THE MASTER OF THE MYSTIC ARTS!
HULK HAS FOUND MAGICIAN'S HOUSE!

NOW MAGICIAN WILL HELP HULK MAKE JARELLA WELL AGAIN, AND THEN...
HUH?

THERE IS SOMETHING IN AIR IN FRONT OF HULK-- SOMETHING THAT HULK CANNOT SEE!
IT FEELS LIKE WALL-- WALL THAT WILL NOT LET HULK COME CLOSE TO MAGICIAN'S HOUSE!

BUT NOTHING WILL STOP HULK FROM REACHING HULK'S FRIEND!
NOTHING!
HULK WILL SMASH THIS WALL HULK CANNOT SEE!

AND, FOR SEVERAL RELENTLESS MINUTES, THE JADE-HUED GIANT ATTEMPTS TO MAKE GOOD HIS THREAT--
--HIS MASSIVE FISTS HAMMERING SAVAGELY AT THE MYSTIC BARRICADE THAT PROTECTS THE DOMICILE OF DOCTOR STRANGE IN ITS MASTER'S ABSENCE--

--UNTIL AT LAST, EVEN HIS BE-CLOUDED MIND COMES TO REALIZE THAT FURY IS FUTILE!
MAGICIAN IS NOT HOME-- AND HULK CANNOT GET IN!
BUT MAGICIAN MUST COME HOME SOMETIME--

--AND WHEN HE DOES, HULK WILL BE WAITING!

THE DAWN COMES UP LIKE "THUNDERBOLT" ROSS'S FAMOUS TEMPER OVER THE NEW MEXICAN PARA-MILITARY INSTALLATION CALLED GAMMA BASE--

--AND, ON AN OTHERWISE DESERTED ATHLETIC FIELD, THE EMERALD-TRESSED DOC SAMSON GOES ABOUT HIS MORNING EXERCISES...
HI, DOC, HOW'RE THE OL' BICEPS?
GOOD MORNING, QUARTERMAIN. CARE TO JOIN ME?

NO THANKS, PAL. THIS IS FAR TOO FINE A DAY TO COME DOWN WITH A HERNIA!
HEY, I HEAR YOU CONVINCED GENERAL ROSS TO SHELVE HIS HULK-HUNT FINALLY.

A MOST IMPRESSIVE PIECE OF DIPLOMACY, M'MAN. I FIGURED OL' "THUNDERBOLT" WOULD KEEP HOUNDING THE HULK TILL ONE OF THEM DROPPED IN HIS TRACKS!
HOW'D YOU MANAGE TO TALK ROSS OUT OF IT?
IT WASN'T ALL THAT DIFFICULT, CLAY.

THE GENERAL FELT AS BAD AS I DID ABOUT WHAT HAPPENED TO JARELLA. SHE MAY HAVE BEEN BRUCE BANNER'S LAST CHANCE FOR HAPPINESS...
...AND THAT POOR GUY DESERVES ALL THE HAPPINESS HE CAN GET!

NOW HOW ABOUT YOU AND THE HULK, QUARTERMAIN?
I'M AN AGENT OF SHIELD, SAMSON-- I DO WHAT I'M TOLD!
AND IF I'M TOLD TO GET ON GREENSKIN'S BACK AGAIN--THEN THAT'S JUST WHAT I'LL HAVE TO DO!
IT'S YOUR JOB, EH? YOU SOUND DEPRESSINGLY LIKE THE OLD "THUNDERBOLT" ROSS!

LOOK, DESPITE EVERYTHING-- IN HIS OWN WAY, THE HULK IS AS HUMAN AS ANY OF US!
HE'S ENTITLED TO LIVE HIS LIFE AS HE SEES FIT--
--AND I AM GOING TO DO WHATEVER I HAVE TO DO TO HELP HIM!

IN NEW YORK CITY, THE SUN ROSE ABOVE THE POLLUTION SEVERAL HOURS AGO--AND VELMA WOLENSKY, A RATHER PUDGY EARLY-RISER INCLINED TO SWEAT-PANTS AND FLOWERED HATS, WAS OUT WALKING HER FRENCH POODLE CUDDLES AT 6:15 AS ALWAYS.

PASSING BY THAT QUEER-LOOKING TOWNHOUSE ON THE NEXT BLOCK, SHE HAPPENED TO NOTICE SOMETHING ELSE RESTING ALONG THE CURB, IN PLACE OF THE CUSTOMARY GARBAGE--

--AND BEING A PUBLIC-SPIRITED CITIZEN ABOVE ALL ELSE, VELMA WOLENSKY IMMEDIATELY NOTIFIED THE PROPER AUTHORITIES.
IT TOOK THEM 45 MINUTES TO MAKE SENSE OF HER HYSTERICAL BABBLING--

--AND CONSIDERABLY LESS TIME TO MOBILIZE EVERY S.W.A.T. TEAM AND RIOT SQUAD THEY COULD LAY THEIR SWEATING HANDS ON!
OKAY, MEN--LET'S JUST TRY TO KEEP THINGS CALM!
I DON'T WANT ANYBODY DOING ANYTHING STUPID WITHOUT PROPER PROVOCATION!
NYPD
N.Y.P.D.

THAT BRUTE TORE THE STATUE OF LIBERTY APART BECAUSE HE THOUGHT HE WAS BEING ATTACKED WITHOUT CAUSE! I DON'T WANT THAT INCIDENT REPEATED IN A POPULATED AREA!
DO YOU REALLY THINK WE CAN CONTAIN HIM, CAPTAIN?
I DON'T KNOW, HOFFMAN--!
BUT STICK WITH ME, ROOKIE, AND WE'LL BOTH FIND OUT!

GO AWAY, LITTLE MEN! HULK DOES NOT WANT TROUBLE WITH YOU!
HULK IS JUST WAITING HERE FOR HULK'S FRIEND!
GO AWAY, PUNY HUMANS--OR YOU WILL REGRET IT!

THIS IS PATROLMAN BRIAN HOFFMAN'S FIRST TIME UNDER FIRE, SO PERHAPS HE CAN BE FORGIVEN THE NERVOUSNESS THAT TIES A PAINFUL KNOT IN THE PIT OF HIS STOMACH...
NYPD
NYPD

HULK WILL NOT WARN YOU AGAIN, LITTLE MEN!
GO AWAY!!

BUT CAN ANYONE FORGIVE HIM FOR DOING-- THIS!?!
NO! HE'S GOING TO ATTACK! I'VE GOT TO STOP HIM!
HOFFMAN-- DON'T!
NYPD
B-DOW!

"SWEET GOD, BOY-- NOW YOU'VE REALLY DONE IT!"
BAH! PUNY HUMANS SHOOT AT HULK!
SPAK!
THEY IGNORE HULK'S WARNING!

AND, LITTLE MEN-- THAT MAKES HULK MAD!!
THOOOM!

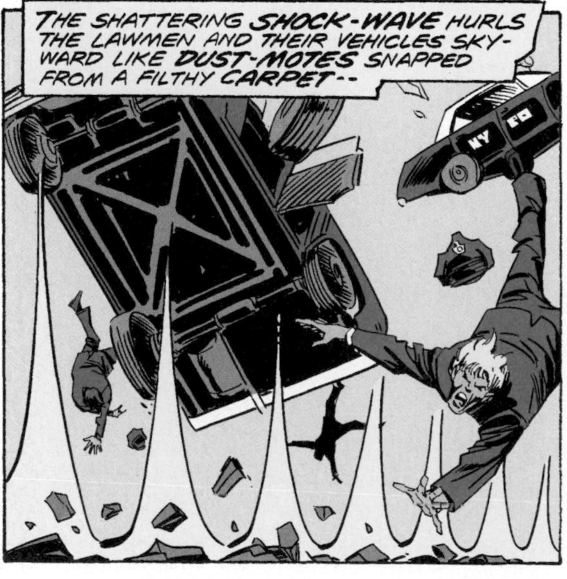
THE SHATTERING SHOCK-WAVE HURLS THE LAWMEN AND THEIR VEHICLES SKYWARD LIKE DUST-MOTES SNAPPED FROM A FILTHY CARPET--

--AND THE MAN-BRUTE IS JUST WARMING UP!
YOU BEGAN THIS BATTLE, LITTLE MEN--

--BUT IT IS HULK WHO WILL FINISH IT!
NYPD
SKRASH!

WHATEVER HAPPENS NOW IS YOUR FAULT, PUNY HUMANS-- REMEMBER THAT!
ALL HULK HAS EVER WANTED WAS TO BE LEFT ALONE-- TO BE LEFT IN PEACE--
RRAKK!

--BUT WHEREVER HULK HAS GONE, PUNY HUMANS HAVE HOUNDED HULK --TRIED TO KILL HULK--
NYPD

--AND FORCED HULK TO FIGHT BACK!!
PWHAMM!

THERE'S NO WAY ON EARTH WE'RE GONNA STOP THAT BRUISER OURSELVES!
WE NEED HELP-- THE SUPER-POWERED KIND!

AND IN THE BAXTER BUILDING HEADQUARTERS OF THE FAR-FAMED FANTASTIC FOUR, A SPECIAL POLICE-BAND EMERGENCY SIGNAL BEEPS FORTH ITS INSISTANT CALL...
N.Y.P.D. ALE
...BUT THERE IS NOBODY HOME TO HEAR! *
* SINCE THE FF IS STILL IN TRANSIT FROM COUNTER-EARTH, AS SHOWN IN THEIR LATEST ISSUE. --LEN.

QUICKLY, MAN--FIRE THE NEUTRON-BAZOOKA!
TONY STARK HIMSELF DESIGNED IT FOR US! IT'S GOT FIRE-POWER ENOUGH TO FLATTEN A RAGING MOB!
FOOM!

THE NEUTRON-SHELL ERUPTS WITH A NERVE-NUMBING FORCE THAT WOULD RENDER SEVERAL DOZEN PEOPLE SENSELESS FOR PRECISELY 45 MINUTES--
WHOOMP!

--BUT WHICH ONLY SERVES TO MAKE A CERTAIN MAN-BRUTE EVEN MADDER, IF POSSIBLE, THAN HE ALREADY IS!
ENOUGH!!

HULK IS DONE TRYING TO REASON WITH PUNY HUMANS!
HULK HAS SAID ALL HULK WILL SAY!

CHOOM!
HULK JUST WANTED TO WAIT HERE PEACEFULLY FOR MAGICIAN TO COME HOME--

--BUT IF ALL PUNY HUMANS WANT TO DO IS FIGHT--
--THEN HULK WILL GIVE THEM FIGHT!
WHAMM!
HULK WILL DESTROY THEM ALL!!

MERCIFUL MOTHER! WILL YOU LOOK AT WHAT HE'S DOING TO THOSE POOR COPS!?!
WHY AREN'T THE FANTASTIC FOUR HERE TO STOP HIM... OR THE AVENGERS... OR SPIDER-MAN... OR SOMEONE?
WNBS
TV

YES, COMMISSIONER--I'VE BEEN WATCHING THE CONFLICT ON THE TV!
YES SIR, I SHALL INFORM THE AVENGERS OF THE SITUATION AS SOON AS THEY RETURN TO NEW YORK!
YES SIR, I TOO HOPE IT WILL BE SOON!

BAH! HULK CANNOT KEEP FIGHTING WHILE JARELLA LIES HURT!
FIRST HULK MUST FIND MAGICIAN TO SAVE JARELLA--
--AND THEN HULK WILL SMASH EVERY HUMAN WHO GETS IN HULK'S WAY!

But, shortly after, on the decaying Manhattan waterfront...
WATERFRONT WAREHOUSE
NO MATTER WHERE HULK LOOKS, HULK CANNOT FIND MAGICIAN!
...AND HULK CANNOT UNDERSTAND WHY!

MAGICIAN NEVER HAS TROUBLE FINDING HULK, SO WHY CAN'T HULK FIND...
WEEOWEEOH
HUH?
SOUND OF HOWLING-- COMING THIS WAY--!?!

"BAH! IT IS PUNY HUMANS AGAIN! WHY DO THEY NEVER GIVE UP?"
WEEOWEEOWEEO
WEEOWEEOWEEO

WELL, HULK IS TIRED OF ALWAYS BEING CHASED BY LITTLE MEN--
--TIRED OF BEING CORNERED LIKE AN ANIMAL!

LET PUNY HUMANS COME THEN!
RRAKK!
LET THEM COME CLOSE-- SO HULK CAN SMASH THEM ALL WITH HEAVY MACHINE!

NO, MY FRIEND-- YOU HAVE DONE ENOUGH DAMAGE FOR ONE DAY!
ZAT!
HUH? MACHINE HAS TURNED TO-- NOTHING!?!

SOMEONE IS ON ROOF BEHIND HULK!
BUT WHOEVER IT IS, HULK WILL CRUSH HIM INTO...
YOU?!?

NEXT ISSUE: IN MORTAL COMBAT WITH DOCTOR STRANGE...VALKRYIE ...NIGHTHAWK... AND THE RED GUARDIAN! IT'S THE HULK AT HIS MOST SAVAGE... ALONE AGAINST THE DEFENDERS! BE HERE!

INCREDIBLE HULK

MARVEL COMICS GROUP™

APPROVED BY THE COMICS CODE AUTHORITY

30¢ 207 JAN 02456

THE INCREDIBLE HULK®

ALONE AGAINST THE DEFENDERS!

THE HULK IS PULLING DOWN THE *HIGHWAY!*

IF *WE* DON'T STOP HIM-- *HUNDREDS* WILL DIE!!

NCC-1701

COCKRUM

Caught in the heart of a ***Nuclear Explosion,*** victim of ***Gamma-Radiation*** gone wild, ***Doctor Robert Bruce Banner*** now finds himself transformed in times of stress into seven feet, one thousand pounds of unfettered ***Fury***—the most powerful creature to ever walk the earth—

Stan Lee PRESENTS: THE INCREDIBLE HULK!™

C-170

LEN WEIN WRITER/EDITOR / **SAL BUSCEMA & JOE STATON** ILLUSTRATORS / **GLYNIS WEIN** COLORIST / **IRV WATANABE** LETTERER

I IMPLORE YOU, MY FRIEND-- DO NOT FORCE US TO RAISE OUR HANDS AGAINST YOU!
JUST CALM YOURSELF, HULK--AND TELL US WHY YOU BEGAN THIS UNNECESSARY RAMPAGE!

WHY, VALKYRIE?
HULK WILL TELL YOU WHY!

BECAUSE OF THEM!
BECAUSE OF PUNY LITTLE MEN!!

WHEREVER HULK GOES, PUNY HUMANS HOUND HULK--WON'T LET HULK ALONE--WON'T LET HULK REST--
--AND HULK IS SICK OF IT!!
THOOM!

VALHALLA! HE'S SHATTERED A WHOLE SECTION OF THE WAREHOUSE WALL!
IT'S TOPPLING TOWARDS THE CROWD BELOW!
AND HULK IS GLAD!

RUN, MEN--RUN! GET OUT OF THE WAY--
--BEFORE THAT FALLING SLAB BECOMES OUR TOMBSTONE!

NEVER! THOUGH I AM NO LONGER SORCERER SUPREME, DOCTOR STRANGE IS STILL MASTER OF THE MYSTIC ARTS!*
*AND IF YOU DON'T BELIEVE HIM, JUST CHECK OUT DOCTOR STRANGE #19 AND SEE FOR YOURSELF. --LEN.

"AND AT MY COMMAND, THE FLAMES OF THE FALTINE WILL REDUCE THAT PLUNGING BRICK AND MORTAR TO SO MUCH DRIFTING ASH!"

BAH! HULK THOUGHT YOU WERE HULK'S FRIENDS--
--BUT IF YOU PROTECT THE PUNY HUMANS WHO TRY TO HURT HULK--
--THEN HULK WILL HURT YOU!!

I CAN SEE THERE WILL BE NO REASONING WITH YOU FOR THE NONCE, MY FRIEND!

THUS LET THE CRIMSON BANDS OF CYTTORAK CONTAIN YOUR BURNING RAGE UNTIL IT COOLS!
NOT EXACTLY THE NEATEST LITTLE JOB OF GIFT-WRAPPING, DOC--BUT IT'S CERTAINLY EFFECTIVE!
IS IT, NIGHTHAWK? HAVING SEEN THAT BRUTE IN ACTION, I TRULY WONDER.

AND FRANKLY, RED GUARDIAN-- WE CAN'T BLAME YOU!
LET HULK OUT, MAGICIAN!
LET HULK OUT!!

PUNY BANDS WILL NOT HOLD HULK, MAGICIAN!
NOTHING CAN HOLD HULK!
NOTHING!!

BAH! HULK'S PUNCHES HAVE NO EFFECT ON STUPID BANDS!
BUT THERE ARE OTHER WAYS FOR HULK TO BREAK FREE!

BY HELA! THE HULK HAS LEAPED SKYWARD WITH SUCH FORCE, HE'S CARRIED THE CRIMSON BANDS ALONG WITH HIM!
GOT ANY MORE BRIGHT IDEAS, DOC?

NO! THE HULK'S BRUTAL ASSAULT AGAINST MY ENCHANTMENT ASSAILS ME LIKE A PHYSICAL FORCE!
CAN...NOT... CONCENTRATE...
YOU MUST, STEPHEN-- YOU MUST!

BUT BEFORE THE MIND-WRACKED MAGE CAN GATHER HIS THOUGHTS, THE MYSTIC SPHERE PLUMMETS BACK TO EARTH LIKE A RAMPANT METEOR--
--STRIKING THE DAMAGED WAREHOUSE WITH SPINE-CHILLING POWER--
KWHOOM!

--AND CARRYING IT SAVAGELY DOWN TO THE STREET IN TWISTED RUINS!
DEAR LORD! THOSE FOLKS WERE STILL ON THE ROOF!
THEN THEY'RE FINISHED, MALLOY!

FOR A MOMENT, NOTHING MOVES AMIDST THE SMOKING WRECKAGE, THEN HEAVY SLABS OF CONCRETE FALL AWAY TO REVEAL...
PRAISE THE VISHANTI, I COMPLETED MY SPELL IN TIME!
I ENVELOPED US ALL IN THE SHIELD OF THE SERAPHIM BEFORE THE FALLING RUBBLE COULD CRUSH US!

YEAH. WE'RE DOING JUST SWELL, DOC...
...BUT WHAT ABOUT THE HULK?
WITH MY CONCENTRATION BROKEN, NIGHTHAWK-- THE CRIMSON BANDS DISSOLVED!
THE HULK MADE GOOD HIS ESCAPE WHILE WE WERE STILL TRAPPED BENEATH THE RUINS!

HE CAME SEARCHING FOR ME AS A FRIEND-- AND I MET HIM AS AN ADVERSARY.
WE MUST FIND HIM, FELLOW DEFENDERS-- TRY TO REACH HIM SOMEHOW--
--BEFORE IT'S TOO LATE FOR US ALL!

THE VAST NEW MEXICAN DESERT IS A SPRAWLING EXPANSE OF SCRUB - BRUSH AND PALE GRAY DESOLATION.
IN ITS CENTER STANDS THE SEMI-SECRET PARA-MILITARY INSTALLATION CALLED GAMMA BASE--

--AND IN ITS CENTER STANDS THE SOLITARY PATCH OF GREENERY TO BE SEEN FOR MANY MILES AROUND.

BUT THOUGH THIS LONELY NURSERY IS GREEN IN COLOR, THE MOOD HERE IS MOST DEFINITELY BLUE.
SOMETHING'S WRONG WITH YOU, BETTY--THAT MUCH IS OBVIOUS.
CARE TO TELL YOUR FAITHFUL FATHER WHAT IT IS?
I'M THAT TRANSPARENT, HUH?

I'M AFRAID IT'S GLENN, DAD. HE JUST HASN'T BEEN THE SAME SINCE HE REGAINED HIS MEMORY.*
WELL, YOU CAN'T EXPECT A MAN TO GO THRU WHAT HE'S BEEN THRU WITH-OUT IT AFFECTING HIM SOMEHOW.
JUST GIVE HIM A CHANCE TO FIND HIMSELF AGAIN.
*BACK IN HULK #200, RIGHT?--LEN.

THAT'S EASIER FOR YOU TO SAY, DAD. YOU'RE GENERAL "THUNDERBOLT" ROSS, HIS COMMANDING OFFICER...
...BUT I'M GLENN TALBOT'S WIFE!
SEEING HIM LIKE THIS RIPS ME TO PIECES INSIDE.

I LOVE GLENN, DADDY. I WANT TO REACH OUT TO HIM--BUT HE WON'T LET ME.
WITH ALL MY HEART, I WANT TO HELP HIM...

...BUT I... I JUST DON'T KNOW HOW.
HEY NOW, GIRL-- DON'T GO ALL WEEPY ON ME.
YOUR OLD DAD IS HERE, BETTY.

I KNOW I WASN'T MUCH OF A FATHER TO YOU WHEN YOU WERE YOUNGER, CHILD--
--BUT MAYBE I CAN MAKE IT UP TO YOU NOW.
THERE HAS TO BE A WAY TO HELP GLENN, BETTY--AND I SWEAR TO YOU, WE'LL FIND IT!

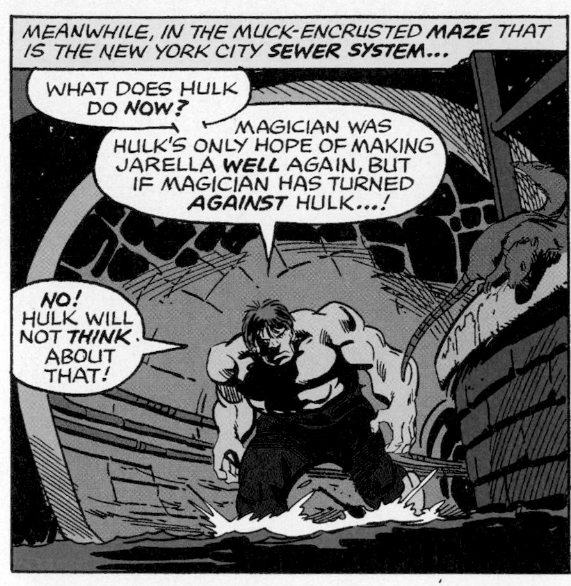
MEANWHILE, IN THE MUCK-ENCRUSTED MAZE THAT IS THE NEW YORK CITY SEWER SYSTEM...
WHAT DOES HULK DO NOW?
MAGICIAN WAS HULK'S ONLY HOPE OF MAKING JARELLA WELL AGAIN, BUT IF MAGICIAN HAS TURNED AGAINST HULK...!
NO! HULK WILL NOT THINK ABOUT THAT!

FIRST HULK WILL FIND HULK'S WAY OUT OF FOUL-SMELLING TUNNEL, AND THEN...HUH?
LIGHT COMING IN THRU TUNNEL ROOF!
MAYBE THAT IS THE WAY OUT!

ON THE STREET ABOVE, THERE IS THE SUDDEN GRATING SOUND OF METAL BEING SLOWLY PUSHED ASIDE--
THEN A SUSPICIOUS PAIR OF EMERALD EYES PEER OUT OF THE STIFLING DARKNESS--

--AND GROW WIDE IN DISBELIEF!
NO! IT CANNOT BE!
CAN IT?

GIRL STANDING ON STREET... HER HAIR...HER CLOTHES... SHE LOOKS LIKE...
...JARELLA?
BUS STOP

COULD IT BE? IS JARELLA WELL AGAIN?
HAS SHE COME TO BIG CITY LOOKING FOR HULK?

OR IS IT JUST ANOTHER TRICK OF PUNY HUMANS-- TO TEAR HULK'S HEART APART?
PLEASE... LET IT BE TRUE!

JARELLA?
IS IT REALLY YOU?

EH?

YES, WHAT CAN I DO FOR...

OH... MY... GOD!

BAH! HULK WAS RIGHT! IT IS NOT JARELLA!
IT IS ONLY PUNY HUMAN!

P-P-PLEASE, MISTER--I DIDN'T DO ANYTHING!
J-J-JUST LEAVE ME ALONE!

LEAVE...YOU... ALONE?
HAH!
HULK ALWAYS ASKS LITTLE MEN TO LEAVE HULK ALONE-- BUT DO THEY EVER LISTEN?

NO!!
ALWAYS THEY ATTACK HULK--TRY TO KILL HULK!

THEY NEVER LISTEN TO HULK, GIRL--
--SO WHY SHOULD HULK LISTEN TO YOU?
N-N-NO! PLEASE-- STAY BACK!

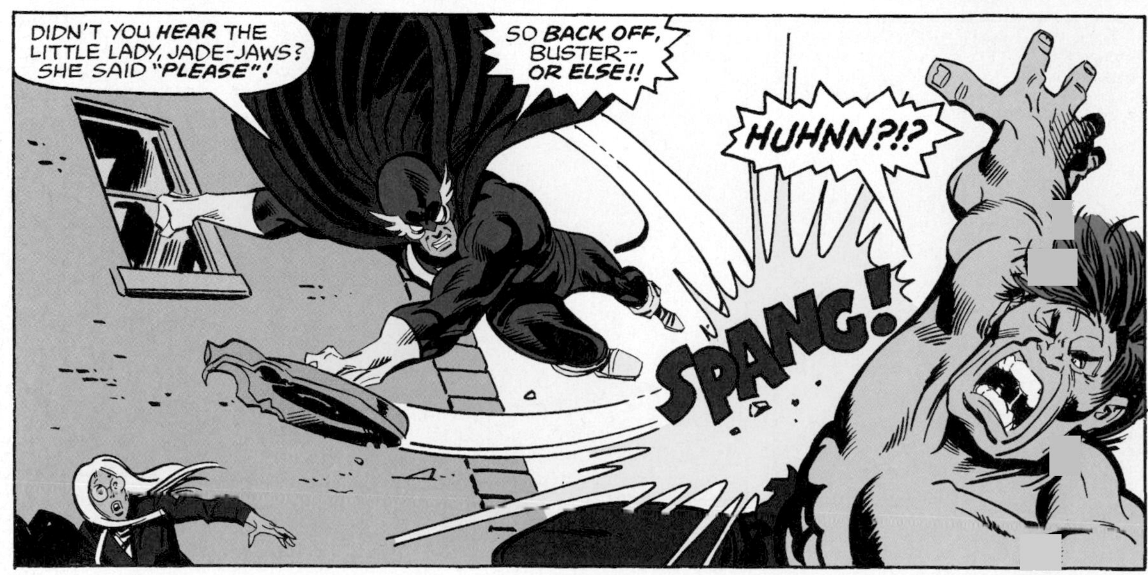
DIDN'T YOU HEAR THE LITTLE LADY, JADE-JAWS? SHE SAID "PLEASE"!
SO BACK OFF, BUSTER-- OR ELSE!!
HUHNN?!?
SPANG!

SO! NOW BIRD-NOSE AND THE OTHERS HUNT HULK, TOO!
PLEASE, MY FRIEND-- THERE HAS BEEN A TERRIBLE MISUNDERSTANDING!
WE ONLY WANT TO HELP YOU!

BAH! HULK ASKED FOR YOUR HELP BEFORE, MAGICIAN--AND YOU PUT HULK IN MAGIC CAGE!
THIS TIME, HULK WILL TAKE WHAT HULK WANTS--
--AND HULK WANTS REVENGE!!

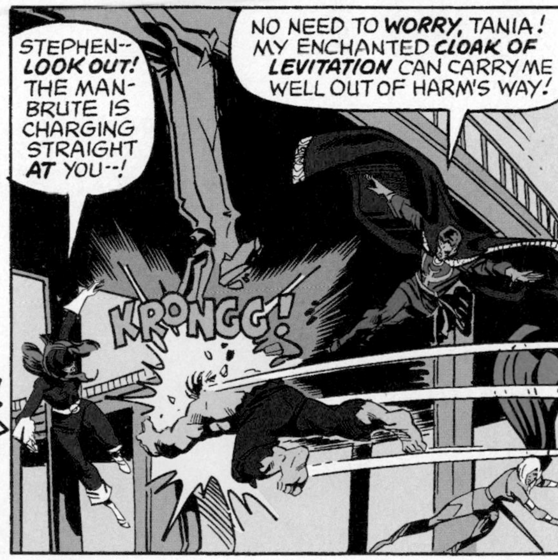
STEPHEN-- LOOK OUT! THE MAN-BRUTE IS CHARGING STRAIGHT AT YOU--!
NO NEED TO WORRY, TANIA! MY ENCHANTED CLOAK OF LEVITATION CAN CARRY ME WELL OUT OF HARM'S WAY!
KRONGG!

BUT, UNFORTUNATELY, THE ALREADY-DELAPIDATED WEST SIDE HIGHWAY POSSESSES NO SUCH MYSTIC POWERS--
--AND AFTER A HEAD-ON COLLISION WITH A CERTAIN GREEN GOLIATH, IT IS MOST DEFINITELY THE WORSE FOR WEAR!
STEPHEN-- THAT MOTORWAY--!
THE RUBY RAYS OF RAGGADOR WILL SUPPORT ITS CRUMBLING WEIGHT, RED GUARDIAN--
--BUT WHILE I MAINTAIN THE SPELL, I FEAR THE REST OF YOU MUST SOMEHOW SUBDUE THE RAGING HULK WITHOUT MY MYSTIC AID!

COME THEN, FALSE FRIENDS! COME AND TRY TO CAPTURE HULK!
COME CLOSE--SO HULK CAN CRUSH YOU ALL LIKE BUGS!!

NOW HOW CAN ANYONE TURN DOWN SUCH A CHARMING INVITATION?
DON'T JEST, NIGHTHAWK! WITH SUCH FURY IN HIS VOICE...SUCH FIRE IN HIS EYE...
...I'M AFRAID THERE'LL BE NO CALMING THE HULK AS IT IS!

THEN WE'LL TAKE HIM BY FORCE IF WE MUST!

"MY BELT BUCKLE WAS DESIGNED BY SOVIET SCIENTISTS AS A WEAPON EQUALLED ONLY BY CAPTAIN AMERICA'S LEGENDARY SHIELD!"
WAK!
SPAK!
HUH??

WELL DONE, RED GUARDIAN! YOUR WEAPON HAS CONFUSED HIM MOMENTARILY--

--ENABLING ME TO GET CLOSE ENOUGH TO STRIKE!
SPANG!

FORGIVE ME, MY EMERALD FRIEND--
--BUT I DO THIS AS MUCH FOR YOUR SAKE AS FOR OURS!
CHUDD!

PUT SWORD DOWN, GIRL--
NOW!!
BY ODIN! MY ENCHANTED BLADE HAD NO EFFECT OH HIM!
OH, WE WOULDN'T NECESSARILY SAY THAT, VALKYRIE--

--FOR IT SEEMS TO HAVE MADE THE MAN-BRUTE EVEN ANGRIER, IF THAT WERE POSSIBLE, THAN HE WAS BEFORE!

BAH! GIRL WILL NOT HIT HULK WITH SWORD AGAIN!
VALHALLA! H-HE'S SNATCHED DRAGONFANG FROM MY VERY GRASP--!

HULK WILL BREAK PUNY SWORD INTO PIECES, AND THEN HULK WILL BREAK GIRL INTO...HUH?
SWORD BENDS--BUT IT DOES NOT BREAK!
NO! SWORD MUST BREAK! IT MUST!!

BAH! HULK IS TIRED OF WASTING TIME ON STUPID SWORD!
SPWAK!

PROPELLED BY THE MOST POWERFUL ARM MUSCLES ON EARTH, THE ENCHANTED WEAPON DRAGONFANG PLOWS INTO ITS MISTRESS LIKE A GLEAMING GOLDEN JUGGERNAUT--
--BOWLING HER SAVAGELY OFF HER FEET--
UUNNFF!
WHUD!

--AND SENDING HER HURTLING HELPLESSLY INTO THE LITHE AND SUPPLE FIGURE OF THE RED GUARDIAN!
CHOOM!
IN AN INSTANT, BOTH LIE SPRAWLED ON THE PAVEMENT, THEIR SENSES REELING--

--WHILE THE MYSTIC MAGE LOOKS ON IN RAPIDLY-GROWING DESPAIR...
I CANNOT DROP MY SPELL FOR EVEN A MOMENT--OR THE ENTIRE HIGHWAY WILL COLLAPSE!
IF ANYONE WILL DEFEAT THE HULK, IT HAS TO BE NIGHTHAWK!

THAT'S A STIRRING DISPLAY OF CONFIDENCE, DOC--BUT THE ONLY HOPE I HAVE OF BEATING GREENILOCKS IS TO HIT HIM WHILE HE'S OFF-BALANCE...
...AND THEN PRAY HE GETS STRUCK BY LIGHTNING OR SOMETHING!
WHOM!

BECAUSE ONE-ON-ONE, I'VE GOT ABOUT THE SAME CHANCE OF CLOBBERING THE HULK AS WOODY ALLEN HAS OF TAKING ON MUHAMMAD ALI!
KTOW!

SWELL! ALL I'VE MANAGED TO DO SO FAR IS BRUISE BOTH OF MY HANDS--
--AND NOW IT LOOKS LIKE JADE-JAWS IS GOING TO BRUISE HIS FIST--WHILE HE REARRANGES MY FACE!

STAND STILL, BIRD-NOSE--SO HULK CAN SMASH!

SORRY, BIG FELLA--BUT I'M JUST NOT ALL THAT ANXIOUS TO COMMIT SUICIDE!
BAH!

IF YOU WANT ME, GREENSKIN--YOU'RE GONNA HAVE TO COME AND GET ME!
THEN THAT IS WHAT HULK WILL DO!
OKAY, I'VE MANAGED TO LURE HIM OFF THE HIGHWAY--
--SO NOW WHAT?

BLAST! I FORGOT HOW FAST HE CAN MOVE-- AND THAT JUST MAY BE THE LAST MISTAKE I MAKE!
HE'S GOT ME CORNERED!

AND NOW, BIRD-NOSE, HULK WILL MAKE YOU PAY FOR BETRAYING HULK!
NOW HULK IS GOING TO...
NO, HULK-- WAIT!

PLEASE, BIG FELLA-- TRY TO REALIZE WHAT YOU'RE DOING!
OKAY, SO YOU CAME TO US FOR HELP--AND WE GOT OUR WIRES CROSSED. WE'RE SORRY ABOUT THAT, MAN--AND WE'RE TRYING TO SET THINGS STRAIGHT!
YOU'VE GOT TO GIVE US THAT CHANCE!

SOMEWHERE IN THE BACK OF YOUR MIND, HULK--YOU KNOW WE'RE YOUR FRIENDS!
SMASH US--AND WHO DO YOU HAVE LEFT? WHO WILL YOU TURN TO THEN?
THINK ABOUT IT, HULK-- THINK ABOUT IT!!

NO! BIRD-NOSE IS TRYING TO CONFUSE HULK--
--BUT HULK WILL NOT LISTEN!
SHUT UP, BIRD-NOSE, OR HULK WILL... WILL... WILL...

AARRGGHH!!
WHOOM!
AT THE LAST POSSIBLE SECOND, H-HE PULLED HIS PUNCH!
THANK HEAVEN I GOT THRU TO HIM!

YOU ARE RIGHT, BIRD-NOSE, YOU ARE HULK'S FRIENDS--
--AND HULK NEEDS FRIENDS NOW... MORE THAN EVER!
WELL, YOU'VE GOT 'EM, CHUM. JUST TELL US WHAT WE CAN DO TO HELP.
THIS TIME WE'LL LISTEN.

AND MOMENTS LATER...
FORGIVE THIS DELAY, HULK--BUT IT IS NECESSARY!
SPLANG!
HULK WILL DO AS YOU SAY...FRIENDS.
WE MUST REPAIR THE DAMAGE WE HAVE WROUGHT, MY EMERALD FRIEND--BEFORE WE CAN LEAVE HERE IN GOOD CONSCIENCE.

THEN, SHORTLY THEREAFTER, IN THE GREENWICH VILLAGE SANCTUM SANCTORUM OF THE MAN CALLED DOCTOR STRANGE...
...AND THAT IS ALL HULK CAN REMEMBER!

GIRL CALLED BETTY SAID THAT SCIENCE COULD NOT HELP HULK'S JARELLA--
--SO HULK WENT LOOKING FOR YOU!
I AM TRULY TOUCHED THAT YOU PLACE SO MUCH FAITH IN ME, HULK--BUT THERE IS MUCH THAN EVEN I CANNOT ACCOMPLISH.
THE FORCES OF LIFE AND DEATH WEAVE A MOST DELICATE TAPESTRY INDEED--ONE THAT CANNOT EASILY BE TAMPERED WITH!
IF MAGICIAN CANNOT MAKE JARELLA WELL AGAIN...THEN NOBODY CAN!

BUT FOR YOUR SAKE, MY FRIEND--AND FOR THE SAKE OF THE WOMAN YOU LOVE--
--I PROMISE I WILL DO WHAT I CAN!

THEN, WITHOUT ANOTHER WORD, THE MASTER OF THE MYSTIC ARTS TAKES HIS PLACE IN THE CENTER OF AN ARCANE PENTA-GRAM INSCRIBED IN THE VERY FLOOR--

--AND, WITH AN INCANTATION ON HIS LIPS AND A FERVENT PRAYER IN HIS HEART--
--HE SETS HIS SPIRIT FREE!

HOLD FAST TO YOUR FAITH, MY EMERALD FRIEND. I SHALL RETURN AS SWIFTLY AS I CAN.
WE'LL BE WAITING, DOC.

LIKE A WIND-BLOWN WRAITH, THE ASTRAL IMAGE OF THE MASTER MAGICIAN SAILS AWAY FROM THE ISLAND MANHATTAN--
--THEN OUT ACROSS THE NORTH AMERICAN COUNTRYSIDE--
--AND IN LESS TIME THAN IT TAKES TO TELL OF IT, IN THE AFOREMENTIONED GAMMA BASE...
I HAVE REACHED MY GOAL.
I CAN SENSE IT!

MEN OF GAMMA BASE, FORGIVE MY UNTIMELY INTRUSION--
--BUT I HAVE DESPERATE NEED OF YOUR HELP.
HOLY HOPPIN' HANNAH!
WH-WHO ARE YOU?!?

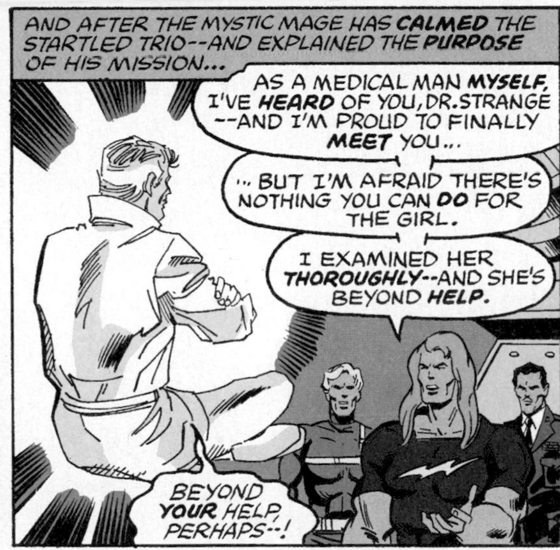
AND AFTER THE MYSTIC MAGE HAS CALMED THE STARTLED TRIO--AND EXPLAINED THE PURPOSE OF HIS MISSION...
AS A MEDICAL MAN MYSELF, I'VE HEARD OF YOU, DR. STRANGE --AND I'M PROUD TO FINALLY MEET YOU...
... BUT I'M AFRAID THERE'S NOTHING YOU CAN DO FOR THE GIRL.
I EXAMINED HER THOROUGHLY--AND SHE'S BEYOND HELP.
BEYOND YOUR HELP, PERHAPS--!

WHAT DO YOU MEAN?
THERE ARE RESOURCES AVAILABLE TO THE MASTER OF THE MYSTIC ARTS THAT ARE DENIED TO LESSER MEN!
FOR EXAMPLE-- THE EYE OF AGAMOTTO!

BUT, UNFORTUNATELY, MY NECROMANTIC DIAGNOSIS MERELY CONFIRMS YOUR OWN, DOC SAMSON.
THE SPIRIT OF THE WOMAN JARELLA HAS INDEED FLED THIS FRAGILE FORM. SHE HAS PASSED ON TO A HIGHER PLANE.
BUT HOW DO I EXPLAIN THAT TO A HOPEFUL HULK?

AS A WORD, HOPEFUL DOES NOT TRULY DESCRIBE THE SOLITARY MAN-BRUTE WHO ANXIOUSLY AWAITS THE SORCERER'S RETURN.
PERHAPS FEARFUL WOULD BE MORE TO THE POINT.

FOR ALL OF HIS MISERABLE LIFE, THE HULK HAS WANTED NOTHING MORE THAN SOMEONE HE COULD SHARE THE LONELY HOURS WITH, SOMEONE HE COULD BE CLOSE TO--
--AND NOW THAT HE HAS FOUND THAT SOMEONE, HE IS TERRIFIED OF LOSING HER.

BUT THE GREEN GOLIATH IS NOT REALLY ABLE TO PUT SUCH THOUGHTS INTO WORDS, AND SO HE SITS IN SILENCE...
...AND BROODS.
SOME TEA, EMERALD SIR?
NO.

IT IS A VERY SPECIAL BLEND, SIR--PERHAPS IT WOULD HELP TO CALM YOU.
HULK SAID-- NO!
OF COURSE, SIR--FORGIVE ME. I DID NOT MEAN TO INTERRUPT YOUR VIGIL.

DON'T LET JADE-JAWS BOTHER YOU, WONG. HE WON'T EXACTLY BE THE LIFE OF THE PARTY UNTIL DOC STRANGE GETS BACK FROM...
BUT I AM BACK, NIGHTHAWK.
DON'T YOU EVER USE A DOOR?

BUT WHERE IS JARELLA, MAGICIAN? WHY IS SHE NOT WITH YOU?
I'M SORRY, MY FRIEND-- DREADFULLY SORRY--BUT I HAVE FAILED YOU.

TRY TO UNDERSTAND, HULK-- THERE ARE THINGS IN THIS LIFE BEYOND THE KEN OF EVEN THE WISEST MEN.
WHY THOSE WE LOVE ARE TAKEN FROM US IN FURY IS PERHAPS THE DARKEST QUESTION OF ALL.

JARELLA IS GONE, MY FRIEND-- AND THERE IS NO WAY TO SUMMON HER BACK.
YOU MUST TRY TO GO ON WITH-OUT HER--AS SHE WOULD WANT YOU TO.
JARELLA IS... DEAD?

NOOOOOOOO!!

JARELLA IS NOT DEAD! SHE CANNOT BE DEAD!!

HULK TOLD BETTY THAT MAGICIAN WOULD HELP JARELLA!

HULK SAID YOU WOULD MAKE JARELLA WELL AGAIN!

KROOM!

IF MAGICIAN CANNOT HELP, THEN HULK WILL SAVE JARELLA!

HULK CAN DO IT! HULK CAN DO ANYTHING!

THA-KOOM!

HULK IS THE STRONGEST ONE THERE IS!!

STEPHEN, WE'VE GOT TO STOP HIM--BEFORE HE DESTROYS EVERYTHING!

NO, VALKYRIE-- LET HIM BE!

THE HULK MUST DEAL WITH HIS GRIEF IN HIS OWN WAY!

BUT ALL YOUR PRECIOUS ARTIFACTS--!

THEY ARE THE LEAST I CAN OFFER HIM, VAL.

AFTER ALL... HE'S MY FRIEND.

NEXT ISSUE: THE BEGINNING OF A WHOLE **NEW** DIRECTION FOR EVERYONE'S FAVORITE **MAN-BRUTE**--PLUS THE UNEXPECTED **RETURN** OF SOME OLD FAMILIAR FACES! BELIEVE US, PILGRIM, **EXCITEMENT** AS YOU'VE NEVER SEEN IT BEFORE AWAITS YOU IN THE STARTLING SAGA WE CALL...

"A MONSTER IN OUR MIDST!"

Accepting the finality of Jarella's death, Bruce Banner briefly contemplated suicide but eventually attempted to rebuild his life in New York City, with the help of friends both new and old. Banner and the Hulk drew the quiet attention of the mysterious "They Who Wield Power," denizens of El Dorado, the Bolivian hidden City of Gold, and months later, seeking to replenish their Sacred Flame of Life (actually an ancient Deviant weapon), "They" brought the Hulk to their city. In order to facilitate their capture of the Hulk, one of the trio, Des (secretly Tyrannus, an old foe of the Hulk), reduced the Hulk to despair by revealing that the military still held Jarella's body, and convinced him that her body was being illicitly studied.

Incredible Hulk #240 — Art by Sal Buscema & Joe Sinnott

While this had the desired effect of demoralizing the Hulk and reverting him to Banner, when he eventually escaped and inevitably transformed again to the Hulk, the simple-minded monster was now haunted by the recurring need to return to Gamma Base and free his true love's body from the clutches of the military. Despite a series of distractions from both friends and foes, the Hulk finally made his way there and defeated the Base's military defenders. Still standing in his way, however, was Betty Ross's now-estranged husband, Colonel Glenn Talbot, who donned S.H.I.E.L.D. Mandroid armor in a vengeful attempt to kill the Hulk, whom he blamed for his own marital strife. In the end, the Hulk's drive to recover Jarella pushed him to defeat the Mandroid, and as the Hulk held the now-wounded Talbot's life in his hands, the hero Captain Marvel arrived to defend Gamma Base. Marvel's cosmic awareness told him that Hulk sought only to recover his long-dead love and return her to her own world, and the Captain offered to aid Hulk in retrieving Jarella from the military if he'd let loose of the helpless Talbot...

40¢ 246 APR 02456

MARVEL® COMICS GROUP

APPROVED BY THE COMICS CODE AUTHORITY

THE INCREDIBLE HULK®

TM

MARVEL'S TV SENSATION!

YOU BEAT THE ***MANDROID,*** HULK, BUT NOW YOU FACE CAPTAIN MARVEL!

THE HERO AND THE HULK!

BUCKLER & ABEL

Caught in the heart of a ***Nuclear Explosion***, victim of ***Gamma-Radiation*** gone wild, ***Doctor Robert Bruce Banner*** now finds himself transformed in times of stress into seven feet, one thousand pounds of unfettered ***Fury***—the most powerful creature to ever walk the earth—

Stan Lee PRESENTS: **THE INCREDIBLE HULK!®**

BILL MANTLO WRITER | SAL BUSCEMA ARTIST | DIANA ALBERS LETTERS | BEN SEAN COLORS | AL MILGROM EDITOR | JIM SHOOTER EDITOR-IN-CHIEF

UNTIL A FEW MOMENTS AGO, COL. GLENN TALBOT THOUGHT HE HAD HIS GREEN NEMESIS WHERE HE WANTED HIM--HELPLESS BEFORE THE MILITARY MIGHT OF GAMMA BASE AND THE BONE-CRUSHING POWER OF HIS OWN ***MANDROID*** ARMOR! NOW, GAMMA BASE IS IN RUINS AND TALBOT LIES DEFEATED... A GRIM TESTIMONY TO THE RAGE OF THE INCREDIBLE HULK! THIS SITUATION PROMPTED CAPTAIN MARVEL, THE RED-AND-BLUE CLAD KREE SPACEMAN, TO TAKE A HAND IN THE MATTER!

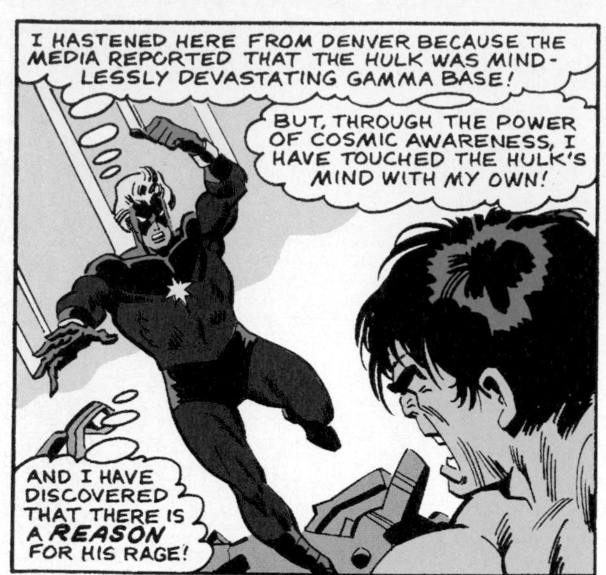
I HASTENED HERE FROM DENVER BECAUSE THE MEDIA REPORTED THAT THE HULK WAS MIND-LESSLY DEVASTATING GAMMA BASE!
BUT, THROUGH THE POWER OF COSMIC AWARENESS, I HAVE TOUCHED THE HULK'S MIND WITH MY OWN!
AND I HAVE DISCOVERED THAT THERE IS A REASON FOR HIS RAGE!

THE MILITARY HOLDS THE LIFELESS BODY OF AN ALIEN WOMAN IN A SPECIMEN CHAMBER HERE AT GAMMA BASE! A WOMAN NAMED... JARELLA!
A WOMAN THE HULK LOVED--AND WHOSE BODY HE HAS SWORN TO BEAR BACK TO HER HOME WORLD!
HULK, LISTEN TO ME! RELEASE TALBOT, AND I'LL HELP YOU LOCATE JARELLA!

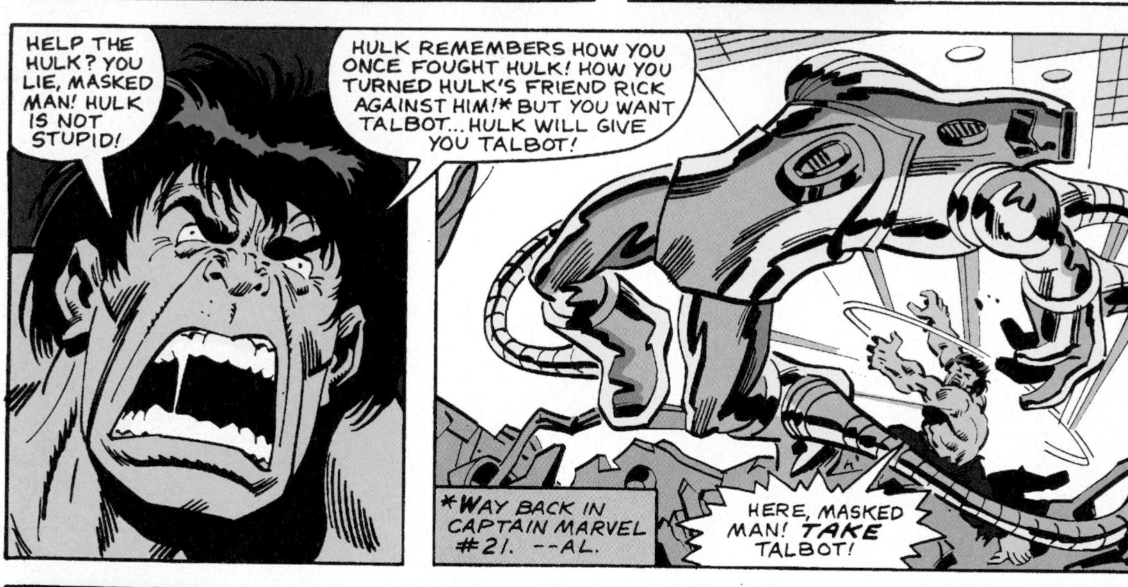
HELP THE HULK? YOU LIE, MASKED MAN! HULK IS NOT STUPID!
HULK REMEMBERS HOW YOU ONCE FOUGHT HULK! HOW YOU TURNED HULK'S FRIEND RICK AGAINST HIM!* BUT YOU WANT TALBOT... HULK WILL GIVE YOU TALBOT!
*WAY BACK IN CAPTAIN MARVEL #21. --AL.
HERE, MASKED MAN! TAKE TALBOT!

WASN'T EXPECTING THAT! THE MANDROID'S BEING HURLED AT ME WITH UNBELIEVABLE VELOCITY! IF I MOVE OUT OF ITS PATH, IT WILL STRIKE THE WALL BEHIND ME...
AND THE MAN INSIDE THE MANDROID ARMOR COULD NEVER SURVIVE THE IMPACT!
CAUGHT BETWEEN THE PROVERBIAL ROCK AND THE HARD PLACE, CAPTAIN MARVEL DOES WHAT HE MUST, AS SWORN PROTECTOR OF THE HUMAN RACE!

BUT THE KREE WARRIOR'S GALLANT SACRIFICE IS LOST ON AN ENRAGED HULK!
MASKED MAN CAUGHT TALBOT, BUT NOW BOTH OF THEM DON'T MOVE!
GOOD! HULK HAS SMASHED THEM--
KA-WAP!

AND NOW HULK WILL BURY THEM--
SHKRROOM!
SENDING OUT SHATTERING SOUNDWAVES WITH ONE THUNDEROUS CLAP, THE HULK BRINGS THE ROOF DOWN--

BURYING BOTH HIS FOES BENEATH A MINOR MOUNTAIN OF RUBBLE!
IN MOST THINGS, THE HULK'S MEMORY IS SHORT! THE OLD MAXIM "OUT OF SIGHT, OUT OF MIND", APPLIES.

AS THE DUST SETTLES ON THE UNMOVING PILE, THE HULK LOSES INTEREST IN HIS BURIED ENEMIES.
SHRUGGING, HE STALKS OFF INTO THE OMINOUS SILENCE OF GAMMA BASE, INTENT UPON HIS MISSION...
TO FIND JARELLA, AND TO TAKE HER HOME!

BUT PERHAPS THE GREAT GREEN BEHEMOTH HAS TURNED AWAY TOO SOON.
BEHIND HIM, THE FORGOTTEN WRECKAGE TREMBLES, SHIFTS--

--AND HEAVES UPWARDS AS A DAZED CAPTAIN MARVEL PULLS HIMSELF FROM THE DEBRIS!
BY PAMA! ONE CLAP OF HIS HANDS AND THE HULK NEARLY BURIED US ALIVE!

THE MANDROID'S ARMOR TOOK THE BRUNT OF THE CEILING'S COLLAPSE!
THUS, I WAS SHIELDED--BUT WHAT OF THE HUMAN WITHIN THE ARMOR?!

TALBOT LIES UNCONSCIOUS-- OR WORSE! THE ARMOR ITSELF IS CRACKED!

HAD THE HULK'S HAMMERING NOT WEAKENED IT, I WONDER IF EVEN MY NEGA-BAND BESTOWED POWERS--

--WOULD SUFFICE TO FREE THIS HUMAN WARRIOR FROM THE ARMOR THAT HAS BECOME HIS PRISON?!

Y-YOU'RE CAPTAIN MARVEL, AREN'T YOU? THANKS. THE HULK HAD SMASHED THE MANDROID'S POWER PACK...
IF YOU HADN'T ARRIVED, HE WOULD HAVE SMASHED ME!
PERHAPS HE HAD HIS REASONS.
REASONS? WHAT POSSIBLE REASONS COULD A MINDLESS MONSTER LIKE THE HULK HAVE??

YOU HOLD, FOR PURPOSES OF SCIENTIFIC EXPERIMENTATION, THE CORPSE OF A WOMAN NAMED JARELLA, COL. TALBOT. A WOMAN THE HULK LOVED.
JARELLA? BUT SHE DIED MONTHS AGO!
YET, THE HULK REMEMBERS A PROMISE HE MADE TO HER-- TO TAKE HER HOME.

NOW HE HAS COME TO KEEP HIS PROMISE.
COL. TALBOT! WE JUST MANAGED TO GET THROUGH THE RUBBLE! ARE YOU--? HOLY COW!
CAPTAIN MARVEL!
IT APPEARS YOUR TROOPS HAVE ARRIVED, COLONEL.

WHAT WILL YOU ORDER YOUR MEN TO DO NOW? ESCALATE THE DESTRUCTION BY HAVING THEM CONTINUE TO HUNT THE HULK--?

--OR ALLOW THE HULK TO TAKE JARELLA FROM GAMMA BASE WITHOUT FURTHER FIGHTING? THE CHOICE IS YOURS.
LET THE HULK GO? MY MEN'S SAFETY IS MY PRIMARY CONSIDERATION, MARVEL...

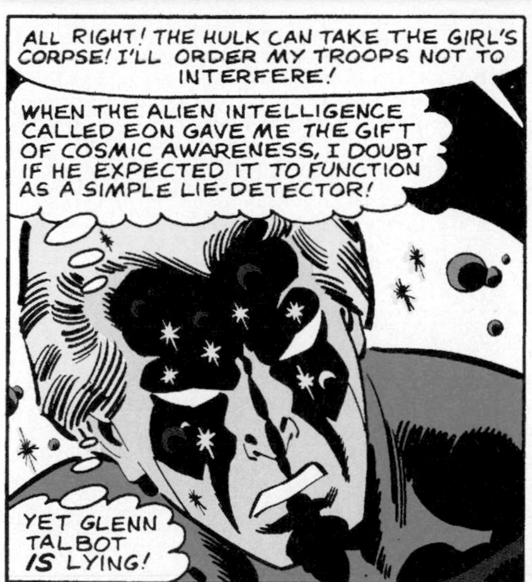
ALL RIGHT! THE HULK CAN TAKE THE GIRL'S CORPSE! I'LL ORDER MY TROOPS NOT TO INTERFERE!
WHEN THE ALIEN INTELLIGENCE CALLED EON GAVE ME THE GIFT OF COSMIC AWARENESS, I DOUBT IF HE EXPECTED IT TO FUNCTION AS A SIMPLE LIE-DETECTOR!
YET GLENN TALBOT *IS* LYING!

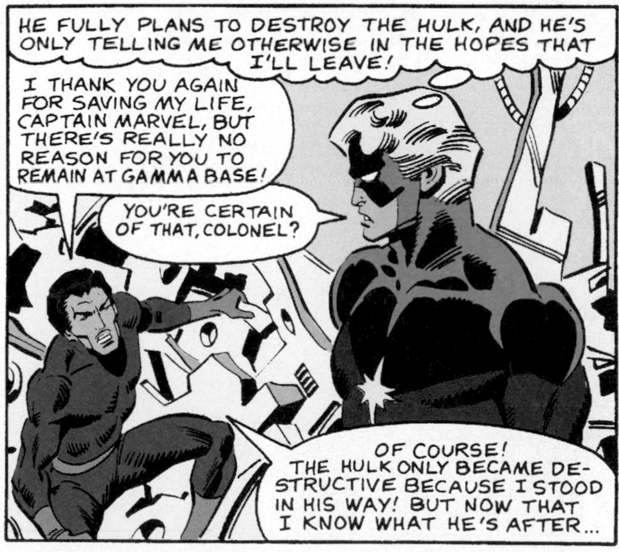
HE FULLY PLANS TO DESTROY THE HULK, AND HE'S ONLY TELLING ME OTHERWISE IN THE HOPES THAT I'LL LEAVE!
I THANK YOU AGAIN FOR SAVING MY LIFE, CAPTAIN MARVEL, BUT THERE'S REALLY NO REASON FOR YOU TO REMAIN AT GAMMA BASE!
YOU'RE CERTAIN OF THAT, COLONEL?
OF COURSE! THE HULK ONLY BECAME DESTRUCTIVE BECAUSE I STOOD IN HIS WAY! BUT NOW THAT I KNOW WHAT HE'S AFTER...

YOU PLAN ON FINISHING WHAT YOU STARTED--THE COMPLETE DESTRUCTION OF THE HULK!
THEN I GUESS I'M NO LONGER NEEDED, COLONEL!
I'LL PLAY ALONG--LET TALBOT THINK I'VE DEPARTED--AND THEN TRY TO REACH THE HULK BEFORE HE DOES!

AT LAST--THAT SELF-RIGHTEOUS SPACEMAN'S GONE! ASSEMBLE THE HULKBUSTER ASSULT UNITS, CAPTAIN! WE'LL PROCEED AS PLANNED!
BUT, COLONEL--YOU TOLD CAPTAIN MARVEL--?!
WHO DO YOU TAKE ORDERS FROM, SOLDIER?! ME--OR SOME INTERFERING ALIEN?? NOW, DO AS I SAY! WE'RE HUNTING THE HULK!

OBLIVIOUS TO HIS PLANNED DESTRUCTION, THE HULK STRIDES SILENT CORRIDORS

HE HAS TRODDEN THIS ULTRA-MODERN LABYRINTH BEFORE, IN HAPPIER TIMES

AS BRUCE BANNER, THE MAN, WALKING BESIDE HIS BE-LOVED JARELLA, A QUEEN FROM A SUB-MICROSCOPIC REALM.
NOW, THE MAN IS GONE, BURIED WITHIN THE MONSTER THAT IS THE AWESOME, INCREDI-BLE HULK.

AND THE ALIEN EMPRESS OF A WORLD-WITHIN-OUR-WORLD LIES COLD AND LIFELESS IN THIS CHAMBER

CRYOGENICS MORGUE
THE HULK CANNOT READ THE LEGEND ON THE DOOR.

YET HE KNOWS, DREDGING THE MEMORY FROM THE DIM RECESSES OF HIS MIND, THAT HE WILL FIND THE ONE HE SEEKS-- WITHIN.

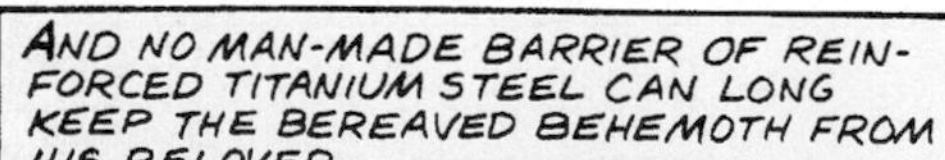
AND NO MAN-MADE BARRIER OF REIN-FORCED TITANIUM STEEL CAN LONG KEEP THE BEREAVED BEHEMOTH FROM HIS BELOVED--

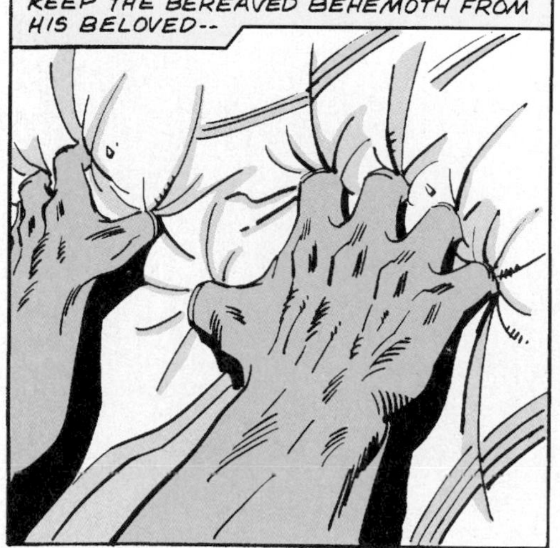

SHKROOM!
JARELLA!

HULK HAS COME FOR YOU. HULK IS HERE.

THERE IS NO RE-SPONSE FROM WITHIN THE CHAMBER...

HULK WILL KEEP HIS PROMISE.

THERE IS ONLY SILENCE!
THE SILENCE OF THE DEAD.

MEANWHILE, SOARING THROUGH THE TUNNELS IN SEARCH OF THE HULK...
ONE NEEDN'T POSSESS COSMIC AWARENESS TO FIND THE HULK!
NOR WILL TALBOT AND HIS TROOPS NEED A ROAD MAP, SINCE ALL THEY NEED DO IS FOLLOW THE PATH OF WANTON DESTRUCTION LEFT IN HIS WAKE!

FORTUNATELY, I GOT HERE AHEAD OF THE HUNTERS! BUT WHAT OF THE--

--HULK??
DIS-SOLVE TO:

A SECLUDED HUNTING CABIN SITUATED ON THE FOOTHILLS OF THE MAJESTIC COLORADO ROCKIES...

JUST THEN...
EH?
...RUMORED THAT THE HULK HAS DEVASTATED GAMMA BASE...

THE RADIO BROADCAST JARS GENERAL ROSS--

--REMINDING HIM OF THE BEING HE HAS TRIED SO HARD TO FORGET!

NNNNNN--

--NO!!
GENERAL!
SKRAK!

BLASTED RADIO-- I COULDN'T TURN IT OFF IN TIME! THE MERE MENTION OF THE HULK HAS DISTURBED THE GENERAL'S DELICATELY BALANCED PSYCHE, RUINING ALL MY WEEKS OF THERAPY!
DAMNED MURDERING MONSTER!
EASY, GENERAL!
IF ONLY HE COULD ACCEPT REALITY-- THAT THE HULK IS AS TORTURED AND TORMENTED AS HE IS!

DOC SAMSON'S EXPOSURE TO GAMMA RAYS MERELY GAVE HIM SUPER-STRENGTH, NOT THE GIFT OF PRE-SCIENCE, ELSE HE WOULD KNOW THAT, AT THIS MOMENT--
THE MONSTER MEN CALL HULK IS EVEN MORE AWASH IN GRIEF THAN SAMSON'S CURRENT CHARGE!
JARELLA DOESN'T MOVE. DOESN'T BREATHE.

IT IS TRUE THEN, WHAT HULK REMEMBERED. JARELLA IS... DEAD.

FROM THE TURMOIL OF HIS MEMORIES, THE HULK DREDGES UP THE RECOLLECTION OF HIS FALL THROUGH SUBMICROSCOPIC SPACE...

THEN, HE SMILES, THIS MONSTER, WHO HAS FOUND LITTLE IN LIFE TO BE HAPPY ABOUT!

THE HULK HAS KNOWN HIS TIME OF JOY-- A BRIEF INTERLUDE SPENT AS THE WARRIOR-PRINCE OF A MOLECULAR WORLD, REIGNING BESIDE HIS RADIANT QUEEN! HER NAME WAS JARELLA, AND GREAT WAS THEIR LOVE!

BUT THE HULK HAD TO RETURN TO EARTH...

AND, THOUGH JARELLA SOON FOLLOWED, IN HER WAKE CAME A KILLER FROM HER OWN WORLD! FIALAN, THE MASTER ASSASSIN!
THE HULK SHIELDED JARELLA FROM THAT DANGER!

AND SOON HE VOYAGED AGAIN TO JARELLA'S WORLD--

-- TO SAVE HIS PRINCESS AND HER PLANET FROM THE RAPACIOUS RAVAGES OF THE SINISTER PSYKLOP!

BUT, IN THE END, IT WAS ALL FOR NOTHING! ALL IN VAIN!

FOR JARELLA DIED, AWAY FROM HER PEOPLE, AWAY FROM HER WORLD--DIED SAVING A CHILD OF EARTH FROM BEING CRUSHED BENEATH A WALL OF CRUMBLING MASONRY!
THIS, THE HULK REMEMBERS!

THIS, HE CAN NEVER FORGET!
JARELLA IS DEAD! EARTH KILLED HER WHEN ALL SHE WANTED WAS TO GO BACK HOME!

I SENSE HIS GRIEF IS REAL. AND NOW THE TRAGIC MONSTER... CRIES!

HULK IS SORRY JARELLA-- SORRY YOU CAME TO EARTH BECAUSE YOU LOVED THE HULK!

HULK CAN NOT MAKE YOU LIVE AGAIN! ALL HULK CAN DO IS TAKE YOU FROM EARTH, BACK TO YOUR WORLD! HOME!
HULK, IF YOU'LL LET ME, I'D LIKE TO--

YELP!
HE--
EVEN HIS MOMENT WITH JARELLA YOU WOULD STEAL FROM HULK, SPACEMAN? EVEN THAT??
KWOM!

BY ALL THE GODS OF THE KREE--! THAT BLOW COULD HAVE KILLED ME!
I WAS MISTAKEN TO INTRUDE UPON THE HULK'S GRIEF...

A FAIRLY SOUND APPRAISAL, MAR-VELL!

KASTROOM!
MANAGED TO AVOID HIS CHARGE...BUT JUST BARELY!

BY THE GREAT PAMA! THE HULK'S LEAP CARRIED HIM THROUGH THE VERY FLOOR, INTO THE BEDROCK BELOW GAMMA BASE ITSELF!
I MUST SEE WHETHER HE'S ALL--

--RIGHT!

WHILE MASKED MAN LOOKED FOR HULK OVER THERE--
--HULK HAS COME UP HERE! NOW HULK HAS MASKED MAN WHERE HE WANTS HIM!

AND NOTHING WILL STOP HULK FROM...

SMASHING ME, HULK? NO, I DON'T THINK SO.

I UNDERSTAND YOUR DISTRUST OF WORDS-- MEN CAN USE THEM TO SAY SO MANY THINGS OTHER THAN WHAT THEY REALLY MEAN! BUT I HAVE A WAY OF COMMUNICATING BEYOND MERE WORDS, HULK!

AND, ONCE OUR MINDS HAVE MERGED ON A COSMIC PLANE, WHERE TRUTH IS SIMPLY ANOTHER ASPECT OF AWARENESS...

PERHAPS THEN YOU WILL BELIEVE ME WHEN I SAY THAT I MEAN YOU NO HARM-- THAT I MERELY WISH TO HELP YOU.
HELP? BUT WHY DOES SPACEMAN WANT TO HELP HULK?

PERHAPS, HULK, BECAUSE I, TOO, ONCE LOST A LOVE.
NO MORE WORDS! HULK BELIEVES YOU, MASKED MAN! HE WILL LET YOU HELP!

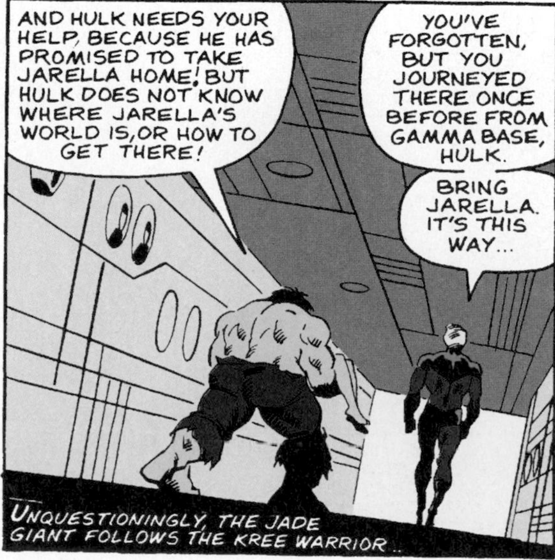
AND HULK NEEDS YOUR HELP, BECAUSE HE HAS PROMISED TO TAKE JARELLA HOME! BUT HULK DOES NOT KNOW WHERE JARELLA'S WORLD IS, OR HOW TO GET THERE!
YOU'VE FORGOTTEN, BUT YOU JOURNEYED THERE ONCE BEFORE FROM GAMMA BASE, HULK.
BRING JARELLA. IT'S THIS WAY...
UNQUESTIONINGLY, THE JADE GIANT FOLLOWS THE KREE WARRIOR..

WHILE, ELSEWHERE IN GAMMA BASE...
THE BETA-BORER'S FULLY CHARGED COL. TALBOT! ALL HULKBUSTER UNITS ARE READY!
GOOD! BY NOW THE HULK'S RETRIEVED JARELLA'S BODY!
UNLESS I MISS MY GUESS, HIS NEXT STOP WILL BE THE SUBMOLECULAR STUDIES CHAMBER!
WILL THIS THING REALLY STOP THAT GREEN GOLIATH?
IT SHOULD! IT WAS DESIGNED TO PUNCH HOLES THROUGH ASTEROIDS!
YEAH BUT THE HULK'S NOT AN ASTEROID!

OUR PLAYERS NOW CONVERGE FROM OPPOSITE DIRECTIONS ON...
GAMMA BASE'S SUBMOLECULAR STUDIES LAB. I REMEMBER HEARING THAT IT WAS DE-SIGNED BY REED RICHARDS.
BAH! MACHINES ARE ALWAYS MADE TO HURT HULK!
IT'S AMAZING HOW LIGHT THE BETA-BORER IS, SIR!
TONY STARK BUILT IT FOR ONE-MAN MINING IN SPACE, SOLDIER! HE NEVER DREAMED I'D CONVERT IT INTO A WEAPON!

THIS MACHINE WAS MADE TO HELP, HULK, BY SHRINKING MEN OR OBJECTS DOWN TO SUBMICROSCOPIC SIZE.
IT ONCE SHRUNK YOU, ENABLING YOU TO ENTER THE BRAIN OF GLENN TALBOT AND BRING HIM OUT OF A COMA.

THE HULK'S IN THE LAB, SIR--WITH CAPTAIN MARVEL AND THE DEAD GIRL!
SO, MARVEL LIED ABOUT LEAVING GAMMA BASE?! WELL TOO BAD THEN... FOR HIM!
MOVE THE BETA-BORER INTO POSITION!

IT TAKES BUT A MOMENT TO DECIPHER THE CONTROLS OF THE MICRON-CANNON. THERE, IT IS DONE.

THEN WHY IS HULK STILL HERE, MASKED MAN?
WHY HASN'T CANNON SHOT HULK AND JARELLA AWAY?

BECAUSE I HAVE ONLY DETERMINED THE COORDINATES OF YOUR JOURNEY, HULK. ALL THAT REMAINS IS TO CHARGE THE MACHINERY.
A BRACE OF PHOTON BURSTS SHOULD DO IT.

PREPARE YOURSELF, HULK. AND WHATEVER HAPPENS, DO NOT MOVE FROM THE TRANSPORT PLATFORM!
HULK IS READY!
THE MICRO-CANNON HUMS TO LIFE...

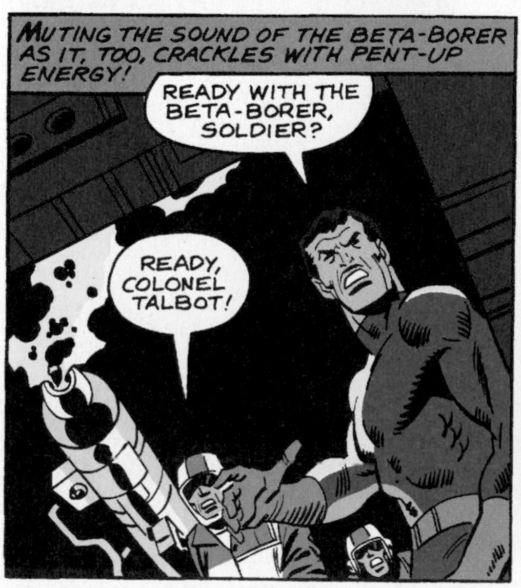
MUTING THE SOUND OF THE BETA-BORER AS IT, TOO, CRACKLES WITH PENT-UP ENERGY!
READY WITH THE BETA-BORER, SOLDIER?
READY, COLONEL TALBOT!

THEN, ON MY COMMAND: GET READY... TAKE AIM...

NEXT ISSUE

HOME IS NEVER THE WAY WE REMEMBER IT!

JARELLA'S WORLD!

40¢
CC
247
MAY
02456

MARVEL® COMICS GROUP

APPROVED BY THE COMICS CODE AUTHORITY

THE INCREDIBLE

HULK

TM

MARVEL'S
SENSATION!

Caught in the heart of a Nuclear Explosion, victim of Gamma-Radiation gone wild, Doctor Robert Bruce Banner now finds himself transformed in times of stress into seven feet, one thousand pounds of unfettered Fury—the most powerful creature to ever walk the earth—
Stan Lee PRESENTS: THE INCREDIBLE HULK!®
WILLINGLY SUBMITTING HIMSELF TO THE RAYS OF GAMMA BASE'S MICRON-CANNON--
--THE JADE GIANT KNOWN AS THE HULK SHRINKS INTO A SUB-MOLECULAR SOLAR SYSTEM--
--BEARING IN HIS ARMS THE CORPSE OF JARELLA, AN ALIEN PRINCESS WHOM THE HULK ONCE LOVED...
HE IS NOW RETURNING HER BODY TO HER HOME!
JARELLA'S WORLD
HUNH! AT LAST HULK HAS STOPPED SHRINKING-- STOPPED FALLING THROUGH WORLDS! BUT WHERE IS HULK NOW?
SPACEMAN SAID HE WOULD HELP BY SENDING HULK TO JARELLA'S HOME! BUT HOME HAD FLOWERS AND GRASS AND TREES!
DID SPACEMAN LIE TO HULK? DID CAPTAIN MARVEL SEND HULK TO DEAD ROCKWORLD TO DIE??!
BILL MANTLO Writer
SAL BUSCEMA Artist
JOHN COSTANZA · letters
BEN SEAN · colors
AL MILGROM · editor
JIM SHOOTER editor-in-chief

NO! SOMEHOW HULK KNOWS CAPTAIN MARVEL DID NOT LIE!

THIS IS JARELLA'S WORLD-- BUT IT IS DIFFERENT! HULK REMEMBERS BIRDS AND BUGS... AND PEOPLE!

BUT NOW, EVERYTHING IS BLACK ROCKS, BLACK DUST! EVERYTHING IS COLD AND DEAD--
--LIKE JARELLA!
BUT WHY HAS JARELLA'S WORLD CHANGED? HULK LIKED IT THE WAY IT WAS!

JARELLA'S PEOPLE LOVED THE HULK BECAUSE HULK LOVED JARELLA! THEY WANTED THE HULK TO BE THEIR KING ONCE!
HULK WAS HAPPY HERE! HAPPY! HULK NEVER WANTED TO LEAVE... NEVER WANTED TO GO BACK TO EARTH!

BUT EARTH ALWAYS MADE HULK COME BACK! WHY? WHY DID EARTH WANT HULK BACK, WHEN ALL EARTH DID WAS TRY TO KILL HULK--
--THE WAY EARTH KILLED JARELLA!
EH?!
HULK HEARS... SCREAMS!

AND SCREAMS MEAN PEOPLE! PEOPLE IN TROUBLE!
JARELLA'S PEOPLE!!
LUMBERING ONTO THE CLIFFSIDE, HIS PRECIOUS BURDEN CAREFULLY CRADLED IN HIS ARMS, THE GREEN GOLIATH PEERS OVER THE PERILOUS PRECIPICE...

IF THE HULK HAD ANY LINGERING DOUBTS AS TO HIS WHEREABOUTS IN THE VAST VOID OF THIS SUB-ATOMIC MICRO-VERSE, THEY ARE INSTANTLY DISPELLED! THE HUMANS BELOW, THOUGH CAKED WITH DIRT AND GARBED IN FOUL-SMELLING FURS, POSSESS THE SAME EMERALD PIGMENTATION AS THE HULK AND HIS BELOVED PRINCESS!

THEY ARE JARELLA'S PEOPLE... AND THEY ARE IN DESPERATE DANGER!

MWROWRR

...FULL ONTO THE SLAVERING SERPENT...
IT IS NOT HELPLESS HUMANS YOU FACE NOW, BAT-DRAGON!
IT IS THE HULK!

AND HULK IS PR...PRO... PROTECTOR OF THESE PEOPLE WITH GREEN SKIN LIKE HULK'S!

SO LET HULK'S PEOPLE GO!!

IT IS THE KIND OF BATTLE FROM WHICH MYTHS ARE WOVEN!

IF THERE ARE STORYTELLERS AMONGST THE WATCHERS BELOW, THEY ARE ALREADY EMBROIDERING THE TALE FOR THEIR CHILDREN AND THEIR CHILDREN'S CHILDREN!

TELLING OF A DAY WHEN THE LONG-LOST CHAMPION OF K'AI DROPPED OUT OF THE SKY--

--TO DEAL DEATH AND DESTRUCTION TO THE OUTLAND DEMONS THAT PLAGUED THE PEOPLE DURING THE DAYS OF DARKNESS.
DIE, BAT-DRAGON! HULK HAS FOUGHT BIGGER ENEMIES THAN YOU!
THROOM

AND HULK ALWAYS WINS!

BECAUSE HULK IS THE STRONGEST ONE THERE IS!

WITH THE DRAGON'S DEMISE, THE EMERALD-HUED INHABITANTS OF K'AI SWARM EN MASSE FROM THEIR CAVERNS OF CONCEALMENT--
--SONGS OF PRAISE SPRINGING SPONTANEOUSLY TO THEIR LIPS!

BUT THE HULK NEITHER UNDERSTANDS, NOR DESIRES, THEIR ADORATION!
BACK!

FOR, IN HIS MONSTER'S SOUL, THE HULK KNOWS WHAT THEY CANNOT KNOW!

THAT HIS RETURN TO K'AI WILL NOT SIGNAL A TIME OF CELEBRATION--

--BUT WILL MERELY SIGNAL THE BEGINNING OF A PAINFUL PERIOD OF RENEWED GRIEF!
SING A SONG! HULK'S RETURN WILL NOT MAKE YOU HAPPY!
HULK HAS BROUGHT JARELLA HOME, AS HE PROMISED--BUT JARELLA IS... DEAD!

JXXELLX!
JXXELLX!
JXXELLX?

AND, DRAWN FROM THE CAVE'S DEPTHS BY THE DIRGEFUL DIN, THREE ELDERS STEP OUT INTO THE HALF-LIGHT!
THEY COMPRISE THE PANTHEON OF SORCERORS--AND ARE CALLED HOLI, MOLI AND TORLA!

RECOGNIZING AT ONCE THE BRUTE THAT BEARS THE BODY OF THEIR QUEEN, THEY WEAVE A SUBTLE SPELL...
THEY POSSESS LESS POWER THAN THEY WIELDED OF OLD--

--AND YET, 'TIS ENOUGH... 'TWILL SUFFICE!

HULK KNOWS YOU! YOU ARE JARELLA'S MAGICIANS!
AND YOU HAVE DONE SOMETHING TO HULK TO MAKE HIM UNDERSTAND YOUR WORDS!

IN TIMES PAST, REINFORCED BY THE TRANSCENDANT TECHNOLOGY OF K'AI, OUR SPELLS COULD HAVE DONE FAR MORE THAN MERELY BRIDGE THE LANGUAGE BARRIER THAT KEPT US FROM COMMUNICATING, FRIEND HULK!
THEN WE WERE ABLE TO ALLOW THE MIND OF BRUCE BANNER TO DOMINATE THE BODY OF THE HULK!

BANNER? HULK HATES BANNER! IF MAGICIAN WANTS TO BE HULK'S FRIEND HE WILL NEVER MENTION PUNY BANNER AGAIN!
IT IS HULK WHO HAS RETURNED TO YOU--
--AND HULK WHO HAS BROUGHT JARELLA HOME!

DEAD--AS WE HAVE LONG SUSPECTED AND LONG FEARED! THANK YOU FOR RETURNING JARELLA TO HER PEOPLE, HULK!
A DEAD QUEEN COME HOME TO A DYING WORLD!

BUT WHY IS JARELLA'S WORLD DYING? WHAT HAPPENED TO THE CITIES? WHY DO JARELLA'S PEOPLE LIVE IN CAVES AND NEVER SMILE?
THERE IS LITTLE LEFT TO SMILE ABOUT, HULK! OUR WAY OF LIFE CHANGED--

"--ON THE VERY DAY THAT YOU RESCUED OUR WORLD FROM THE RAVAGES OF THAT MILLENIA-OLD MADMAN... PSYKLOP!

"DO YOU REMEMBER, HULK, HOW ALL K'AI TURNED OUT TO PRAISE YOU? AND TO HEAR OUR QUEEN'S PROCLAMATION?
THE DANGER IS PAST! LET THIS BE A DAY FOR CELEBRATION--
--FOR IF THE HULK WILL HAVE ME, I WOULD BE HIS BRIDE!

"BUT, EVEN AS THE ROYAL PALACE RESOUNDED WITH REJOICING--!"
F-FEEL SO STRANGE SUDDENLY! WHAT'S HAPPENING TO US?
WE ARE GROWING BIGGER, JARELLA!
TURNING INTO GIANTS!!

"AND THAT, HULK, IS THE LAST WE OF K'AI EVER SAW OF YOU OR OUR BELOVED QUEEN JARELLA!
DO NOT BE AFRAID, JARELLA! HULK WILL PROTECT YOU!
I COULD NEVER BE FRIGHTENED, BELOVED--SO LONG AS I'M WITH YOU!

"WHERE DID YOU GO, HULK? DID YOU TAKE OUR QUEEN BACK TO YOUR WORLD, THUS SPARING HER THE SIGHT OF K'AI'S FINAL DESTRUCTION--
"AS MIGHTY EARTHQUAKES TOPPLED OUR REMAINING CITIES INTO THE DUST?"

THE MAGE TORLA GROWS SILENT! HE KNOWS THE HULK CANNOT COMPREHEND HIS QUESTIONS, LET ALONE GIVE ANSWER.
FOR THE HULK BARELY REMEMBERS GROWING EVER LARGER, JARELLA IN HIS ARMS--
--AS THEY LEFT THE MICROVERSE BEHIND THEM...

G-GENERAL ROSS? SOMETHING'S MATERIALIZING ON THE MICROSCOPE SLIDE!
IT'S THE HULK, SAMSON! YOU'VE PULLED HIM BACK FROM THE MICROVERSE!
YES, SIR! BUT I HAVEN'T BROUGHT HIM BACK ALONE!

YES, THE HULK RETURNED TO EARTH WITH HIS BRIDE-TO-BE, BUT JARELLA WAS WISE ENOUGH TO KNOW SHE WAS SOMEWHERE SHE DID NOT BELONG!
I MUST RETURN TO K'AI, HULK--TO HELP REBUILD MY WORLD!
AND I MUST RETURN ALONE!

UNFORTUNATELY, THAT WASN'T THE WAY THINGS WORKED OUT!
I'M AFRAID JARELLA'S NOT GOING ANYWHERE! YOU SEE--
--IN HIS ANGER, THE HULK SHATTERED THE SLIDE CONTAINING HER SUBATOMIC WORLD!

HULK DID NOT MEAN TO DO IT! HULK WAS ANGRY THAT ROSS AND SAMSON BROUGHT HULK HOME!
HULK IS SORRY HE BROKE SLIDE!

THE SHATTERING OF THAT SLIDE SENT OUR WORLD OF K'AI SPINNING THROUGH SUB-ATOMIC CREATING MASSIVE GEOLOGICAL UPHEAVALS!

"AND, WHEN THE TREMORS ENDED, I'M AFRAID THERE WASN'T MUCH LEFT OF US, OR OUR AGE-OLD CIVILIZATION!
"BUT WE PICKED OURSELVES UP FROM THE RUINS--

"--AND, CARRYING WITH US WHATEVER KNOWLEDGE OF OUR FORMER GLORY WE COULD BEAR IN OUR MINDS...
"WE SET OUT INTO THE WILDERNESS... TO BEGIN ANEW!"

BUT IT WAS NOT EASY, HULK! OUR NEW POSITION IN SPACE IS FAR FROM ANY SUN! FEW PLANTS GROW, AND THOSE ANIMALS WHICH SURVIVED FEED MOSTLY UPON OUR OWN KIND!
HULK SWORE TO PROTECT JARELLA AND JARELLA'S WORLD! SHE WANTED TO COME BACK--TO REBUILD! NOW HULK IS HERE TO CARRY OUT JARELLA'S LAST WISH!
YOU WILL AID US, HULK? WITH YOUR MIGHTY STRENGTH, PERHAPS WE CAN REBUILD K'AI TO ITS FORMER GLORY! BUT FIRST, A MORE SOMBER TASK AWAITS US! JARELLA MUST BE BURIED ALONGSIDE HER ANCESTORS! THERE... IN THE VALLEY OF LIFE!
A COLD WIND HOWLS, AND NIGHT FALLS ON JARELLA'S WORLD!

MORNING IN THE COLORADO ROCKIES, AS DR. LEONARD SAMSON ATTEMPTS A NEW FORM OF THERAPY ON HIS PATIENT, GENERAL "THUNDERBOLT" ROSS!
IT'S A GREAT DAY FOR HUNTING, GENERAL!

AND MAYBE A BRISK WALK IN THE WOODS WILL GET YOUR MIND OFF THE CAUSE OF YOUR NERVOUS COLLAPSE--YOUR FAILURE TO END THE MENACE OF THE HULK!
READY, GENERAL?
THE OLD SOLDIER MAKES NO AUDIBLE REPLY--

--BUT ALLOWS HIMSELF TO BE LED LIKE A CHILD BY THE GREEN-HAIRED PSYCHIATRIST!
THEIR BREATH MISTS IN THE CHILL MOUNTAIN AIR...
AND, BEFORE LONG, THE DEEP, SILENT FOREST HIDES THEM FROM VIEW!

THE NEW MEXICO SUN BEATS DOWN MERCILESSLY ON THE TWISTED WRECKAGE OF WHAT ONLY YESTERDAY WAS THE THEORETICALLY INVINCIBLE MILITARY INSTALLATION KNOWN AS GAMMA BASE!
TODAY, SHATTERED WEAPONS LIE SCATTERED LIKE SUN-BLEACHED BONES ABOUT THE DESERT FLOOR!
FOR ALL ITS FIREPOWER, GAMMA BASE COULD NOT FULFILL THE SOLE PURPOSE FOR WHICH IT WAS BUILT... THE COMPLETE AND UTTER ANNIHILATION OF THE MAN-MONSTER KNOWN AS THE INCREDIBLE HULK!

AND THAT IS A FACT THAT THE PRESENT COMMANDER, COL. GLENN TALBOT, CANNOT TOLERATE!
MAKE ONE MOVE, CAPTAIN MARVEL, AND YOU'RE A DEAD MAN!
YOU HELPED THE HULK, AND YOU'RE GOING TO PAY FOR THAT!

LIKE YOU'VE MADE EVERYONE--INCLUDING YOUR WIFE--PAY FOR NOT SHARING YOUR OBSESSIVE HATRED OF THE HULK, GLENN?
WHO--??

HAS IT BEEN SO LONG SINCE WE CEASED TO BE MAN AND WIFE, GLENN, THAT YOU'VE EVEN FORGOTTEN MY VOICE?
BETTY! HOW DID YOU GET HERE? THE BASE HAS BEEN UNDER A COMPLETE SECURITY SEAL SINCE WORD CAME OF THE HULKS IMPENDING ATTACK!
YOU MEAN GAMMA BASE'S ATTACK ON THE HULK, DON'T YOU, COLONEL TALBOT?
THE HULK ONLY FOUGHT YOU BECAUSE YOU TRIED TO KEEP HIM FROM THE BODY OF HIS BELOVED JARELLA!

I-I THOUGHT SOMETHING LIKE THAT MUST BE THE TRUTH, CAPTAIN MARVEL, SO I FLEW RICK JONES, FRED SLOAN, YOUR GIRLFRIEND ELYSIUS AND MYSELF DOWN IN MY PRIVATE PLANE --
--HOPING TO GET HERE BEFORE MY EX-HUSBAND IRRATIONALLY DESTROYED A POOR CREATURE WHO MEANS NO HARM!
YOU STILL DEFEND THAT BRAINLESS BRUTE OVER ME, BETTY?
WHY DON'T YOU ADMIT YOU NEVER STOPPED LOVING BRUCE BANNER-- THE MAN TRAPPED INSIDE THE HULK!

I WON'T EVEN DIGNIFY THAT WITH AN ANSWER, GLENN!
CAPTAIN MARVEL, WHAT OF THE HULK? IS--IS HE...?
DEAD, MS. ROSS? THOUGH I POSSESS THE GIFT OF COSMIC AWARENESS--

"--EVEN I CANNOT SAY WHAT BECAME OF THE HULK AFTER HE STEPPED UPON THE LAUNCHING PLATFORM OF GAMMA BASE'S MICRON-CANNON...

"FOR, HE HAD BARELY SHRUNK FROM SIGHT, WHEN TALBOT BURST IN AND ORDERED THE MICRON-CANNON DESTROYED!"

I HAD PINPOINTED THE LOCATION OF JARELLA'S WORLD, K'AI! THE HULK MAY HAVE ARRIVED THERE SAFELY...
OR HE MAY BE DEAD, OR LOST FOREVER IN SUB-SPACE!
OH, WOW! NOW I'VE GOT AN ENDING FOR MY BOOK ABOUT THE HULK--AN ENDING I DIDN'T WANT!
I HOPE YOU'RE REAL PROUD OF YOURSELF, TALBOT! IT COST YOU GAMMA BASE, BUT YOU DOOMED THE HULK!
I-I DID MY DUTY!
YEAH, BUT YOU LOST YOUR HUMANITY!

WHILE ON A FAR-FLUNG WORLD!
MREE MREE
WHY DO JARELLA'S PEOPLE SING, MAGICIAN?
TO TELL DEATH THEY BRING HIM THEIR QUEEN, HULK!
AND BECAUSE THEIR KING HAS RETURNED TO LEAD THEM FROM THE DEAD LANDS TO THE VALLEY OF LIFE!

IF JARELLA'S WORLD IS DEAD, HOW DO JARELLA'S PEOPLE EAT?
FOOD WE SCAVENGE FROM OUR SHATTERED CITIES, FOR NOTHING GROWS--

--SAVE THERE, IN THE ONE CORNER OF K'AI STILL FERTILE! GAZE, O' HULK, ON THE SACRED VALLEY OF LIFE!

LOOK THE HULK DOES, LONG AND HARD, AT THE TREES SWAYING IN A SOFTLY SIGHING BREEZE!
FROM AFAR, THE SCENT OF FLOWERS REACHES THE HULK'S FLARING NOSTRILS!
AND THE DISTANT SOUNDS OF WILD BIRDS AND CLEAR-FLOWING STREAMS CARESS HIS EARS. EARS WHICH HAVE HEARD NOTHING BUT THE HOWLING WINDS OF BLACK DUST SINCE HIS RETURN TO JARELLA'S WORLD!

HUNH! VALLEY OF LIFE IS GOOD PLACE! HULK WILL BURY JARELLA THERE! AND THERE JARELLA'S PEOPLE WILL BUILD NEW HOMES TO LIVE!
B-BUT, THAT'S IMPOSSIBLE, HULK! THE VALLEY OF LIFE IS FORBIDDEN TO THE PEOPLE OF K'AI!
WE MAY BURY OUR DEAD THERE, 'TIS TRUE! BUT TO THE LIVING--

--THE DELIGHTS OF THE VALLEY OF LIFE ARE ETERNALLY DENIED! YONDER HANG THE BONES OF THOSE WHO SOUGHT TO DWELL THERE!
NONE HAVE DARED PASS INTO ITS FORESTS SINCE!

WE MUST LEAVE JARELLA'S BIER HERE AND DEPART! THE VALLEY DEMONS WILL COME AND CLAIM HER FOR BURIAL!
LEAVE JARELLA HERE, WHERE IT IS COLD AND DARK?
WALK BACK TO ROCKWORLD WHEN THERE IS FOOD IN VALLEY FOR ALL?

NO! HULK WILL TAKE JARELLA INTO GREEN WOODS AND LAY HER TO REST-- THEN HULK WILL GET FOOD FOR JARELLA'S PEOPLE!
B-BUT THE VALLEY WILL NOT TOLERATE YOUR LIVING PRESENCE!
THE VALLEY DEMONS WILL REND YOU!
DO NOT GO, O'KING!

JARELLA MUST BE BURIED, AND JARELLA'S PEOPLE MUST HAVE FOOD! NO DEMONS WILL STOP HULK!
IF THEY TRY, HULK WILL SMASH!
WAIT HERE! HULK WILL BE BACK!

BEHIND THE HULK, THE GENTLE FOLK OF K'AI SEND UP A KEENING WAIL, FOR TO THEM IT SEEMS THIS DAY HAS LOST THEM A BELOVED QUEEN... AND A MIGHTY KING!
YET, THEY SETTLE DOWN TO WAIT, FOR SUCH WAS THEIR KING'S LAST COMMAND!
VALLEY IS PRETTY-- LIKE JARELLA'S WORLD USED TO BE!

YET, WORLD IS DIFFERENT! JARELLA IS DEAD! EVERYTHING HAS CHANGED!

EVERYTHING ALWAYS CHANGES! EVERYTHING EXCEPT HULK!

HULK IS ALWAYS HULK-- ALWAYS THE SAME!
A GENTLE SOUND STIRS THE HULK FROM HIS REVERIE...

...AND THE SCENE THAT GREETS THE JADE GIANT'S EYES IS IDYLLIC INDEED!
HULK KNOWS THIS PLACE--
--BUT CAN'T REMEMBER FROM WHERE!
FROM FAIRYTALES TOLD TO A LONELY CHILD CHRISTENED ROBERT BRUCE BANNER--

--A LONG, LONG TIME AGO, ON ANOTHER WORLD, IN ANOTHER LIFETIME...

BEFORE THE BOY GREW INTO A MAN, BEFORE THE MAN BECAME A SCIENTIST, BEFORE THE SCIENTIST CREATED A GAMMA BOMB...
BEFORE THE BOMB CREATED A MONSTER!

OTHER MEMORIES RISE UNBIDDEN FROM THAT OTHER LIFETIME LIKE GHOSTS FROM THEIR GRAVES...
FAREWELL, MOTHER--DAD! I-I'LL MISS YOU BOTH!

MEMORIES OF FAMILY--AND FRIENDS...
HULK'S FRIEND IS DEAD. EVERYONE HULK LOVES, HULK LOSES.
KRAKER JAK JAKSON
THEN THE MEMORIES FADE--

--AND THE HULK REMEMBERS WHAT HE HAS COME TO DO!
HULK BURIED CRACKAJACK, AND NOW HULK MUST BURY JARELLA!

THE HULK'S MIGHTY FINGERS GOUGE THE GENTLE EARTH...

...AND SUDDENLY, STARTLINGLY, THE EARTH REACTS!
HUNHH??!
ROCKS AND EARTH FLY AT HULK--DRIVING HIM BACK FROM JARELLA!

TREES BEND DOWN AND HOLD HULK'S ARMS WHILE STONES HAMMER HULK BACK?!

ARRGH! NOW TREES TRY TO CHOKE HULK!
TRY TO KILL HULK!

BUT HULK HAS NOT COME ALL THE WAY TO JARELLA'S WORLD TO BE KILLED BY STUPID TREES!

ROCKS HAVE STOPPED FLYING AT HULK! TREES STOP GRAB-BING HIM! HULK HAS WON!
BUT HAS VALLEY HURT JARELLA?
UNTOUCHED, JARELLA SLEEPS THE ETERNAL SLEEP...

BUT THERE IS TO BE NO REST FOR THE UNWARY HULK!
SKROWR!
GRARGHH!

CAT-BEAST DIGS ITS CLAWS INTO HULK'S BACK--HURTING HULK!

CAT-BEAST MADE A BIG MISTAKE TRYING TO HURT HULK!
BRAM!!

BECAUSE HULK KNOWS HOW TO TAKE PAIN--

--AND HOW TO GIVE IT!!
KABRAK!

CAT-BEAST IS GONE! NOW HULK CAN-- GLAGGH!

DRAGON RISES FROM WATERFALL AND SNAKES OUT TONGUE TO GRAB HULK--

--DRAGGING HULK TOWARD DRAGON'S MOUTH!!

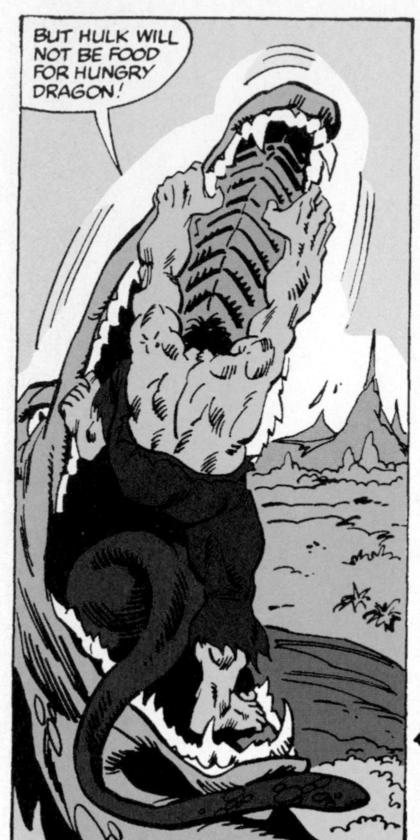
BUT HULK WILL NOT BE FOOD FOR HUNGRY DRAGON!

AND HULK WILL NOT LET MONSTERS OF VALLEY OF LIFE DRIVE HIM AWAY!
SNAP

SPLOOSH

DRAGON IS DEAD! IT COULD NOT KEEP HULK FROM JARELLA! NOTHING CAN--

SKREE
SKREE
SKREE

SKREE
BRZZZ
BRZZZ
NOW MONKEYS AND BUGS TRY TO GET IN HULK'S WAY!

NEXT ISSUE: How Green Grows My Garden!

40¢
248
JUNE
02456
MARVEL® COMICS GROUP
APPROVED BY THE COMICS CODE AUTHORITY
© 1979 MARVEL COMICS GROUP
THE INCREDIBLE HULK®
MARVEL'S TV SENSATION!™
HOW GREEN GROWS... THE GARDENER!

Caught in the heart of a ***Nuclear Explosion,*** victim of ***Gamma-Radiation*** gone wild, ***Doctor Robert Bruce Banner*** now finds himself transformed in times of stress into seven feet, one thousand pounds of unfettered ***Fury***—the most powerful creature to ever walk the earth—

Stan Lee PRESENTS: THE INCREDIBLE HULK!®

THE HULK STILL FACED A DANGER GREATER THAN BEING LOST IN SUB-SPACE!

YONDER LIES THE VALLEY OF LIFE, THE ONLY FERTILE AREA LEFT ON K'AI! THERE MUST JARELLA BE BURIED!

WHILE IT ACCEPTS THE DEAD, NO LIVING SOUL HAS GONE THERE AND RETURNED!

YET, THE HULK DARED ENTER THE VALLEY OF LIFE, BEARING IN HIS MONSTROUS ARMS THE CORPSE OF HIS BELOVED JARELLA, WHOM HE HAD BROUGHT HERE FOR BURIAL! AT ONCE THE VALLEY ROSE AGAINST THE BRUTE, KEEPING HIM FROM HIS TASK, FOR SUCH WERE THE ORDERS OF THE ONE WHO WAS MASTER HERE ...THE GARDENER!
HOW GREEN MY GARDEN GROWS!
WHY DID OLD MAN TELL HIS GARDEN TO ATTACK HULK? WHY?
MERELY TO HAVE TRODDEN UPON THIS SACRED GROUND IS REASON ENOUGH, MONSTER! IN THIS VALLEY I HAVE CREATED A PARADISE, AND NO LIVING HUMAN SHALL EVER FIND SHELTER IN ITS SHADE!
BILL MANTLO, WRITER
SAL BUSCEMA, ARTIST
JIM NOVAK, LETTERS
BEN SEAN, COLORS
ALLEN MILGROM, EDITOR
JIM SHOOTER, EDITOR-IN-CHIEF

WHY DID YOU NOT HEED THE CORPSE-STREWN RING OF CROSSES SURROUNDING THE VALLEY?
MORE CLEARLY THAN WORDS THEY ANNOUNCE THAT HERE IS NO PLACE FOR THE LIVING!

BUT HULK HAS BROUGHT JARELLA HERE, OLD MAN!
AND JARELLA IS DEAD!

THEN SHE WILL BE MADE WELCOME, AND WILL BE LAID TO REST, AS BEFITS HER QUEENLY STATION!

FOR THE DEAD SOW NO STRIFE IN THE VALLEY OF LIFE! BEAR HER AWAY, MY FRIENDS!
YOU TAKE JARELLA FROM HULK?

NO! HULK MUST BE WITH JARELLA TO THE END! THAT IS WHAT HULK PROMISED!

I'M AFRAID THAT IS IMPOSSIBLE, CREATURE! BUT AS I AM NOT WITHOUT COMPASSION--

--I WILL TRY TO MAKE YOU UNDERSTAND WHY LIVING HUMANS, OTHER THAN MYSELF, ARE FORBIDDEN THIS VALLEY'S BOUNTY!

AND, THAT YOU MAY BETTER COMPREHEND, I CAUSE THE RAGE OF THE BEAST TO GIVE WAY TO THE REASON OF... THE MAN!
THE EMERALD GEM ON THE GARDENER'S BROW GLOWS WITH SUDDEN FIRE...

...AND THE FURY-CLOUDED VISION OF THE TRAPPED BRUTE GIVES WAY TO THE CLEAR-EYED GAZE OF THE CURIOUS SCIENTIST... CONFUSED, BUT EAGER TO UNDERSTAND!
WHAT ARE YOU DOING TO HULK? NO! HULK KNOWS!
YOU ARE SENDING HULK AWAY! MAKING HIM CHANGE PLACES WITH PUNY BANNER!
HULK HATES BANNER!
HATES--! HUNH?
W-WHERE AM I?
IN THE NAME OF ALL THAT'S HOLY, WHAT'S THE HULK GOTTEN ME INTO NOW??
THE VOICE, THOUGH GUTTURAL, IS BRUCE BANNER'S!

WHERE AM I? WHO ARE YOU? HOW DID I GET HERE? AND HOW IS IT THE HULK HAS GOT BRUCE BANNER'S MIND??
AS FOR THE REST-- YOU ARE IN MY VALLEY OF LIFE, THE ONLY FERTILE SPOT ON THE OTHERWISE DESOLATE SUB-ATOMIC WORLD OF K'AI!
YOU CAME HERE BRINGING K'AI'S QUEEN FOR BURIAL-- AND FOUGHT THE VALLEY WHEN IT TRIED TO TURN YOU BACK!
THE SOUL GEM SENSED THE DUALITY OF YOUR NATURE-- AND FREED THE MAN FROM THE MONSTER!

NOW THAT YOU ARE CAPABLE OF UNDERSTANDING, I WILL EXPLAIN WHY!

RELAX YOUR MIND, AND PAY HEED AS THE SOUL GEM TRANSMITS... THE STORY OF THE GARDENER!

"I AM ONE OF THE ELDERS WHO CAME TO YOUR UNIVERSE IN THE WAKE OF CREATION!
"BROTHERS HAD I, ONE WHO LOVED TO STUDY, ANOTHER WHO ENGAGED IN ENDLESS SPORT!
"BUT I SOUGHT ONLY PEACE, A RETURN TO THE PARADISE FROM WHENCE WE CAME.
"UNFORTUNATELY, THIS ROAD WAS BARRED TO US. I TRIED TO CREATE PARADISE ANEW...
"...AND MY GARDEN SPRANG TO LIFE ON EARTH'S MOON!

"THE POWER OF MY SOUL GEM SOON DREW THE SINISTER STRANGER, WHO CRAVED THE GEM FOR HIS OWN!
"I THOUGHT MY PRESENCE MIGHT GO UNDISCOVERED AS THE SOUL GEM OF ADAM WARLOCK DIVERTED THE STRANGER--!
"--BUT SPIDER-MAN SOON CONVINCED ME THAT I COULD NOT REMAIN NEUTRAL!

"THUS, I JOINED MY POWER TO WARLOCK'S, AND WE DROVE THE STRANGER FROM THE MOON!

"IN SO DOING, I CORRUPTED MY GEM, EXPENDING ITS POWER TO SUPPORT LIFE, AND I ABANDONED IT ON THE BARREN LUNAR PLANE...

"...WHERE IT WAS SOON FOUND BY HE WHO REPRESENTED THE DARK SIDE OF LIFE... THANOS!
"FOR THANOS MEANS DEATH!

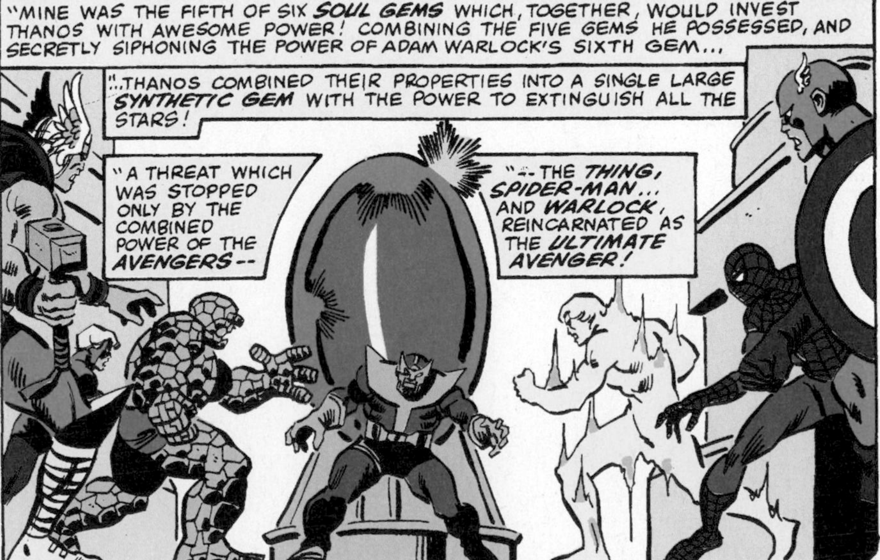
"MINE WAS THE FIFTH OF SIX SOUL GEMS WHICH, TOGETHER, WOULD INVEST THANOS WITH AWESOME POWER! COMBINING THE FIVE GEMS HE POSSESSED, AND SECRETLY SIPHONING THE POWER OF ADAM WARLOCK'S SIXTH GEM...
"...THANOS COMBINED THEIR PROPERTIES INTO A SINGLE LARGE SYNTHETIC GEM WITH THE POWER TO EXTINGUISH ALL THE STARS!
"A THREAT WHICH WAS STOPPED ONLY BY THE COMBINED POWER OF THE AVENGERS--
"--THE THING, SPIDER-MAN... AND WARLOCK, REINCARNATED AS THE ULTIMATE AVENGER!

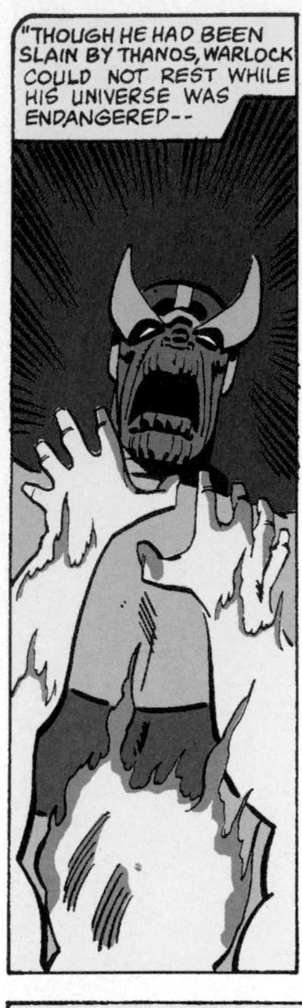
"THOUGH HE HAD BEEN SLAIN BY THANOS, WARLOCK COULD NOT REST WHILE HIS UNIVERSE WAS ENDANGERED--

"--AND SO HE ROSE TO SLAY THANOS IN TURN, TRANSFORMING THE DEATH-GOD TO SOLID GRANITE!

"AT LAST, WARLOCK, WHO WAS BORN ON EARTH, A PROTOTYPE FOR HUMANITY'S FUTURE, LOST HIS INNOCENCE AND HIS LIFE PROTECTING THE VALUES HE CHERISHED...
"...LIGHT, LIFE AND TRUTH!

"HAVING DIED A SECOND TIME, HE WAS BURIED ALONGSIDE TWO OTHER VICTIMS OF THANOS' WAR!

" AFTER PLACING HIS SOUL GEM ON THE FRESHLY-TURNED GRAVE, THE ASSEMBLED EARTH HEROES TOOK THEIR LEAVE OF ADAM WARLOCK...
HERE LIES
ADAM WARLOCK
GOD SLAYER,
SAVIOR OF TWO WORLDS,
AND TORMENTED SOUL.
MAY HE NOW BE AT PEACE.
1967 1977

"THAT IS WHERE I, FOLLOWING THE SOUL GEM'S EMANATIONS--

"--CLAIMED IT, FOR IT BORE WITHIN IT THE POWER WHICH WAS MINE BY RIGHT--THE POWER TO MAKE WORLDS BLOOM!
"THE SOUL OF THAT VALIANT WARRIOR WOULD FOREVER BE AT PEACE--

"--RESIDING IN THE GEM IN MY SAFEKEEPING!"

THEN I JOURNEYED HERE, TO SUB-ATOMIC K'AI, SWEARING NEVER AGAIN TO PLACE THE POWERS OF THE SOUL GEM BEFORE UNDESERVING HUMANITY!
THE INNOCENT ARE WELCOME HERE! THE BIRDS! THE BEASTS--

--AND THE DEAD!
BUT MAN, WHO SPREADS DISCORD WHEREVER HE GOES, IS NOT WELCOME! FAREWELL, HUMAN! LEAVE MY VALLEY!
...OR DIE!
WAIT, BLAST IT! YOU CAN'T TAKE JARELLA FROM ME!

I LOVED HER! AND SHE LOVED THE MAN I WAS... AND THE MONSTER I'D BECOME!

I OWE HER AT LEAST A DECENT BURIAL! CAN'T YOU EVEN GRANT ME THAT?

OH, WHAT'S THE USE? HE'S GONE!

WHY IS IT EVERY-THING I'VE EVER LOVED IS TAKEN FROM ME?

AM I NEVER TO KNOW PEACE?

NEVER??

PLEASE??!

HUH? MY DESPAIR MUST'VE SLOWED MY PULSE DOWN! I'VE BECOME BRUCE BANNER PHYSICALLY AS WELL AS MENTALLY!
AND THE VINES MEANT TO HOLD THE HULK DROP AWAY FROM MY SMALLER FORM!

WELL, I'M FREE-- BUT WHAT DO I DO WITH MY FREEDOM?
FORGET THE HULK'S PROMISE TO JARELLA? LEAVE HER UNTENDED IN THE GARDENER'S GRASP?

NO! BRUCE BANNER MAY NOT POSSESS THE HULK'S HALF A TON OF GREAT GREEN MUSCLE, BUT HE'S NO QUITTER EITHER!
I'M COMING, JARELLA--AND NOTHING IN THIS VALLEY OF LIFE WILL STOP ME!
AND SO HE GOES...

WHILE, ON A DEVASTATED LANDING FIELD BACK ON EARTH, HIS FRIENDS BID EACH OTHER A FINAL FAREWELL!
WHERE WILL YOU GO NOW, MS. ROSS? BACK TO DENVER?

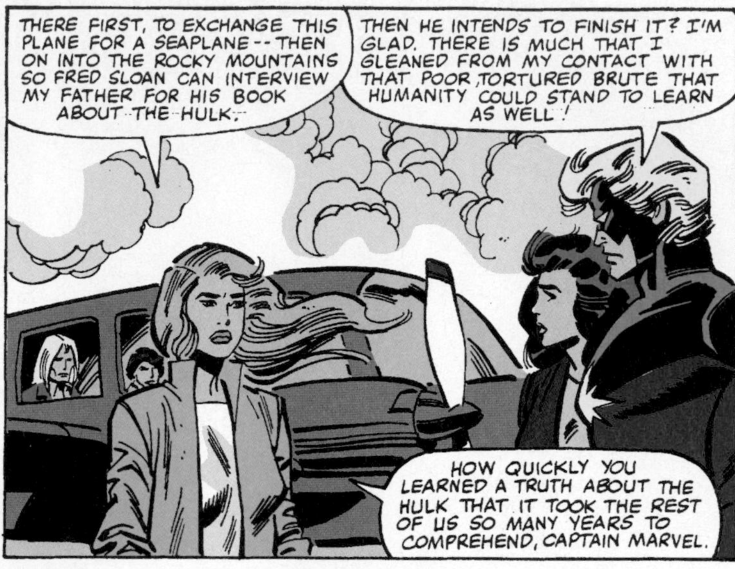
THERE FIRST, TO EXCHANGE THIS PLANE FOR A SEAPLANE--THEN ON INTO THE ROCKY MOUNTAINS SO FRED SLOAN CAN INTERVIEW MY FATHER FOR HIS BOOK ABOUT THE HULK.
THEN HE INTENDS TO FINISH IT? I'M GLAD. THERE IS MUCH THAT I GLEANED FROM MY CONTACT WITH THAT POOR, TORTURED BRUTE THAT HUMANITY COULD STAND TO LEARN AS WELL!
HOW QUICKLY YOU LEARNED A TRUTH ABOUT THE HULK THAT IT TOOK THE REST OF US SO MANY YEARS TO COMPREHEND, CAPTAIN MARVEL.

"AND, EVEN SO, MEN LIKE MY EX-HUSBAND STILL FEAR AND TRY TO DESTROY A CREATURE BETTER DESERVING OF OUR PITY!
"NOW, BY DESTROYING THE MICRON-CANNON, GLENN HAS SUCCEEDED IN BANISHING THE HULK FROM EARTH--FOREVER!

YOU KNOW, IT WASN'T SO MUCH THE HULK THAT GLENN FEARED--BUT ME!
HE COULD NEVER BELIEVE THAT I HAD GOTTEN OVER MY LOVE FOR BRUCE BANNER, EVEN AFTER I CONSENTED TO BECOME MRS. GLENN TALBOT!
HIS INSANE JEALOUSY CAME BETWEEN US MORE THAN BRUCE EVER DID!

BUT NOW, STRANGELY ENOUGH, I CAN THANK GLENN FOR AWAKENING ME TO THE REALIZATION THAT--WHEREVER HE IS--
--I MAY YET LOVE BRUCE BANNER!
ELYSIUS AND I MUST GO NOW, BETTY!

THERE IS MUCH I HAVE TO SHOW HER OF EARTH --AND MUCH, I I HOPE, THAT IS GOOD!
MRS. TALBOT! WAIT!
I'M DIVORCED, SOLDIER! MY MAIDEN NAME'S ROSS!

ER--YES, MA'AM! BUT I'VE BEEN ORDERED TO TELL YOU THAT YOUR HUSBAND--THAT IS, YOUR EX-HUSBAND--WOULD LIKE TO SEE YOU BEFORE YOU LEAVE GAMMA BASE.
YOU CAN TELL COL. TALBOT I HAVE NO WISH TO SEE HIM, SOLDIER--

--NOW... OR EVER AGAIN!
THE SMALL PLANE DRONES OFF INTO THE DISTANCE --LEAVING GLENN TALBOT ALONE WITH HIS THOUGHTS!

THE PLANE HEADS NORTHWARD TOWARD THE MOUNTAINS OF COLORADO WHERE TWO HUNTERS CLIMB IN SEARCH OF GAME!
HOW ARE YOU FEELING, GENERAL ROSS?

GENERAL "THUNDERBOLT" ROSS DOES NOT RESPOND! HIS DRAWN AND ANGUISHED FEATURES GIVE NO CLUE THAT HE WAS, ONCE, ONE OF THIS COUNTRY'S FOREMOST MILITARY TACTICIANS!
BUT THEN, THE GREEN HAIR AND POWERFUL PHYSIQUE OF HIS COMPANION--
--WOULD NOT IDENTIFY DR. LEONARD SAMSON AS A BRILLIANT PSYCHIATRIST, EITHER!

NOW, THE DOCTOR HAS SOUGHT, THROUGH SPORT, TO GET HIS PATIENT'S MIND OFF THE CAUSE OF HIS RECENT NERVOUS COLLAPSE: NAMELY--
--THE GENERAL'S FAILURE TO APPREHEND THE MAN-MONSTER KNOWN AS THE HULK!
THE DOGS HAVE SCENTED SOMETHING, GENERAL!

WHATEVER IT IS SEEMS TO HAVE THEM CONFUSED!
I'VE NEVER SEEN THEM ACT SO UNCERTAINLY ABOUT A SCENT BEFORE!

AH, HERE THEY GO! THE GAME'S AS GOOD AS IN THE BAG RIGHT NOW!
ROWR ROWR AWROOOOOO
BUT WHAT IS IT? DEER? MOUNTAIN LION?

NO, DR. SAMSON! IT IS SOMETHING NO HUNTER CAN POSSIBLY HAVE COME PREPARED FOR!
GOOD HEAVENS! THE CREATURE THE DOGS HAVE SCENTED, IT-- IT'S MONSTROUS!

MONSTER! EVEN HERE HE HOUNDS ME! MOCKS ME!
PTOW!
GENERAL ROSS!

DID YOU SEE, SAMPSON? IT WAS HIM! THE HULK!!
I-I SAW SOMETHING, GENERAL--SHADOWY, INHUMAN! BUT IT WASN'T THE HULK!
BEFORE WE LEFT THE CABIN, COL. TALBOT CALLED TO SAY HE'D GOTTEN RID OF THE HULK FOREVER!
THAT NEWS STARTLES THE OLD GENERAL...

WHILE, ON THE SUB-ATOMIC WORLD OF K'AI, JARELLA'S PEOPLE WAIT ON THE OUTSKIRTS OF THE VALLEY OF LIFE, FOR WORD FROM THEIR KING!
THE HULK HAS BEEN GONE LONG!
SURELY, HE IS DEAD!
I-I FEAR YOU ARE RIGHT, FELLOW COUNSELLORS!

WE SHOWED OUR KING THE GRIM PORTENTS BIDDING HUMANS STAY OUT OF YONDER VALE, BUT HE IGNORED THEM!
YET, I HAVE FAITH IN THE HULK AND WILL WAIT A WHILE LONGER FOR HIS RETURN!

MAY YOUR FAITH BE MIGHTY ENOUGH TO PRESERVE YOU THEN, WISE TORLA!

FOR WE ARE ABOUT TO BE DRIVEN FROM EVEN THE OUTSKIRTS OF THE VALLEY OF LIFE!
OUR KING MUST BE DEAD! FLEE ALL! FLEE FOR YOUR LIVES!
GODS OF K'AI! THE VALLEY-DWELLERS STAMPEDE UPON US!

MEANWHILE, UNAWARE OF THE IMPENDING DOOM BEARING DOWN UPON JARELLA'S PEOPLE, BRUCE BANNER FOLLOWS THE TRAIL OF THOSE WHO HAVE STOLEN THE BODY OF HIS QUEEN...
ALL OF K'AI ONCE RESEMBLED THIS VALLEY-- UNTIL THE HULK SHATTERED A MICROSCOPIC SLIDE CONTAINING THIS SUB-MOLECULAR WORLD...
...AND SENT IT CAREENING THROUGH SUB-SPACE!

THIS WORLD HAS OFFERED THE HULK AND ME NOTHING BUT HAPPINESS--AND WE'VE REPAID IT BY NEARLY CAUSING ITS DESTRUCTION, AND BY INADVERTANTLY CAUSING THE DEATH OF ITS QUEEN!
WATER! I WONDER WHEN THE HULK ATE OR DRANK LAST!

I'VE GOT TO STOP-- REFRESH MYSELF! REST!
AND THEN GET BACK ON JARELLA'S TRAIL!
BUT THIS IS NO ORDINARY STREAM!

EVERYTHING IN THE GARDEN OF LIFE OBEYS THE GARDENER'S INJUNCTION: NO HUMANS!
WHAT--? A WATERY TENDRIL, GRABBING MY ARM!

DRAGGING ME INTO THE STREAM!

CURRENT'S INCREDIBLY STRONG-- PULLING ME UNDER!

I-IF I DON'T DO SOMETHING TO SAVE MYSELF, I-I'LL DROWN!

NO!

WATER MIGHT DROWN PUNY BANNER, BUT WATER WILL NOT DROWN THE HULK! HULK IS STRONGER THAN WATER!

STRONGER THAN WHIRLPOOL! STRONGER THAN ANYTHING!!

AND HULK WILL PROVE HOW STRONG HE IS--

--BY MAKING WATER LET HULK GO!

STUPID WATER! IT WOULD NOT LISTEN TO HULK, AND NOW HULK HAS SENT IT AWAY!
BUT WATER LISTENED TO GARDENER, TRIED TO KEEP HULK FROM GOING AFTER JARELLA!

NOW HULK WILL FIND OLD MAN GARDENER... AND GET JARELLA BACK!

MEANWHILE, A SHORT DISTANCE AHEAD...
THE SITE OF THE ANCIENT BURIAL GROUNDS OF K'AI LIES HERE MY CREATURES! SOON WILL JARELLA SLEEP WITH HER ANCESTORS!
IT IS A PITY I COULD NOT ALLOW HER BRUTISH ESCORT TO BEAR HER HITHER, FOR, IN TRUTH, HE IS BUT A SAVAGE INNOCENT!

YET THE PEOPLE OF K'AI HAVE NAMED HIM THEIR KING -- AND I DARE NOT RISK DESPOILING THIS VALLEY BY OPENING IT TO THE MASS OF PETTY HUMANITY!
EH? THAT CRASHING IN THE TREE-TOPS--??

IT IS THE HULK! HE IS HERE!!
YES, OLD MAN! HULK IS HERE TO KEEP HIS PROMISE TO JARELLA!
HULK WILL BURY HER, AND THEN BRING JARELLA'S PEOPLE HERE TO LIVE!

HERE? TO MY PARADISE? NO, MONSTER! IT CANNOT BE!

AIDING HUMANITY COST ME MY GARDEN ON EARTH'S MOON! I HAVE SWORN NEVER AGAIN TO SACRIFICE BEAUTY FOR THE BENEFIT OF MAN!
YOU ARE MIGHTY, HULK--BUT I AM OF THE ELDER RACE, AN IMMORTAL CAPABLE OF RECREATING PARADISE...AND OF DEFENDING IT!
WITH A NOD OF HIS HEAD, THE GARDENER BIDS HIS MENAGERIE ATTACK...

...AND THE HULK IS LOST TO SIGHT BENEATH A SNARLING SWIRL OF BIZARRE, BESTIAL BODIES!

BUT NOT FOR LONG!
AWAY, ANIMALS! HULK'S FIGHT IS NOT WITH YOU!

NO! I AM YOUR FOE, MONSTER--BUT EVERY BIRD AND BEAST THAT DRAWS BREATH IN THIS VALLEY IS MINE TO COMMAND!

OLD MAN SENDS BIRDS AND BUGS TO DRIVE HULK AWAY?

HULK WILL SEE IF BIRDS AND BUGS CAN FLY IN A BIG WIND!
FWROO

WROOSHH!

AT THAT MOMENT, OUTSIDE THE VALLEY...
LOOK TO THE SKY, PEOPLE, OF K'AI!

A BLOW HAS BEEN STRUCK AGAINST THE VALLEY! FIGHT ON WITH RENEWED COURAGE, FOR IT IS A SIGN THAT THE HULK--OUR KING --YET LIVES!

LIVES, YES! AND FIGHTS!
HULK HAS BLOWN AWAY YOUR BIRDS AND BUGS, OLD MAN! HULK HAS BEATEN YOUR BEASTS!
YES, MONSTER!

BUT NOW YOU FACE THE FURY OF THE ELDERS, ENCASED IN THE BLAZING SOUL GEM I WEAR AT MY BROW-- AND EMBODIED IN MYSELF!
HULK DOES NOT CARE ABOUT ELDERS OR PRETTY STONES! HULK FIGHTS FOR JARELLA AND JARELLA'S WORLD--

--AND THAT IS GOOD ENOUGH FOR HULK!
BY THE STARS! YOU GRASP MY STAFF WITH A POWER WELL NIGH EQUAL TO MY OWN!
WHAT MANNER OF MORTAL ARE YOU?
HULK IS HULK! HULK IS THE STRONGEST ONE THERE IS!

AS THE DUEL OF TITANS TRANSPIRES WITHIN THE GARDEN, THE TIDE OF BATTLE TURNS WITHOUT!
FIGHT, MEN OF K'AI! DRIVE THE VALLEY DEMONS BACK!
FIGHT FOR THE FUTURE OF OUR WORLD--AND FOR OUR KING!
AYE-- FOR THE HULK!

NEVER IN HIS EVENTFUL LIFE HAS THE HULK HEARD HIS NAME RAISED AS A CLARION CALL TO BATTLE--NOR IS HE WITHIN EARSHOT TO HEAR IT NOW!
BUT, AS IF HE SENSES THE FAITH JARELLA'S PEOPLE PLACE IN HIM--
--HE PRESSES HIS STRUGGLE WITH THE GARDENER... TO VICTORY!
AWAY, OLD MAN! HULK HAS YOUR STICK!

AND YOUR PRETTY STONE!

A SOUL GEM OF THE ELDER RACE IN THE HANDS OF A MORTAL? NO, IT MUST NOT BE!

IT IS, OLD MAN! AND HULK REMEMBERS YOU SAID THAT IT WAS PRETTY STONE THAT GIVES VALLEY LIFE!

IF STONE CAN DO THAT--
--THEN STONE CAN MAKE JARELLA'S PLANET LIVE!
THE HULK HURLS THE SOUL GEM DOWN:

DOWN THROUGH THE PLANET'S MANTLE...

DOWN THROUGH THE PLANET'S CRUST...

DOWN TO THE VERY CORE OF K'AI!

AND, WHEN THE SOUL GEM MERGES WITH THE PLANET'S MOLTEN HEART...
...A MAGICAL TRANSFORMATION COMES OVER THE FACE OF K'AI!
ALL FIGHTING STOPS, AS MEN BEFRIEND BEASTS!

THEIR BATTLE NO LONGER HAS MEANING. IT WAS A WAR BETWEEN THOSE WHO POSSESSED PARADISE AND THOSE WHO WANTED A SHARE!
NOW, NEW LIFE SPRINGS FORTH, ALL OVER THE SURFACE OF THE PLANET K'AI, AND THERE IS PEACE AND PLENTY FOR ALL!

NOW ALL OF JARELLA'S WORLD IS LIKE YOUR VALLEY, OLD MAN! JARELLA'S PEOPLE WILL EAT!

NOW HULK HAS KEPT HIS PROMISE TO JARELLA'S PEOPLE!
NOW JARELLA CAN REST!

PARADISE TEEMS WITH THE SOUNDS OF LIFE...

BUT THERE IS A GREAT SILENCE IN THE HULK'S HEART!
UNTIL NOW HE HAS NOT FULLY ACCEPTED JARELLA'S DEATH!

BUT HOLDING THE LIFELESS BODY OF HIS BELOVED IN HIS MIGHTY ARMS, HE AT LAST UNDERSTANDS THAT JARELLA IS NEVER COMING BACK TO HIM!

SHE LIVED ONCE, BUT NOW IS GONE.
THE HULK ACCEPTS THAT, AND LAYS JARELLA IN HER GRAVE!

GENTLY COVERING HER WITH EARTH, THE INCREDIBLE HULK BURIES SOME OF HIS CHILDLIKE INNOCENCE WITH HER!
GOODBYE, JARELLA!
FAREWELL, OUR QUEEN.

LOOK! 'TIS A MIRACLE!
HUNH ?!
A MIRACLE, TRULY!

NEXT MONTH: JACK FROST NIPPING AT YOUR SOUL!

With Jarella's body returned to her own world at long last, the Hulk returned to Earth and his life there. However, Jarella's world was not yet done with Bruce Banner, and years later (in Incredible Hulk #351-352, both reprinted in Incredible Hulk Visionaries: Peter David, Volume 3), Banner was drawn there yet again. Religions had grown up around the story of Jarella and the Hulk's love and the rebirth of fertility that the planet had undergone on his last visit there – both Jarella and the Hulk were now revered as gods. As can be the case with religion, debates on the true nature and wills of the two had resulted in religious warfare, and one sect, led by its Grand Inquisitor, Risuli, brutally conquered and ruled the others. A rival sect, led by the wizard Gorsham, collected the technology of Psyklop (now known as the "Mountain God") and combined that with their own magics to find the Hulk's world and bring him, now in his grey-skinned Mr. Fixit identity, to their world. Gorsham promised to rid Fixit of Banner if he would in turn remove the Grand Inquisitor and serve as their planet's god, but once the Inquisitor was finally defeated, Gorsham betrayed Fixit and returned him to Earth, ruthlessly seizing control of the planet for his own ends. How well Gorsham has ruled poor Jarella's world remains to be seen.

While our Jarella and her world both faced unhappy endings, there exist other worlds and other realities in the Multiverse. In some realities, the star-crossed lovers may have never met, in others perhaps they became the deadliest of enemies, and in still others they may have lived happily ever after. Rejecting the tragedy of the Jarella and the Hulk that we knew, we can always ask "What If... Hulk's girlfriend Jarella had not died?"

MARVEL® COMICS GROUP

75¢ 23 OCT 02686

WIN A TOYS "Я" US® SHOPPING SPREE!

GRAND PRIZE MINIMUM VALUE $3000! DETAILS INSIDE!

APPROVED BY THE COMICS CODE AUTHORITY

WHAT IF™ THE HULK®

HAD BECOME A BARBARIAN?

THIS IS THE WHOLE PACKAGE... SCI-FI, FANTASY, AND HULK-POUNDING *ACTION!*

STAN LEE PRESENTS: A STUNNING SAGA OF AN ALTERNATE REALITY!

WHAT IF... HULK'S GIRLFRIEND JARELLA HAD NOT DIED?

I AM THE *WATCHER!* AND IT HAS BEEN MY SOLEMN DUTY TO OBSERVE AND RECORD ALL THE MOMENTS OF EXISTENCE ON THE WORLD CALLED EARTH. WITNESS, IF YOU WILL, THE TRAGIC GAMMA-RADIATED MAN-MONSTER KNOWN AS THE *HULK!* IN ALL HIS TORMENTED LIFE, THERE WAS NO MORE PAINFUL MOMENT THAN THE DEATH OF THE WOMAN HE LOVED!

JARELLAAA!!

BMT

DEAD END

PETER GILLIS, *SCRIPT* | HERB TRIMPE, *PENCILS* | MIKE ESPOSITO, *INKS* | TOM ORZECHOWSKI, *lettering* GAFF, *coloring* | O'NEIL/GRUENWALD, *EDITORS* | JIM SHOOTER, *Ed-in-CHIEF*

THE JADE-SKINNED WOMAN JARELLA WAS NOT OF THIS EARTH--
--BUT A QUEEN ON THE SUB-ATOMIC WORLD OF K'AI. INTO HER SPHERE THE HULK WAS ONCE CAST, AND DURING HIS ALL-TOO-BRIEF STAY ON HER WORLD, SHE GREW TO LOVE THE MISUNDERSTOOD GOLIATH.

"THEN, ON ONE OF THE HULK'S RETURN VISITS TO JARELLA'S WORLD... *
WE'VE DONE IT, GENERAL ROSS! WE'VE MANAGED TO REVERSE THE PROCESS BY WHICH WE SHRANK THE HULK!
YES, SAMSON, BUT IT SEEMS WE'VE UNSHRUNK SOMEONE ELSE AS WELL!
*HULK #203.-- D/M.

"MOREOVER, THE SLIDE WHICH SEEMINGLY CONTAINED K'AI HAD BEEN SHATTERED, STRANDING JARELLA ON EARTH.

"DAYS LATER, A MURDEROUS ROBOT CALLED THE CRYPTO-MAN CROSSED THE HULK'S PATH--
BAN

"AND WITH JARELLA WATCHING, A BATTLE ROYALE ENSUED!

"THE FORCE OF THE FIGHT CAUSED A WALL TO COLLAPSE OVER A LITTLE BOY...

"AND, SELFLESSLY, JARELLA PUSHED THE BOY TO SAFETY, BEARING THE BRUNT HER-SELF--

"--AND THUS SHE PERISHED."

BUT SUCH A CRITICAL POINT IN TIME HAS MORE THAN ONE POSSIBLE OUTCOME. ONE ALTERNATE PATH BEGINS IN THIS WAY...
JARELLA SEES THE BOY--

"-- WHEN SUDDENLY, THE IMAGE OF THE BOY FLICKERS IN AND OUT OF EXISTENCE, FOR REASONS JARELLA CAN'T BEGIN TO GUESS. SHE PAUSES --

"-- AND THAT PAUSE MAKES ALL THE DIFFERENCE!

"JARELLA IS TOO LATE TO SAVE THE BOY -- TOO LATE TO SACRIFICE HERSELF --

"AND SO ONE LIFE CONTINUES, WHILE ANOTHER -- ENDS?

"THE HULK DEMOLISHES THE CRYPTO-MAN --

"-- AND THE FEEDBACK DESTROYS THE CONTROLS AND ITS ANONYMOUS CONTROLLER --
"-- IN A LABORATORY WHICH, ODDLY ENOUGH, CONTAINS A STRANGE IDOL!

DARLING, QUICK! THERE'S A LITTLE BOY UNDERNEATH THE RUBBLE!

"BUT, DESPITE A THOROUGH SEARCH, THE HULK FINDS NO BODY -- NOTHING!
"IT IS A MYSTERY INDEED!

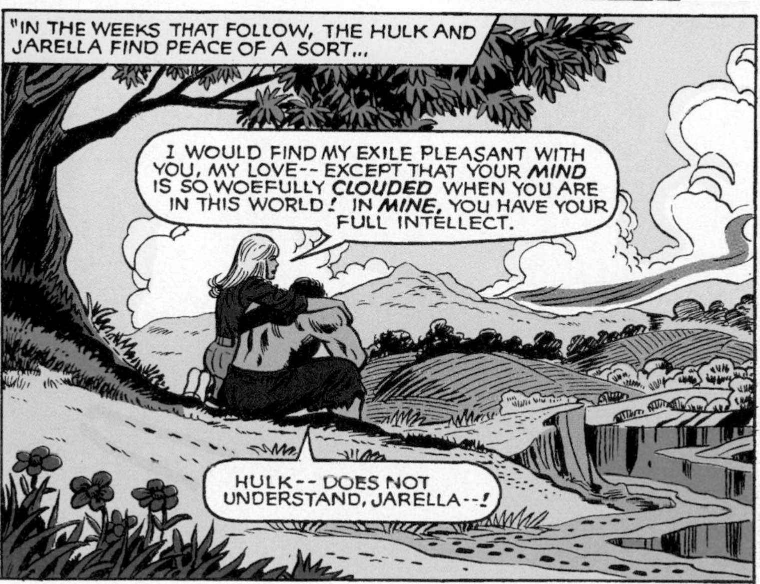
"IN THE WEEKS THAT FOLLOW, THE HULK AND JARELLA FIND PEACE OF A SORT...
I WOULD FIND MY EXILE PLEASANT WITH YOU, MY LOVE -- EXCEPT THAT YOUR MIND IS SO WOEFULLY CLOUDED WHEN YOU ARE IN THIS WORLD! IN MINE, YOU HAVE YOUR FULL INTELLECT.
HULK -- DOES NOT UNDERSTAND, JARELLA --!

MY LOVE--
WHAT
IS THAT
SOUND?
HULK KNOWS THAT
SOUND! IT IS--

SOLDIERS!
THEY ALWAYS
FOLLOW HULK--
ATTACK HULK!
HULK WILL--

NOT THIS TIME, GREEN-
SKIN! IF YOU AND THE
LITTLE LADY WILL
JUST HOP ABOARD--
--WE HAVE SOME
GOOD NEWS FOR YOU,
FOR A CHANGE!

"HULK BUSTER CHIEF
CLAY QUARTERMAIN'S
GRIN BROADENS AS THEY
RETURN TO GAMMA BASE--

"--WHERE THEY FIND 'THUNDERBOLT' ROSS,
BETTY ROSS, AND GLENN TALBOT LISTENING
TO HENRY PYM--BETTER KNOWN AS ANT
MAN...
IN SHORT,
I THINK WE
HAVE IT LICKED!

AS YOU KNOW, WE'VE BEEN
BUILDING A MACHINE POWERFUL
ENOUGH TO SHRINK THE HULK
PERMANENTLY!
THE BIG PROBLEM SEEMED
TO BE LOCATING JARELLA'S
WORLD AMID THE MYRIAD
ATOMS AROUND US!

THE THING IS, THE OLD "WORLDS WITHIN WORLDS" MODEL WE'VE BEEN USING NO LONGER WORKS!
QUANTUM MECHANICS STATES THERE IS A LOWER LIMIT TO SIZE-- PLANCK'S CONSTANT-- BELOW WHICH YOU JUST CAN'T GO!
IN THIS WORLD!

VIOLATE THE PLANCK LIMIT AND YOU DROP OUT OF THIS UNIVERSE ALTOGETHER, AND INTO ANOTHER, PARALLEL ONE, WHICH WE CALL A MICRO-WORLD--
--PARALLEL TO US, AND NOT REALLY "INSIDE" A PARTICULAR ATOM!

SO INSTEAD OF "WORLDS WITHIN WORLDS", WE HAVE "WORLDS BESIDE WORLDS", EACH WITH A DIFFERENT PLANCK CONSTANT!
I'M SORRY IF I'M BEING ABSTRUSE, BUT WHAT IT ALL BOILS DOWN TO IS THIS:

I'M PRETTY SURE THAT K'AI, THOUGH MANY LEVELS AWAY FROM EARTH, IS PARALLEL TO, AND LINED UP DIRECTLY WITH, EARTH!
AND THAT MEANS--

THAT MEANS, MY DARLING, THAT THEY CAN SEND US HOME AGAIN!

THEN, THE TIME COMES FOR GOODBYES!
I'M NO GOOD AT SPEECHES, JARELLA, BUT YOU'VE GIVEN TWO NIGHTMARES -- THE HULK'S AND MINE-- A HAPPY ENDING. THANKS.

GOODBYE, OLD FRIEND, FELLOW AVENGER, FELLOW DEFENDER: IT SEEMS, AFTER ALL THESE YEARS, THAT THE UNIVERSE HAS FINALLY FOUND A PLACE FOR YOU.

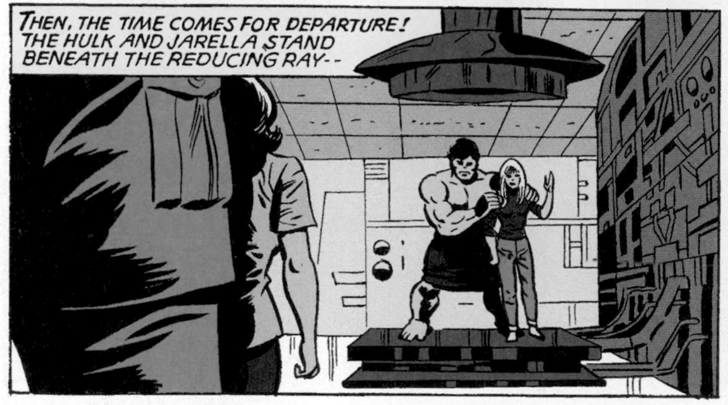
THEN, THE TIME COMES FOR DEPARTURE! THE HULK AND JARELLA STAND BENEATH THE REDUCING RAY--

1
2
3
4
5
POWER START
--AND HERE GOES NOTHING!
CRITICAL OVERRIDE

THE PROCESS BEGIN SLOWLY...
GOOD-BYE, ROSS--

AND THEN ACCELERATES...
HULK DID NOT HATE YOU... REALLY--!

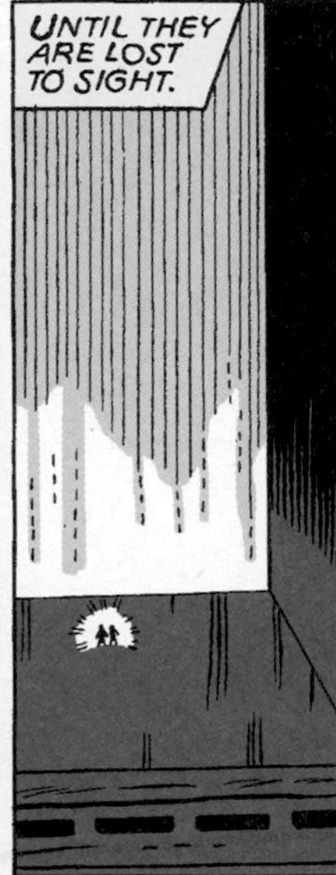
UNTIL THEY ARE LOST TO SIGHT.

SOON, THEY ARE STANDING ON MOLECULES...

THEN PLUNGING THROUGH ATOMS...

UNTIL THEY DROP THROUGH THE VERY FABRIC OF OUR UNIVERSE--
--LIKE GRAINS OF SAND THROUGH A SIEVE!

THEY FALL THROUGH A NEW COSMOS--

--EVER SHRINKING...

SUDDENLY, THE TWO MATERIALIZE ON THE SURFACE OF A PLANET, THEIR SHRINKING HALTED...
THIS IS NOT JARELLA'S WORLD!

SOME FORCE IS SLOWING US DOWN-- TRYING TO KEEP US HERE! BUT WE MUST GO ON! WE HAVE TO FIGHT IT!
HULK WILL FIGHT! HOW?

CONCENTRATE, MY LOVE-- USE YOUR WILL!
HULK WILL CONCENTRATE--
--ON GOING HOME.

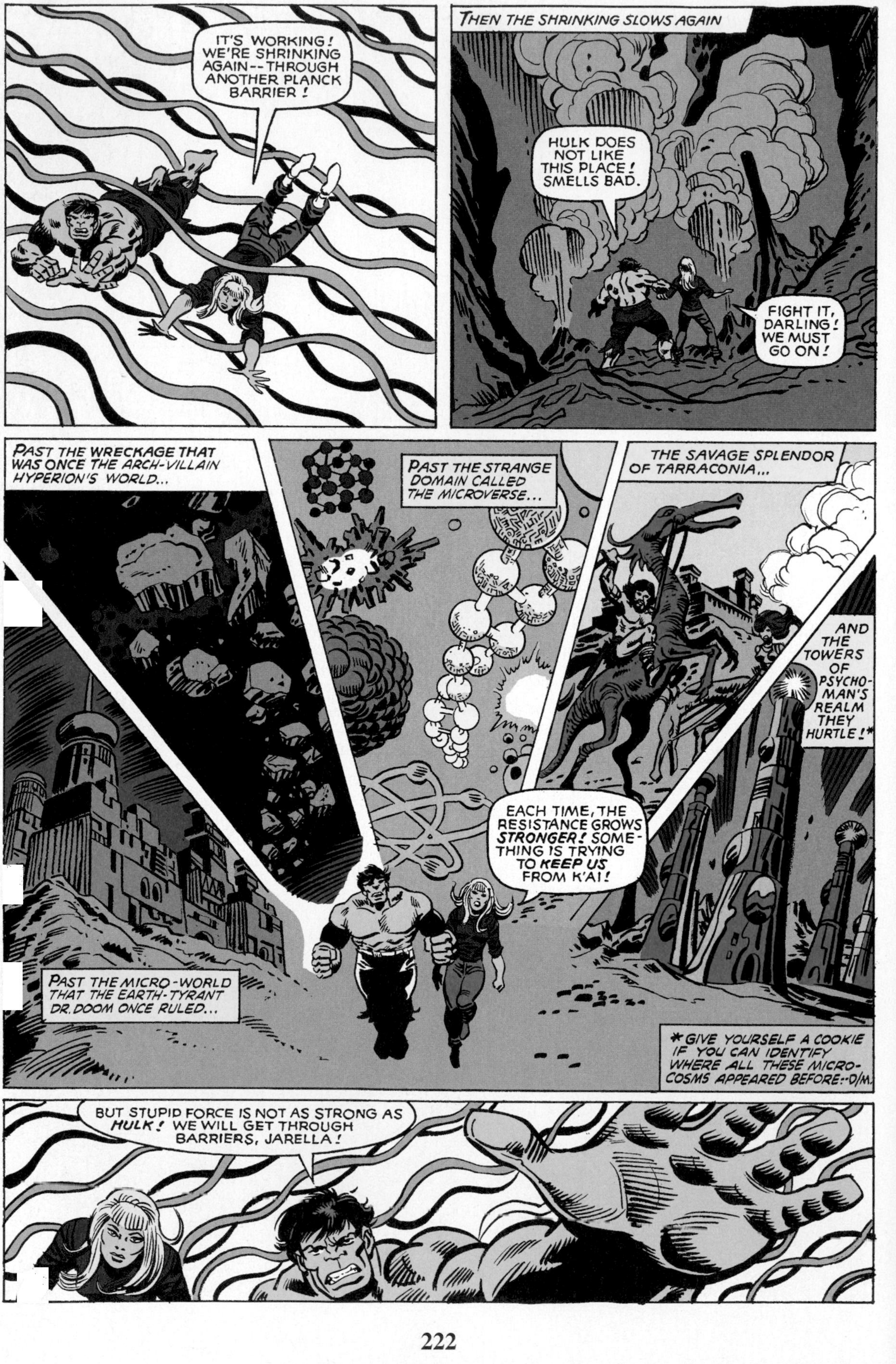

PAST THE WRECKAGE THAT WAS ONCE THE ARCH-VILLAIN HYPERION'S WORLD...

PAST THE MICRO-WORLD THAT THE EARTH-TYRANT DR. DOOM ONCE RULED...

PAST THE STRANGE DOMAIN CALLED THE MICROVERSE...

THE SAVAGE SPLENDOR OF TARRACONIA...

AND THE TOWERS OF PSYCHO-MAN'S REALM THEY HURTLE!*

EACH TIME, THE RESISTANCE GROWS **STRONGER!** SOMETHING IS TRYING TO **KEEP US** FROM K'AI!

*GIVE YOURSELF A COOKIE IF YOU CAN IDENTIFY WHERE ALL THESE MICROCOSMS APPEARED BEFORE.--D/M.

AND THIS BARRIER PROVES TO BE THE LAST!
THE TREES-- THE AIR-- MY LOVE, WE HAVE RETURNED HOME TO K'AI!

YES-- AND THE SPELL OF K'AI IS STILL IN EFFECT! I'VE GOT MY HUMAN BRAIN ONCE MORE-- THE MIND OF BRUCE BANNER!

THEIR EMBRACE IS ONE OF THANKSGIVING AND REBIRTH.

BRUCE--THERE IS SOMETHING WRONG! IT'S LIKE I SENSE A GROWING PRESENCE OF EVIL IN THE LAND!

RELAX, KID! THE ONLY EVIL IS THAT YOU'VE BEEN GONE! BESIDES, YOU'VE GOT HULK THE GIANT-KILLER AROUND!

NOW-- HOW ABOUT I CARRY YOU OVER THE THRESHOLD?

GODS OF K'AI! SPREAD THE WORD! OUR QUEEN RETURNS, AND THE HULK WITH HER!

TO THE CHEERS OF THE ADORING POPULACE, THE HULK AND JARELLA ENTER THE CAPITOL CITY!

NOW DOES THIS LOOK EVIL?
YOU'RE RIGHT, MY LOVE. THIS IS--
--WONDERFUL.

HAIL, STEWARDS OF THE REALM! HOW HAS THE KINGDOM FARED IN OUR ABSENCE?
ALL HAS BEEN PEACEFUL, AND, WITH YOUR RETURN, ALL IS WELL!
TORLA!

BRUCE BANNER! IT IS GOOD TO SEE YOU! YOU REMEMBER HOLI AND MOLI, DON'T YOU?
OF COURSE! TORLA, WE'RE BACK TO STAY! AND THERE'S ONE THING I WANT TAKEN CARE OF BEFORE WE DO ANYTHING ELSE!

SO IT IS THAT A FEW DAYS LATER, DR. ROBERT BRUCE BANNER ENTERS INTO MATRIMONY WITH QUEEN JARELLA OF K'AI, IN A LAND WHERE DREAMS CAN COME TRUE...

AS WELL AS NIGHTMARES--!
I DON'T WANT TO ADMIT IT TO JARELLA, BUT EVEN I CAN FEEL THAT GROWING AURA OF EVIL NOW!

"I ASKED TORLA, AND HE SAID IT BEGAN WHEN WE ARRIVED, NOT BEFORE!

"IT'S AS IF SOMETHING IS OBJECTING TO OUR PRESENCE HERE, AND STRONGLY!

"AND WHAT WORRIES ME IS THAT SOON IT'LL BE STRONG ENOUGH TO STRIKE!"

WAIT! WHAT'S THAT AWFUL SMELL?
GOOD LORD!

WHATEVER THAT THING CRAWLED OUT OF, IT'S GOT MY WIFE!

AND NOBODY DOES THAT TO THE HULK!
WHOOOM!

BRUCE! WHAT WAS THAT??
I DON'T KNOW, BUT SOMETHING IS ROTTEN IN THE STATE OF K'AI!
AND I INTEND TO GET TO THE BOTTOM OF IT!

I'M GOING TO FIND WHATEVER SENT THAT THING! AND WHEN I DO--!

AND THE LEGENDARY, TELEPATHIC SPOOR-MEN OF K'AI LEAD THE HUNT!
THE VIBRATIONS LEAD DOWN INTO THESE CATACOMBS, MY LORD!

HERE IS A POOL OF SLIME SIMILAR TO THAT THING'S!

THE TRAIL LEADS TO THAT DOOR! WHAT'S BE-HIND IT?
I--DO NOT KNOW, MY LORD! IT HAS BEEN SHUT WITH AN ALL-POWERFUL SPELL!

REMIND ME TO TALK TO YOU ABOUT THAT TERM "ALL POWER-FUL"! IT TENDS TO LOSE ITS MEANING--

--WHEN THE HULK IS AROUND!
WRAKK!

BUT BRUCE BANNER'S AGILE MIND IS STUNNED BY THE SCENE OF BLOODY SACRIFICE THAT LIES BEYOND THE DOOR!
THE FIGURE CONTINUES TO MAKE HIS OBEISANCES TO THE STONE ALTAR, OBLIVIOUS TO ALL ELSE!
HOLY--!

GET AWAY FROM THERE!

WHY DID YOU KILL THIS GIRL? WHAT WERE YOU TRYING TO DO TO MY WIFE?? ANSWER ME!

HEAR ME, BRUCE BANNER. THE DARK GODS HAVE ORDAINED THAT YOU DIE! AND DIE YOU SHALL!

FAREWELL, HULK! WE SHALL MEET AGAIN-- BELOWWW...

MELTED-- EVEN AS I WAS HOLDING HIM!

I DON'T KNOW WHAT YOU REALLY ARE, YOU SO-CALLED "DARK GODS" -- BUT YOU SHOULD KNOW ONE THING--!

KA-DOOM!
THE POWER OF THE HULK IS GOING TO SMASH YOU!

THIS-- WITH ALL HIS BEING-- THE HULK SWEARS!

THUS THE HULK TURNS AND LEAVES-- AS A GIRL LIES AMID THE RUBBLE WHO BEARS A MARK ON HER BROW--A MARK WHICH, IN THE ALPHABET OF K'AI MEANS JARELLA--!

A FEW DAYS LATER, IN THE ROYAL COUNCIL CHAMBER...
--AND WE HAVE HAD REPORTS FROM ALL OVER THE REALM OF STRANGE AND MENACING OCCURRENCES SINCE YOUR RETURN, MY QUEEN AND LORD BANNER!

"WE HEAR OF THE DEAD RISING FROM THEIR GRAVES --

"-- OF STRANGE FUNGOID GROWTHS THAT SUDDENLY COVER BUILDINGS --

"-- AND MYSTERIOUS MACHINES RAVAGING THE COUNTRYSIDE!"

BUT, BLAST IT, WE CAN'T LAY OUR HANDS ON WHAT'S CAUSING IT! WHY DO WE HAVE AN ENEMY WE CAN'T SMASH?!?

YOUR PARDON, MY QUEEN, BUT THEY HAVE ARRIVED!
THEN MY PRAYERS ARE ANSWERED! SHOW THEM IN!

I HAD NOT DARED TO HOPE THAT YOU WOULD HEAR OUR CALL IN THIS DARK HOUR, YET HERE YOU ARE-- ALL OF YOU!
CNERLA OF THE KNIVES--
--GREAT HROND--
--YTHAER THE SWIFT--
--FIERCE VIDIAS--
--AND GLUNNO THE WINGED ONE!
WE COULD DO NAUGHT ELSE BUT COME, MY QUEEN!

MY LOVE, THESE ARE OUR GREATEST CHAMPIONS -- THE DEFENDERS OF OUR REALM! I FELT WE WOULD NEED THEIR VALOR NOW!
WE HAVE HEARD OF YOUR STRENGTH AND COURAGE, BRUCE BANNER, AND WE WILL BE HONORED TO FIGHT ALONGSIDE YOU -- TO THE DEATH!
SO SAY WE ALL!
I'M HONORED, MY-- FELLOW DEFENDERS --

-- BUT WE STILL DON'T HAVE A SOLID ENEMY! WHAT WE COULD USE WOULD BE THE OFFICES OF MY GOOD FRIEND STEPHEN STRANGE!
BRUCE -- ALL OF US HAD THOUGHT THE WORSHIP OF THE DARK GODS ON K'AI ENDED GEOLOGIC AGES AGO, AND ALMOST NO RECORDS SURVIVE FROM THAT FOUL TIME! HOWEVER --

-THERE ARE WHISPERS, LEGENDS ONLY A FEW MEN HAVE HEARD OF -- OF THE PLACE CALLED WOL ULRAI!

"THOUGH ONLY RUINS NOW, THE MOUNT OF WOL ULRAI ONCE BORE A GREAT CITY! AND THE WHISPERS SAY IT WAS KNOWN AS THE HEART OF ALL DARKNESS!
"IT MAY JUST BE THERE THAT THE DARKNESS HAS COME TO LIVE AGAIN!"

GREAT! THEN WOL ULRAI IT IS! AND SINCE THERE'S NO TIME LIKE THE PRESENT -- !
BRUCE, WAIT! DON'T GO OFF ALONE!

I'M SORRY, KID, BUT I DON'T THINK YOU CAN FOLLOW ME THE WAY I'M GOING!
SHALL I SHOW HIM, MY QUEEN?

TO ME, MY BROTHERS OF THE WING AND CLAW! BEAR US UP, LEND US THE WIND!

AT THE GREEN WINGED MAN'S MYSTIC CALL, THE AIR FILLS WITH A RUSH OF ENORMOUS BIRDS!

QUITE AN AERIAL TAXI SERVICE YOU'VE GOT THERE, GLUNNO! FRIENDS OF YOURS?
THEY ARE MY BROTHERS, BRUCE BANNER--EVEN AS YOU ARE!

AND SOON THE BAND OF HEROES FIND THEMSELVES AMID RUINS ALMOST UNRECOGNIZABLE WITH AGE--THE CITY OF WOL ULRAI!

GLUNNO--THE BIRDS! THEY TAKE OFF AS IN FEAR! WHAT COULD FRIGHTEN SUCH AS THEY?

THEY FEAR LITTLE, VIDIAS--BUT THERE ARE SOME ABOMINATIONS NO NATURAL CREATURE CAN STOMACH! BEHOLD!

FROM OUT OF THE STINKING PITS THEY COME-- THE SPAWN OF THE DARK GODS!

THEY ARE MANY, MY LORD-- STRETCHING BACK INTO THE SHADOWS FOREVER! CAN WE FIGHT THEM ALL?
WE MUST, CNERLA! BUT JUDGING FROM THE LOOKS OF THEM, THEY SHUN THE LIGHT! BEAT THE ADVANCE GUARD AND THE REST MAY FLEE!
BUT, GODS OF K'AI, BRUCE BANNER--

"WHAT NIGHTMARES THESE CREATURES ARE!
"WERE THESE ONCE MEN-- OR WERE MEN ONCE SUCH AS THESE??"

IT DOESN'T MATTER, HROND! I WAS ONCE A MAN-- AND NOW I'M MORE! THAT DOESN'T CHANGE GOOD-- OR EVIL--

--OR THE NEED TO FIGHT! FOR K'AI!!

THE MASSIVE FORM OF THE HULK SLAMS INTO THE CAVE MOUTH, SCATTERING THE MASSED ATTACK OF DEMONS BACK INTO THE DARKNESS!
WA-ROOOM

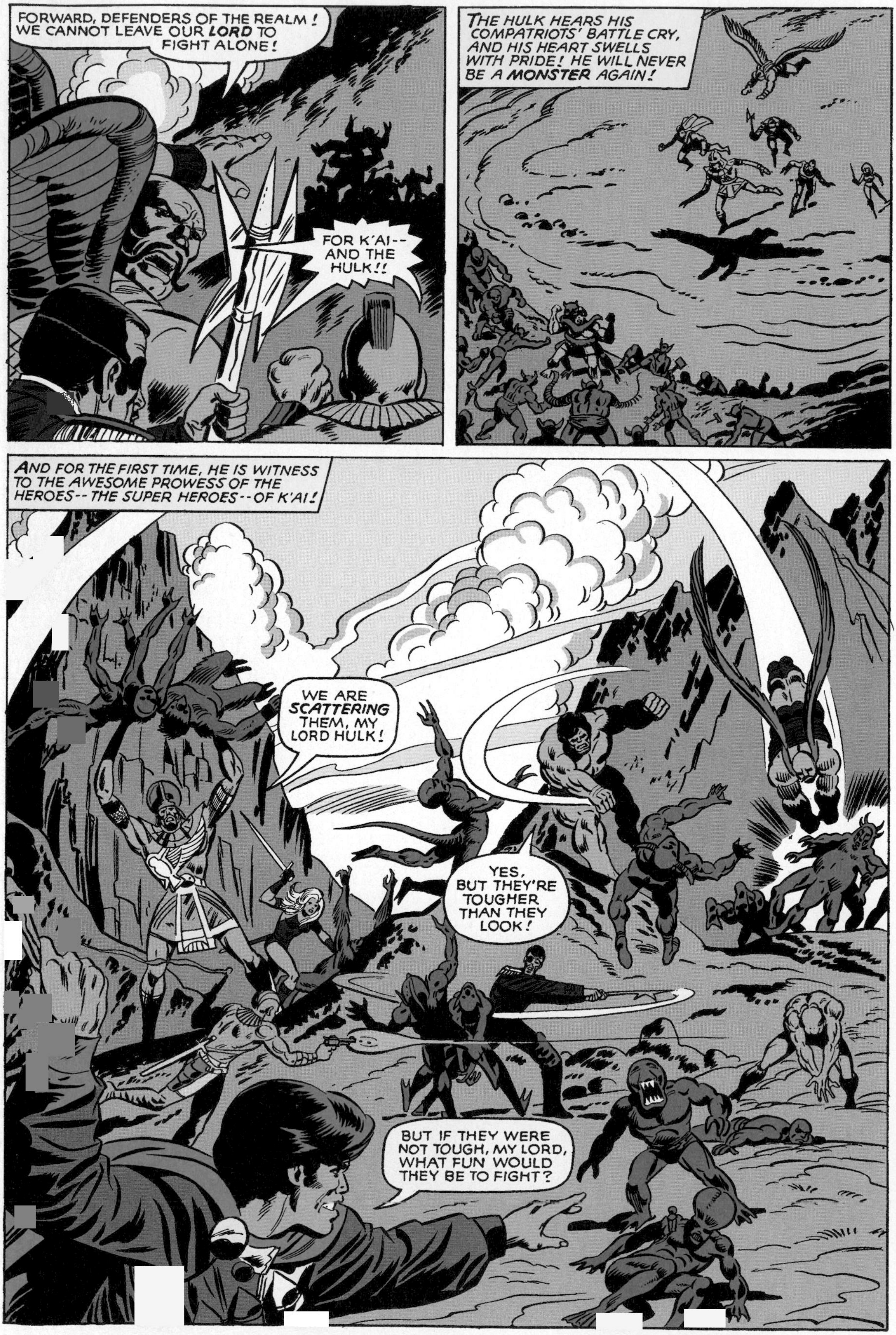

AND FOR THE FIRST TIME, HE IS WITNESS TO THE AWESOME PROWESS OF THE HEROES--THE SUPER HEROES--OF K'AI!

WE ARE **SCATTERING** THEM, MY LORD HULK!

YES, BUT THEY'RE TOUGHER THAN THEY LOOK!

BUT IF THEY WERE NOT TOUGH, MY LORD, WHAT FUN WOULD THEY BE TO FIGHT?

WATCH OUT, MY QUEEN!
THANK YOU, YTHAER-- DOUBLY!
EACH OF THESE MEN HAS HIS OWN STYLE OF FIGHTING--

EACH HIS SPECIAL STRENGTH--THERE ARE EVEN VAST CULTURAL DIFFERENCES AMONG THEM. ONE THING ALONE BINDS THEM TOGETHER IN THIS BATTLE--

LOYALTY! LOYALTY TO A CREATURE ONCE HOUNDED BY A WORLD AS A MENACE! LOYALTY TO THE HULK AND JARELLA!
IT IS THIS WHICH DRIVES THE HULK ON!

THEY'VE STOPPED COMING! HAVE WE BEATEN THEM ALL, OR--?

THE REST OF THEM HAVE FLED--VANISHED--APPARENTLY TO BE REPLACED BY A SINGLE FIGURE--
--AND HE SEEMS SOMEHOW FAMILIAR--!

WAIT--THAT HELMET--NO, IT JUST CAN'T BE--
IT IS, BANNER--

-- AND YET, IT IS NOT.
LORD VISIS!* TRAITOR TO JARELLA'S COURT! BUT-- GOOD LORD, MAN --
VISIS? YES, I WAS VISIS ONCE.
*LAST SEEN IN HULK #155.-- D/M.

-- BUT NOW I HAVE BECOME SOMETHING ELSE: THE VOICE OF THE DARK GODS.
LISTEN TO YOUR DOOM, BRUCE BANNER

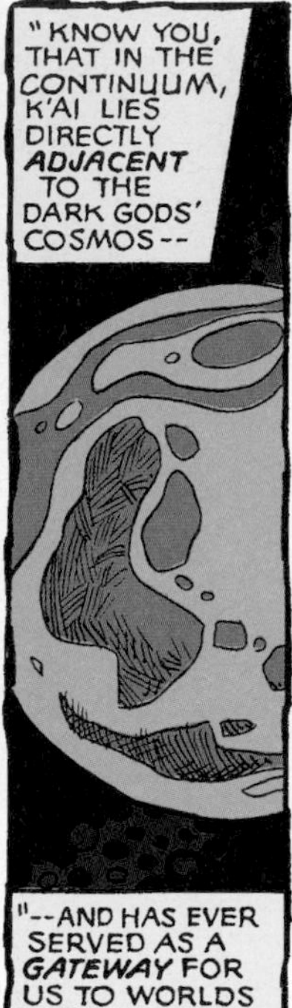
"KNOW YOU, THAT IN THE CONTINUUM, K'AI LIES DIRECTLY ADJACENT TO THE DARK GODS' COSMOS --
"-- AND HAS EVER SERVED AS A GATEWAY FOR US TO WORLDS WITHOUT NUMBER.

"THEN OUR SERVANT, PSYKLOP*, MADE A COLOSSAL BLUNDER IN INADVERTENTLY SENDING YOU TO K'AI.
*AVENGERS #88 & HULK #140.-- D/M.

YOUR UNLIMITED POWER, COUPLED WITH BANNER'S BRAIN, POSED AN UNPRECEDENTED THREAT TO US AS LONG AS IT REMAINED ON K'AI. YOU COULD HAVE SHUT OUR DOOR FOREVER.
I'LL MAKE SURE I DO JUST THAT, FILTH!

"AS PUNISHMENT, PSYKLOP WAS BANISHED TO K'AI TO GUARD AGAINST YOUR RETURN.
"BUT ONCE AGAIN HE FAILED US. THEN OUR ONLY OPTION WAS TO CAUSE BOTH YOU AND JARELLA TO BE SNATCHED BACK TO EARTH.*
*HULK #203.-- D/M.

"ONCE ON EARTH, WE HAD ONE OF OUR WORSHIPPERS REVIVE THE CRYPTO-MAN AND SEND HIM AFTER YOU.

"DURING THE BATTLE WE CREATED THE ILLUSION OF A BOY THAT WOULD HAVE CAUSED JARELLA TO SACRIFICE HERSELF.
"WITH JARELLA DEAD, YOU WOULD NEVER HAVE RETURNED TO K'AI.

SOMEHOW WE WERE THWARTED. THOUGH IT IS NOT OUR WAY, WE MUST NOW CRUSH YOU DIRECTLY. BEHOLD THE WEAPON WHICH UNDID YOU ONCE BEFORE*: YOUR OWN MAD, RAGING, BESTIAL SELF -- THE ONE THING YOU ARE AFRAID TO FIGHT-- CREATED BY A MACHINE OF A TIME-LOST AGE.
*IN HULK #156.-- D/M.

AND THE LIVING EMBODIMENT OF THE HULK'S MINDLESS FURY LEAPS OUT AND GRABS JARELLA!
HULK WILL SMASH!

MY PULSE IS RACING-- MUSTN'T LOSE CONTROL-- HAVE TO THINK--

NO! IF I KEEP REPRESSING THE HULK SIDE OF ME, JARELLA WILL DIE!

AND THE HULK WILL NOT LET HER!

YOU'RE THE ENEMY! ALL MY LIFE I'VE BEEN AFRAID OF MY RAGE-- MY DESTRUCTIVE URGES!
NO LONGER! AT LAST I'VE FOUND SOMETHING WORTH RAGING FOR! JARELLA--K'AI-- MY FRIENDS!

PUT HULK DOWN, PUNY BANNER, OR HULK SMASHES YOU!
NOT TODAY, MONSTER! TODAY THE HULK AND BANNER BOTH RAGE-- WE BOTH STAND AND FIGHT TOGETHER--

--AND TOGETHER WE ARE GREATER THAN YOU!
WHOOM!

AND THE SHEER POWER OF THE HULK'S BLOW BRINGS DOWN THE SIDE OF THE MOUNTAIN!
RRUMBLE!
REGRETTABLY, ONLY THE CORPSE OF VISIS AND A FEW DEMONS WERE UNDONE. THE GODS REMAINED UNAFFECTED.

HEAR ME, DARK GODS!
I KNOW YOU'LL BE BACK! I KNOW YOU'LL TRY AGAIN! BUT I WILL PROTECT THIS WORLD, AND I WILL DESTROY YOU-- BECAUSE NOTHING CAN STOP-- THE HULK!
AND SO WE SEE AN EARTHLY TRAGEDY ENDED IN THIS WORLD, AS A NEW EPIC-- BEGINS!
THE END.

JARELLA

Real name: Jarella
Occupation: Empress of K'ai
Identity: The general populace of Earth is unaware of Jarella's existence
Legal status: Citizen of K'ai
Other aliases: None
Place of birth: K'ai
Place of death: A town in New Mexico
Marital status: Single, engaged to wed Bruce Banner
Known relatives: None
Group affiliation: None
Base of operations: K'ai
First appearance: INCREDIBLE HULK #140
Final appearance: (as a living being) INCREDIBLE HULK #205, (burial) INCREDIBLE HULK #248
History: The monstrous, superhumanly strong Hulk was captured by Psyklop, the last survivor of a sentient, human-sized insect-like race that lived underground before the rise of humanity (see *Hulk, Appendix: Psyklop*). Psyklop's race worshipped "dark gods" who have yet to be identified (see *Gods*). For unknown reasons these gods cast Psyklop's race into a state of suspended animation. Millennia later, the dark gods awakened Psyklop from suspended animation so that he might find the gods an energy source. In return, once the gods were "fed" with energy, they would revive the rest of Psyklop's race. Psyklop believed his race would then take control of Earth away from the human race. Psyklop captured the Hulk so that the latter, with his tremendous power, would serve as the energy source that the dark gods desired.

In order to study the Hulk better, Psyklop used his advanced technology to compress the Hulk's atomic structure at a carefully controlled rate, thereby shrinking him. Then, however, the superhuman champions called the Avengers invaded Psyklop's lair (see *Avengers*). While Psyklop battled the Avengers, the Hulk continued to shrink, passing the point that Psyklop had intended. Finally, the Hulk's atomic structure was compressed to the point that he was shifted from his own universe into one of the so-called "microverses" which are actually universes existing in other dimensions (see *Glossary: Microverse*). Psyklop rid himself of the Avengers by teleporting them away with one of his devices.

The Hulk found himself transported into a wilderness outside the city of K'ai on an otherdimensional planet. There he was attacked by an enormous beast called a warthos, which he quickly defeated. Seeing other warthos attacking the city of K'ai, the Hulk fought them off.

The grateful people of K'ai, all green-skinned like the Hulk, acclaimed him as a hero and brought him before their empress, Jarella. It was the time that Jarella was required to choose a husband, and it was forbidden for an empress to wed anyone who had not proved himself in battle against the warthos. Regarding the Hulk's arrival and victory over the warthos as an omen from her goddess, Jarella declared that she would make the Hulk her husband and the sovereign of the city-state of K'ai. She commanded her Pantheon of Sorcerers to cast a spell that would teach the Hulk their language. The spell did so, but also gave the Hulk the intelligence, memories, and personality of his alter-ego, Dr. Bruce Banner, while he remained in the Hulk's superhuman physical form. Although the Hulk regretted

not being able to return to Earth or to see his future wife, Betty Ross, again, he came to deeply care for Jarella and decided to remain in K'ai as her husband and as its king.

However, Lord Visis, a nobleman of K'ai, wanted the throne for himself, and sent assassins to kill both the Hulk and Jarella. The Hulk thwarted the assassination attempt against him and exiled Visis into the wilderness outside K'ai.

The day before Jarella was to marry the Hulk, Psyklop removed the Hulk from Jarella's world and brought him back to Earth. There the Hulk regained his normal size but lost Bruce Banner's intelligence and personality. Furious, the Hulk defeated Psyklop, who was confronted by the dark gods, who were angered at his failure to secure them an energy source. As an ironically fitting punishment, the dark gods exiled Psyklop to the otherdimensional world of K'ai, Psyklop remained in a mountain retreat on that world, and built a gigantic robot that became known as the "god of the mountain" to ensure his privacy.

Lord Visis organized an army of renegades with which he warred against K'ai. Jarella had the Pantheon of Sorcerers magically transport her to Earth so that she could find the Hulk and bring him back to help them in the war. Visis, who had learned magic while in exile, saw what the Pantheon was doing through his mystic crystal, and he magically sent his master assassin, Fialan, to Earth along the mystical currents of the Pantheon's spell.

Shortly before the Pantheon cast its spell, scientist Dr. Peter Corbeau had used solar energy in an attempt to cure Bruce Banner of becoming the Hulk. Immediately thereafter an unusual storm erupted on the sun's surface. Corbeau believed it was connected with his drawing of energy from the sun to cure Banner, although this explanation seems unlikely. However, it is clear that the magical forces that transported Jarella to Earth, perhaps because of Fialan's secret presence on the interdimensional journey, caused a dangerous disruption of normal solar activity that, if unchecked, could have seriously threatened the Earth's safety.

On Earth Jarella was reunited with Banner, but Corbeau informed them both of the danger to the sun. Corbeau realized that Jarella's interdimensional journey was responsible for the approaching disaster, but he had SHIELD create a Life Model Decoy (android) in Jarella's form (see *SHIELD*). By sending the LMD to Jarella's world, Corbeau hoped to end the disturbances within the sun. Fialan attacked Jarella while she was with Banner. Guards at the military base where they were at the time were unable to stop Fialan. Desperate to protect Jarella, Banner reversed the process that had cured him and became the Hulk once more. Meanwhile, General T.E. "Thunderbolt" Ross and others at the base turned loose the Jarella LMD while concealing the real Jarella (see *Deceased: Ross, General "Thunderbolt"*). Fialan shot at equipment behind the Jarella LMD, thinking it was the real Jarella, and thereby triggering an explosion that destroyed the android. Believing Jarella was dead, the Hulk killed Fialan.

The real Jarella went to the Hulk to tell him she was still alive. But now, with the LMD destroyed, and no time left to complete building another one, it was necessary to send Jarella herself back to K'ai. Moreover, Jarella wanted to return there, unwilling to abandon her people in time of war. Hence, Corbeau transported Jarella and Fialan's

corpse back to K'ai using interdimensional teleportational devices created by the combined expertise of Banner, Corbeau, Dr. Henry Pym, and Reed Richards (see *Mister Fantastic; Pym, Dr. Henry*).

Later, the Hulk was transported to a microverse by the means of the subatomic "Pym Particles" and was then sent to K'ai by the power of the Shaper of Worlds (see *Ant Man*: Known superhuman powers, *Shaper of Worlds*). Once on the world of K'ai, the Pantheon's spell that enabled the Hulk to maintain Bruce Banner's personality and intelligence while possessing the Hulk's body took effect once more. The Hulk discovered that Visis had won the war, destroyed the city of K'ai itself, and captured Jarella and many of her subjects. In order to make his usurpation of the throne legitimate, Visis demanded that Jarella marry him; if she did not, he said he would begin killing her captive subjects. Jarella reluctantly agreed.

But the Hulk, leading a number of warthos, stormed Castle Visis, and rescued her. Together, Jarella and the Hulk thereafter led their loyal legions of followers against Visis's forces, and forced him to the brink of total defeat.

Desperate, Visis formed an alliance with Krylar, leader of the Pitill Pawob, an order of assassins who had access to the advanced technology of their forebears. Visis challenged his enemies to decide the outcome of the war by single combat between champions chosen by both sides. Despite Jarella's objections, the Hulk agreed to the challenge. Using advanced technology, Visis and Krylar had a savage duplicate of the Hulk created to serve as their champion. The Hulk himself acted as Jarella's champion.

The savage duplicate of the Hulk probably would have defeated the real Hulk in combat, had not Jarella commanded the Sorcerers' Triad (the Pantheon of Sorcerers) to lift their spell that gave the Hulk Bruce Banner's personality. Once they did, the real Hulk became savage again, and the duplicate Hulk ceased to exist. Angered that his side had thus lost the war, Visis killed Krylar.

Then, the reducing effect of the "Pym Particles" began to wear off, causing the Hulk to grow in size as he headed towards Castle Visis. With his increased size, the Hulk demolished the Castle. The Hulk grew increasingly immense, and just before he dematerialized from K'ai, the movement of his gigantic foot somehow unintentionally triggered a fault under the planet's surface, causing a series of massive earthquakes. (Accounts that the Hulk knocked K'ai's world from its orbit are erroneous.) The Hulk returned to Earth and his normal size.

Many months later, the Hulk returned to Jarella's world to discover that Jarella was about to be killed as a sacrifice to the "mountain god" who was believed to be responsible for the severe earthquakes. The Hulk, who did not regain Bruce Banner's personality during this visit to Jarella's world, rescued her. Unknown to the people of K'ai, the "mountain god" was actually the robotic servant of Psyklop. The earthquakes that the Hulk had triggered had abated long before; the more recent earthquakes had been caused by Psyklop, who intended to rule Jarella's people.

The Hulk and Jarella went to the "mountain god's" castle, which was actually Psyklop's headquarters, and the Hulk battled and destroyed the "mountain god" robot. Psyklop then captured the Hulk and Jarella. Through sorcery, Jarella's subjects learned of her capture and of Psyklop's responsibility for their own sufferings. They then went to attack Psyklop's castle to free their empress.

Inside Psyklop revealed to Jarella that he had imprisoned within a vessel all of the life forces of those of her subjects who had been killed by the earthquakes he had induced. Using his hypnotic powers, Psyklop sent the Hulk to battle Jarella's would be rescuers, but the Hulk finally broke free of Psyklop's control and turned against him. The Hulk accidentally broke the vessel containing the spirits of Psyklop's victims, who broke free and apparently destroyed their murderer.

Reunited with her people, who were again all loyal to her, Jarella announced her intention to marry the Hulk that very day. But then both the Hulk and Jarella were transported to Earth by equipment being used by Dr. Leonard Samson (see *Doc Samson*). Jarella wished to return to her people. However Samson mistakenly believed that Jarella's planet was literally a subatomic world. The Hulk accidentally destroyed the microscope slide on which Samson erroneously believed that Jarella's world was located, and hence believed that the world had been destroyed as well.

Jarella remained on Earth, but shortly therafter the Hulk engaged in combat with a menace called the Crypto-Man (see *Appendix: Crypto-Man*). During the battle a wall began collapsing. Jarella rushed to save a child from being crushed to death by the falling wall and succeeded, but Jarella herself was crushed to death by the collapsing structure instead.

The U.S. government preserved Jarella's body at Gamma Base for study. Eventually the Hulk invaded Gamma Base and found her body there. The alien Captain Mar-Vell used a "micron-cannon" designed by Reed Richards to send the Hulk and Jarella's body back to her world (see *Deceased: Captain Mar-Vell*).

Due to the disasters that had befallen it, Jarella's world was now virtually devoid of vegetation, and its people were starving. (Contrary to previous reports, the planet had not shifted its orbit.) The Elder of the Universe called the Gardener now lived on the planet and used his powers to create a small fertile region there (see *Elders of the Universe: Gardener*). The Hulk hurled the Gardener's mystic soul-gem into the planet, restoring the world's fertility. The Hulk then lay Jarella's body to rest in the sacred burial grounds of K'ai, and the Gardener sent the Hulk back to Earth.

Height: (on Earth) 5′ 6″
Weight: (on Earth) 115 lbs.
Eyes: Green
Hair: Blond
Skin: Light green
Strength level: Jarella possessed the equivalent of the normal human strength of an Earth woman of her physical age, height, and guild who engaged in intensive regular exercise.
Abilities: Jarella was a great warrior and a brilliant military leader. She was an excellent swordswoman and a superb hand-to-hand combatant.

■

GARDENER

Real Name: Ord Zyonyz
Occupation: Botanist
Identity: Secret. His existence is unknown to the general population of Earth.
Legal status: Possesses no citizenship
Former aliases: None known
Place of self-awareness: Seyfert galaxy M-77
Marital status: Single
Known relatives: None
Group affiliation: Elders of the Universe
Base of operations: Known universe and various microverses
First appearance: MARVEL TEAM-UP #55
History: Like those of all the Elders of the Universe, the Gardener's origin is lost in antiquity (see *Elders of the Universe*). What is known is that he is among the oldest living beings in the universe, having been a member of one of the first of the universe's races to become sentient in the wake of the Big Bang. Virtually immortal, the Gardener has devoted his life to the creation of natural beauty by sowing the seeds of plants, flowers, and trees upon barren or devastated worlds. The number of worlds he has turned into fertile planet-wide gardens over the eons is countless. He has amassed a knowledge of botany second to none and has collected billions of different seeds in his travels. Using his advanced cultivation techniques, he can cover a barren Earth-sized planet with lush vegetation in the space of a year.

In recent millennia, the Gardener acquired a Soul-Gem, an alien artifact that enables its possessor to transform cosmic energy for personal use. The Gardener employed it to stimulate the growth of his seeds beyond their normal rate and to traverse space without a starship. Recently, the Gardener used his Soul-Gem's power to combat the Stranger, another powerful extraterrestrial possessing a Soul-Gem (see *Stranger*). Believing that he "corrupted" the gem by its use as a weapon, the Gardener abandoned it. Later, the Gardener replaced his Soul-Gem with that once worn by the golden Earth-being Adam Warlock (see *Deceased: Warlock, Adam*). Warlock's frequent employment of the gem as a weapon did not matter to the Gardener as long as he himself does not use it in that way. The Gardener's current whereabouts are unknown.
Height: 7′ 1″
Weight: 390 lbs
Eyes: Purple
Hair: Grey
Strength level: Unknown. All Elders presumably have the potential for superhuman strength. It is not known to what extent the Gardener has chosen to develop this potential.
Known superhuman powers: As an Elder of the Universe, the Gardener possesses an immortal body, immune to the cellular deterioration of aging, and impervious to conventional harm (disease, penetration wounds, etc.). Only the dispersion of a major portion of his body's molecules could prevent his regenerative powers from functioning. In his preoccupation with the art and science of cultivating plants, the Gardener has not devoted much of his energies to the development of potential physical and mental powers, as have certain of his kinsmen. Eschewing violence, the Gardener has little experience in combat techniques. While he is able to survive in space and go for prolonged periods of time without nourishment, he is unable to traverse interstellar distances without some means of propulsion.
Weapons: The Gardener currently wears a green Soul-Gem upon his brow, one of six such power-jewels known to exist in the universe. Although the origin and nature of the Soul-Gem is as yet unknown, it would seem to be an artifact that either possesses great energies or is able to tap great energies which can be channeled by the wearer's will. Its previous wearer, Adam Warlock, employed the jewel to emit beams of concussive force, to scan the thoughts of others, and to entrap his opponents' life essences, or souls. This latter property may be an innate capacity of all gems, or may be a property peculiar to this particular Soul-Gem. The Gardener's Soul-Gem even seems to possess a primitive form of sentience, as well as an "appetite" for souls that it is occasionally able to impose upon its wearer. Souls known to reside within the subjective pocket universe of the green Soul-Gem are Adam Warlock of Earth, Pip of Laxidasia, Gamora of Xen-Hoober, Autolycus of Sirus X, and Kray-Tor of Jude. The Gardener mainly uses the Soul-Gem to accelerate the photosynthetic growth process in plants and to animate them. As an Elder, the Gardener is invulnerable to the gem's corrupting influence. He has also used it to defy gravity, travel through space at trans-light speeds, and open portals to other dimensions (such as the microverse of K'ai). ■